SCRIPTURE CENTRAL COMMENTARY ON

The
DOCTRINE
—and—
COVENANTS

VOLUME 2

SECTIONS 41–76

SCRIPTURE CENTRAL  COMMENTARY ON

The
DOCTRINE
— and —
COVENANTS

VOLUME 2
SECTIONS 41–76

CASEY PAUL GRIFFITHS

CFI
An imprint of Cedar Fort, Inc.
Springville, Utah

Paperback ISBN 13: 978-1-4621-4681-9
eBook ISBN 13: 978-1-4621-4836-3

Published by CFI, an imprint of Cedar Fort, Inc.
2373 W. 700 S., Suite 100, Springville, UT 84663
Distributed by Cedar Fort, Inc., www.cedarfort.com

Library of Congress Cataloging Number: 2024936347

Cover design by Shawnda Craig
Cover design © 2024 Cedar Fort, Inc.
Edited and Typeset by Liz Kazandzhy

Printed in the United States of America

10 9 8 7 6 5 4 3 2 1

Printed on acid-free paper

For Acacia, our firstborn child, who changed our lives.

CONTENTS

Introduction to Volume 2

In February 1831 Joseph and Emma Smith moved their family to Kirtland, Ohio, and the second phase of the Restoration began. Only a few months earlier, Joseph received a revelation commanding all of the Saints to gather "to the Ohio" (see Doctrine and Covenants 37). The faithful members of the Church began settling their affairs, selling their homes and farms, and making the immense sacrifice to obey the Lord's command. Partly in return for this amazing sacrifice, they were rewarded with one of the richest seasons of spiritual outpouring in the history of the Church.

Volume 2 of this commentary on the Doctrine and Covenants only covers roughly a year in the life of Joseph Smith, from February 1831 to February 1832. Yet in this single year nearly a quarter of the revelations in the Doctrine and Covenants were received. These revelations cover all manner of subjects, from the implementation of a system of consecration (see Doctrine and Covenants 42), to the development of spiritual gifts (see Doctrine and Covenants 46), to a glimpse into the eternities (see Doctrine and Covenants 76). Found among these revelations are some of the most profound teachings anywhere in scripture.

Why such a rich outpouring in such a small space of time? The first and most prominent factor was Joseph Smith's project to translate the Bible. The translation had nothing to do with ancient languages, which Joseph never claimed to know, or an original manuscript, which Joseph never claimed to have. To Joseph Smith, translation was a form of revelation. It was the Lord's way of getting His prophet to study the scriptures intensely so that the riches of eternity could open before him. The Prophet's project to translate the Bible led to a majestic vision of the afterlife recorded in Doctrine and Covenants 76, where Joseph Smith and Sidney Rigdon beheld the Father and the Son, the different degrees of glory, and the fate of the sons of perdition.

But even as the Saints gazed into eternity, the Lord also shared how to make the world they live in a better place. Doctrine and Covenants 42, known as the law of the Church, challenged the Saints to implement a system of consecration to provide for the poor among them. The first bishop, Edward Partridge, was called around the same time and given the task of using the principles of consecration to provide care for all of the Saints. Church members also continued to come to Joseph Smith with their questions and received divine answers from Jesus Christ through the voice of the Prophet.

In the midst of this busy time in the young Church, the Prophet and a cohort of missionaries were also directed to make a journey of over 800 miles to the edge of the American frontier to identify the location of the city of Zion, or the New Jerusalem. After arriving in Missouri, Joseph and his companions laid the foundation for a temple and a city where all people of good will could find refuge in the latter days. In doing so, they launched a quest still required of Latter-day Saints today: to build Zion. Even though the dreams of Zion eventually crashed into reality, the early Saints discovered that there was much to gain from simply traveling the road to Zion. Along the way, the Lord taught them, blessed them, and enlisted them in a work designed to transform the whole world.

Doctrine and Covenants Section 41

A Bishop unto the Church

Historical Context

EVEN BEFORE JOSEPH SMITH ARRIVED IN KIRTLAND, THE SPIRIT OF GOD was at work among the new converts in the area. Elizabeth Ann Whitney later wrote about a spiritual experience she and her husband, Newel, had that prepared them for the arrival of the gospel and the Prophet to her community. She later recorded:

> It was midnight—as my husband and I, in our house at Kirtland, were praying to the Father to be shown the way, the Spirit rested upon us and a cloud overshadowed the house. . . . The house passed away from our vision. We were not conscious of anything but the presence of the Spirit and the cloud that was over us. . . . A solemn awe pervaded us. We saw the cloud and felt the Spirit of the Lord. Then we heard a voice out of the cloud, saying, "Prepare to receive the word of the Lord, for it is coming." At this we marveled greatly, but from that moment we knew that the word of the Lord was coming to Kirtland.[1]

In early February 1831 a sleigh carrying four people traveled through the streets of Kirtland and stopped in front of the Gilbert and Whitney Store. One of the men in the sleigh, "a young and stalwart personage," jumped out and walked into the store and toward the proprietor, extended his hand "cordially, as if to an old and familiar acquaintance," and proclaimed, "Newel K. Whitney, thou art the man!" Whitney responded, "You have the advantage of me," and as he mechanically shook the man's hand added, "I could not call you by name as you have me." The stranger replied with a smile, "I am Joseph the Prophet." He continued, "You have prayed me here, now what do you want of me?" Joseph explained that he had seen the Whitneys in vision before he came to Kirtland. Newel soon introduced Joseph to his wife, Elizabeth, who later recalled, "I remarked to my husband that this was the fulfillment of the vision we had seen of a cloud, as of glory, resting upon our house."[2]

Joseph dictated the revelation in section 41 the same day he arrived in Kirtland. The Whitneys warmly welcomed Joseph and Emma into their home. Joseph later noted, "I and my wife lived in the family of Brother Whitney several weeks, and received every kindness and attention, which could be expected, and especially from Sister Whitney." Describing conditions among the Saints in Kirtland, Joseph added:

> The branch of the church in this part of the Lord's vineyard, which had increased to nearly one hundred members, were striving to do the will of God, so far as they knew it; though some strange notions and false spirits had crept in among them. With a little caution, and some wisdom, I soon assisted the brethren and sisters to overcome them. The plan of "common stock," which had existed in what was called "the family," whose members generally had embraced the everlasting gospel, was readily abandoned for the more perfect law of the Lord: and the false spirits were easily discerned and rejected by the light of revelation.[3]

The law Joseph refers to is Doctrine and Covenants 42, which was received in two parts, the first portion being received just a few days later on February 9 (Doctrine and Covenants 42:1–73) and the second part a few weeks later on February 23 (Doctrine and Covenants 42:74–93).

Church Historian John Whitmer added a notation to the first part of this revelation when he copied it down a few months later. He explained that the revelation came about because Leman Copley, a new convert from the area, asked Joseph Smith and Sidney Rigdon to live with him and promised to provide them with housing and provisions. This offer prompted Joseph to ask the Lord about the best course of action. In response, the Lord directed the Saints to build a home for Joseph and his family, which would keep him in the midst of the new converts in Kirtland who needed his guidance and direction. This revelation is also significant because it calls, from among the new converts, the first bishop to serve in this dispensation, Edward Partridge.[4]

*V*erse-by-*V*erse *C*ommentary

1 Hearken and hear, O ye my people, saith the Lord and your God, ye whom I delight to bless with the greatest of all blessings, ye that hear me; and ye that hear me not will I curse, that have professed my name, with the heaviest of all cursings.

2 Hearken, O ye elders of my church whom I have called, behold I give unto you a commandment, that ye shall assemble yourselves together to agree upon my word;

3 And by the prayer of your faith ye shall receive my law, that ye may know how to govern my church and have all things right before me.

4 And I will be your ruler when I come; and behold, I come quickly, and ye shall see that my law is kept.

5 He that receiveth my law and doeth it, the same is my disciple; and he that saith he receiveth it and doeth it not, the same is not my disciple, and shall be cast out from among you;

6 For it is not meet that the things which belong to the children of the kingdom should be given to them that are not worthy, or to dogs, or the pearls to be cast before swine.

In the October 1899 general conference, Joseph F. Smith, then a member of the First Presidency, explained that he wanted to share "a few words in relation to the duty which devolves upon the men who have been speaking during this conference." He then read the first four verses of Doctrine and Covenants 41. Commenting on these verses, President Smith stated, "The Lord here especially demands of the men who stand at the head of this

Church and who are responsible for the guidance and direction of the people of God, that they shall see to it that the law of God is kept. It is our duty to do this. . . . The Lord requires of us that we shall see that his law is kept among the people. This is one of the principle reasons why we are talking to you as we are."[5]

The men and women chosen to act as the Lord's representatives to the Church and to the world often come into prominence reluctantly. They are ordinary people with sins, faults, and challenges. Chosen as instruments to speak on behalf of God, they do possess one common attribute—a desire to bless the sons and daughters of God. Keeping the commandments bring blessings, and the burden of stewardship falls upon the shoulders of the men and women chosen to lead.

Speaking of his experience with other Church leaders, Elder David A. Bednar commented, "I have come to know their greatest desire is to discern and do the will of our Heavenly Father and His Beloved Son. As we counsel together, inspiration has been received and decisions have been made that reflect a degree of light and truth far beyond human intelligence, reasoning, and experience. . . . Some people find the human shortcomings of the Brethren troubling and faith diminishing. For me those imperfections are encouraging and faith promoting."[6]

In these verses the Lord provides a simple but profound definition of *disciple* as one "that receiveth my law and doeth it" (verse 5). Those who have covenanted to follow Jesus Christ are obligated to hear His words through imperfect people and then commit to live these commandments as best they can, accepting the Savior's grace as sufficient for their deficiencies.

> 7 And again, it is meet that my servant Joseph Smith, Jun., should have a house built, in which to live and translate.
>
> 8 And again, it is meet that my servant Sidney Rigdon should live as seemeth him good, inasmuch as he keepeth my commandments.
>
> 9 And again, I have called my servant Edward Partridge; and I give a commandment, that he should be appointed by the voice of the church, and ordained a bishop unto the church, to leave his merchandise and to spend all his time in the labors of the church;

10 To see to all things as it shall be appointed unto him in my laws in the day that I shall give them.

11 And this because his heart is pure before me, for he is like unto Nathanael of old, in whom there is no guile.

12 These words are given unto you, and they are pure before me; wherefore, beware how you hold them, for they are to be answered upon your souls in the day of judgment. Even so. Amen.

These verses mark the call of the first bishop to serve in this dispensation, Edward Partridge. At the time, the familiar ward and stake structure of the Church was yet to be revealed, and Partridge's position was more closely aligned with the present-day role of the Presiding Bishop than with the current responsibilities of the bishops who oversee Latter-day Saint congregations. The bishop's duties would be outlined in Doctrine and Covenants 46:27, 29; 58:17; 68:14, 19; 72; and 84:112. The duties of the Presiding Bishop would be outlined further in Doctrine and Covenants 107:13–17, 68–70, 87–88. Revealing the bishop's duties line upon line, the Lord starts with the most important requirement for service as a bishop, or in any role in His kingdom: a heart that is pure (see verse 11).

Speaking directly to those who hold the office of bishop, President Hinckley taught:

We expect you to stand as the presiding high priest of the ward, a counselor to the people, a defender and helper of those in trouble, a comfort to those in sorrow, a supplier to those in need. We expect you to stand as a guardian and protector of the doctrine that is taught in your ward, of the quality of the teaching, of the filling of the many offices which are necessary.

Your personal behavior must be impeccable. You must be a man of integrity, above reproach of any kind. Your example will set the tone for the direction your people follow. You must be fearless in denouncing evil, willing to take a stand for the right, uncompromising in your defense of truth. While all of this requires firmness, it must be done with kindness and love.

You are the father of the ward and the guardian of your people. You must reach out to them in their times of sorrow and sickness and distress. You stand as president of the Aaronic Priesthood, and with your counselors must give leadership to the deacons, and the teachers, and the priests, to see that they grow in "the nurture and admonition of the Lord" (Eph. 6:4).[7]

End Notes

1. Orson F. Whitney, "Newel K. Whitney," *Contributor* 6 (Jan. 1885): 125.
2. Orson F. Whitney, "Newel K. Whitney," 125.
3. Joseph Smith, in History, 1838–1856, volume A-1 [23 December 1805–30 August 1834], 93, josephsmithpapers.org.
4. See "Historical Introduction," Revelation, 4 February 1831 [D&C 41], josephsmithpapers.org.
5. Joseph F. Smith, in Conference Report, Oct. 1899, 41.
6. David A. Bednar, "Chosen to Bear Testimony of My Name," *Ensign* or *Liahona*, Nov. 2015, 129–130.
7. Gordon B. Hinckley, "The Shepherds of the Flock," *Ensign*, May 1998, 53.

Doctrine and Covenants
Section 42
The Laws of the Church of Christ

Historical Context

IN A REVELATION FROM THE LORD, JOSEPH SMITH WAS TOLD TO MOVE TO Ohio, and "there I shall give unto you my law" (Doctrine and Covenants 38:32). The day Joseph arrived in Ohio, he received another revelation promising him that "by the prayer of your faith ye shall receive my law, that ye may know how to govern my church and have all things right before me" (Doctrine and Covenants 41:3). Less than a week later, Joseph Smith received another revelation in the presence of twelve elders. When Church Historian John Whitmer recorded the revelation, he entitled it "The Laws of the Church of Christ."[1] The title was later shortened to "the Law." Shortly after he received the first section of the Law, Joseph Smith wrote to his friend Martin Harris, instructing him to "come here as soon as you can" and informing him, "We have received the laws of the Kingdom, since we came here and the Disciples in these parts have received them gladly."[2]

Several early manuscripts of this revelation have survived. The way the revelation was recorded suggests that "the Law" was originally a compilation of five different revelations received in response to questions posed by the elders present at the meeting. The Church originally thought of just the second section, consisting of Doctrine and Covenants 42:11–69, as "the Law," but in time the entirety of section 42 became known by that title. Joseph Smith received revelatory answers to their questions, ending each section with the words "Even so. Amen." John Whitmer's copy of the revelation, found in Revelation Book 1, includes the questions asked by the elders prior to each section of the revelation.

The first question was "Shall the Church come together into one place or continue in separate establishments?"[3] Second, the elders asked about "the law regulating the Church in her present situation till the time of her gathering."[4] The third question centered on "How the Elders are to dispose of their families while they are proclaiming repentance or are otherwise engaged in the service of the Church." The fourth question concerned the relationship of the Saints with their neighbors of other faiths, asking, "How far it is the will of the Lord that we should have dealing with the world & how we should conduct our dealings with them[?]" Finally, the elders inquired about how to best help the Saints who had been commanded to gather to Kirtland from the East, asking, "What preparations we shall make for our brethren from the East & where & how[?]"[5] The instructions that came as responses to these questions constitute verses 1–72 of section 42.

On February 23 Joseph Smith met with seven elders to inquire "how the elders of the Church are to act upon the points of the Law given by Jesus Christ to the Church."[6] The revelation received on this occasion added three more sections to the Law, making eight in total. The sixth part of the law was prefaced "A commandment how to act in cases of adultery"[7] and covers verses 74–77 in the present text. The remaining sections of the Law were simply "points of the law" and cover verses 78–93 of section 42.[8]

The centerpiece of the Law is the second section, which reiterates and expands on the Ten Commandments given in the book of Exodus (see Doctrine and Covenants 42:18–29; Exodus 20:1–17). The second section then introduces the law of consecration (see Doctrine and Covenants 42:30–42), which is designed to help the poor and the needy gather and find blessings within the kingdom. The Kirtland Saints were already experimenting with consecration before Joseph Smith arrived, and the revelation's focus on this principle appears to have been in answer to the Saints' earnest inquiries. In 1830, before he converted to the Church, Sidney Rigdon stated at a gathering that "our pretension to follow the apostles in all their New Testament teachings, required a community of goods; that as they established this order in the model church at Jerusalem, we were bound to imitate their example."⁹

The law of consecration became a major focus of the following revelations given to Joseph Smith. Estimating conservatively, at least twenty-four revelations in the Doctrine and Covenants concern themselves directly with consecration and the Lord's directions to implement the practice. Doctrine and Covenants 42 provides the foundational principles to carry out one of the most important missions of the Church: "caring for those in need."¹⁰

$\mathcal{V}$erse-by-$\mathcal{V}$erse $\mathcal{C}$ommentary

1 Hearken, O ye elders of my church, who have assembled yourselves together in my name, even Jesus Christ the Son of the living God, the Savior of the world; inasmuch as ye believe on my name and keep my commandments.

2 Again I say unto you, hearken and hear and obey the law which I shall give unto you.

3 For verily I say, as ye have assembled yourselves together according to the commandment wherewith I commanded you, and are agreed as touching this one thing, and have asked the Father in my name, even so ye shall receive.

4 Behold, verily I say unto you, I give unto you this first commandment, that ye shall go forth in my name, every one of you, excepting my servants Joseph Smith, Jun., and Sidney Rigdon.

5 And I give unto them a commandment that they shall go forth for a little season, and it shall be given by the power of the Spirit when they shall return.

6 And ye shall go forth in the power of my Spirit, preaching my gospel, two by two, in my name, lifting up your voices as with the sound of a trump, declaring my word like unto angels of God.

7 And ye shall go forth baptizing with water, saying: Repent ye, repent ye, for the kingdom of heaven is at hand.

8 And from this place ye shall go forth into the regions westward; and inasmuch as ye shall find them that will receive you ye shall build up my church in every region—

9 Until the time shall come when it shall be revealed unto you from on high, when the city of the New Jerusalem shall be prepared, that ye may be gathered in one, that ye may be my people and I will be your God.

10 And again, I say unto you, that my servant Edward Partridge shall stand in the office whereunto I have appointed him. And it shall come to pass, that if he transgress another shall be appointed in his stead. Even so. Amen.

Verses 1–10 of the revelation came in answer to the Saints' questions about the nature of the gathering. Specifically, they had asked if Church members should gather to only one location or remain in separate settlements. The Lord instructs the elders to go forth into the "regions westward" and "build up my church in every region" (verse 8). For the first time in the Doctrine and Covenants, the Lord makes mention of the city of the New Jerusalem. The New Jerusalem, also called Zion, is described in the Book of Mormon as "a new Jerusalem which shall be built up upon this land, unto the remnant of the seed of Joseph" (Ether 12:6). In a revelation given only a few months prior, the Lord gave the first hint of the city's location when He revealed that the city would be built "on the borders by the Lamanites" (Doctrine and Covenants 28:9), or near what was then the boundary of the United States.

Before Joseph Smith arrived in Ohio, he was engaged in the translation of the book of Genesis, which revealed further details about the New Jerusalem. In a prophecy given to the ancient prophet Enoch, the Lord promised that in the latter days, He would send forth righteousness and truth "to gather out mine elect from the four quarters of the earth, unto a place which I shall prepare, an Holy City, that my people may gird up their loins, and be looking forth for the time of my coming; for there shall be my tabernacle, and it shall be called Zion, a New Jerusalem" (Moses 7:62).

Even as Joseph Smith was in Ohio receiving the Law of the Church, Oliver Cowdery was continuing his journey westward toward the US border, eventually arriving in Missouri. A few months after Oliver's arrival, Joseph Smith and several elders of the Church were called upon to travel to Missouri, where the location of the New Jerusalem was designated as Independence, Missouri (see Doctrine and Covenants 57:2).

> 11 Again I say unto you, that it shall not be given to any one to go forth to preach my gospel, or to build up my church, except he be ordained by some one who has authority, and it is known to the church that he has authority and has been regularly ordained by the heads of the church.
>
> 12 And again, the elders, priests and teachers of this church shall teach the principles of my gospel, which are in the Bible and the Book of Mormon, in the which is the fulness of the gospel.
>
> 13 And they shall observe the covenants and church articles to do them, and these shall be their teachings, as they shall be directed by the Spirit.
>
> 14 And the Spirit shall be given unto you by the prayer of faith; and if ye receive not the Spirit ye shall not teach.
>
> 15 And all this ye shall observe to do as I have commanded concerning your teaching, until the fulness of my scriptures is given.
>
> 16 And as ye shall lift up your voices by the Comforter, ye shall speak and prophesy as seemeth me good;
>
> 17 For, behold, the Comforter knoweth all things, and beareth record of the Father and of the Son.

The second part of the Law came in answer to the question of what is "the law regulating the Church in her present situation until the time of her gathering." It discusses nine different topics and consists of Doctrine and Covenants 42:11–69.

The first part of the law could be designated as the law of teaching and authority. The Lord specifies that those who teach and preach in the Church must be ordained by one who has authority (see verse 11). The use of *ordained* here is analogous to the way "set apart" is used in the Church today, and it applied to both men and women who were called to teach (see Doctrine and Covenants 25:7). The men and women called to teach in the Church were expected to draw their instruction primarily from the scriptural canon, which at the time consisted of the Bible and the Book of Mormon.

The Lord also instructs that teachings shall be drawn from the articles and covenants; these are the revelations He was giving to the latter-day prophets of the Church. Parts of these revelations would eventually join the canon as the Doctrine and Covenants and the Pearl of Great Price.

These instructions remain as vital to the Church today as they were in the period of the early Restoration. Remembering them will benefit both members of the Church and our larger society. Elder D. Todd Christofferson warned, "Today the Bible and other scripture are readily at hand, yet there is a growing scriptural illiteracy because people will not open the books." Explaining the importance of the scriptural canon, he added, "Scripture tutors us in principles and moral values essential to maintaining civil society, including integrity, responsibility, selflessness, fidelity, and charity. In scripture, we find vivid portrayals of the blessings that come from honoring true principles, as well as the tragedies that befall when individuals and civilizations discard them. Where scriptural truths are ignored or abandoned, the essential moral core of society disintegrates and decay is close behind. In time, nothing is left to sustain the institutions that sustain society."[11]

> 18 And now, behold, I speak unto the church. Thou shalt not kill; and he that kills shall not have forgiveness in this world, nor in the world to come.
>
> 19 And again, I say, thou shalt not kill; but he that killeth shall die.
>
> 20 Thou shalt not steal; and he that stealeth and will not repent shall be cast out.
>
> 21 Thou shalt not lie; he that lieth and will not repent shall be cast out.
>
> 22 Thou shalt love thy wife with all thy heart, and shalt cleave unto her and none else.
>
> 23 And he that looketh upon a woman to lust after her shall deny the faith, and shall not have the Spirit; and if he repents not he shall be cast out.
>
> 24 Thou shalt not commit adultery; and he that committeth adultery, and repenteth not, shall be cast out.
>
> 25 But he that has committed adultery and repents with all his heart, and forsaketh it, and doeth it no more, thou shalt forgive;

26 But if he doeth it again, he shall not be forgiven, but shall be cast out.

27 Thou shalt not speak evil of thy neighbor, nor do him any harm.

28 Thou knowest my laws concerning these things are given in my scriptures; he that sinneth and repenteth not shall be cast out.

29 If thou lovest me thou shalt serve me and keep all my commandments.

This section of the Law gives commandments to the Church. The commandments here are closely aligned with the Ten Commandments presented to the Israelites in Exodus 20. At the same time, the commandments given in Doctrine and Covenants 42 are a renewal of the law, declared again in the latter days. The Ten Commandments were part of a preparatory law delivered by Moses and later fulfilled by Jesus Christ (see Matthew 5:21–22, 27–28; 3 Nephi 15:2–9; Romans 13:8–10). Though the Ten Commandments were part of the preparatory law, the principles the commandments were based on are eternal, and they were renewed through this revelation to Joseph Smith. The commandments given here also expound and provide further explanation on how the law works.

For instance, in these verses the Lord declares that "he that kills shall not have forgiveness in this world, nor in the world to come" (verse 18). Using other scriptures for a larger context, the word *killing* as used here does not refer to self-defense, legal executions, or taking lives in the course of military service. Rather, it refers to "the shedding of innocent blood" (Alma 39:5). Murderers cannot be saved from the pains of their suffering until the Resurrection. The scriptures speak of murder as an *unforgivable* sin that may be pardoned. The *unpardonable* sin—denial of the Holy Ghost—is later defined clearly in Doctrine and Covenants 76:32–35. Murderers can be pardoned through the Atonement of Jesus Christ once they have answered the full demands of justice.

Speaking on this subject, the Prophet Joseph Smith taught, "A murderer, for instance, one that sheds innocent blood, cannot have forgiveness. David sought repentance at the hand of God carefully, with tears for the murder of Uriah, but he could only get it through hell; he got a promise that his soul should not be left in hell. . . . This is the case with murderers."[12] At a different time, the Prophet added, "If the ministers of religion had a proper understanding of the doctrine of eternal judgment, they would not be found attending the man who had forfeited his life to the injured laws of his country by shedding innocent blood; for such characters cannot be forgiven, until they have paid the last farthing. The prayers of all the ministers in the world could never close the gates of hell against a murderer."[13]

> 30 And behold, thou wilt remember the poor, and consecrate of
> thy properties for their support that which thou hast to impart
> unto them, with a covenant and a deed which cannot be broken.

Doctrine and Covenants 42:30–42 constitute the first instructions given in this dispensation concerning the law of consecration. In some ways, consecration began in the Church as a grassroots effort. When Joseph Smith arrived in Kirtland, he found new converts already attempting to implement a form of communal living. One contemporary observer outside of the Church noted, "Isaac Morley had contended that in order to restore the ancient order of things in the Church of Christ, it was necessary that there should be a community of goods among the brethren; and accordingly a number of them removed to his house and farm, and built houses and worked and lived together, and composed what is here called the 'Big Family,' which at this time consisted of 50 or 60, old and young."[14]

The "family" and other new converts in Kirtland launched these efforts out of a sincere desire to adhere to the scriptures, but a lack of specific direction caused problems to emerge almost immediately. Church Historian John Whitmer recorded, "The disciples had all things in common, and were going to destruction very fast as to temporal things. . . . Therefore they would take each other's clothes and other property and use it without leave, which brought on confusion."[15] When Joseph Smith arrived in Kirtland in February 1831, a number of members clamored to know the Lord's will concerning the practice of communal living. It is likely in response to these requests that the Lord provided these instructions, which revealed the foundational principles of consecration.

The most basic approach to understanding consecration is to examine the meaning of the word itself and how it was used in the time of the early Restoration. An 1828 dictionary defined *consecration* as "the act or ceremony of separating from a common to a sacred use." The entry further adds, "Consecration does not make a person or a thing *holy*, but declares it to be *sacred*, that is, devoted to God or to divine service."[16] This is a broad definition of the term but is perhaps the most useful in comprehending the wide range of practical applications of the law of consecration. Throughout the history of the Church, the terms *law of consecration* and *united order* both refer to attempts to devote the Church's temporal and spiritual resources to assisting the poor and needy. In practice, these attempts took many forms. While for the early Saints in Kirtland or Nauvoo the law of consecration was markedly different than today's practice, Saints in all ages make a covenant to offer their resources to the sacred use of God's kingdom.[17]

> 31 And inasmuch as ye impart of your substance unto the poor, ye will do it unto me; and they shall be laid before the bishop of my church and his counselors, two of the elders, or high priests, such as he shall appoint or has appointed and set apart for that purpose.

> 32 And it shall come to pass, that after they are laid before the bishop of my church, and after that he has received these testimonies concerning the consecration of the properties of my church, that they cannot be taken from the church, agreeable to my commandments, every man shall be made accountable unto me, a steward over his own property, or that which he has received by consecration, as much as is sufficient for himself and family.

> 33 And again, if there shall be properties in the hands of the church, or any individuals of it, more than is necessary for their support after this first consecration, which is a residue to be consecrated unto the bishop, it shall be kept to administer to those who have not, from time to time, that every man who has need may be amply supplied and receive according to his wants.

The Lord's instructions for consecration begin, "Behold thou shalt consecrate *all* thy properties that which thou hast unto me with a covenant and deed which cannot be broken and they shall be laid before the Bishop of my church."[18] The inclusion of the word *all* leads the reader to believe that every single item of an individual's property must be turned over to priesthood leaders. The Prophet and his associates clarified this wording in later revisions of the revelation, most significantly in the 1835 edition of the Doctrine and Covenants, which changed the passage to instruct the Saints to "consecrate *of* thy properties." The change in wording first appeared in *The Evening and the Morning Star* in July 1832. It has remained consistent in every published version of the revelation down to the present day.[19] Consecration of properties denotes a sacrifice of resources to benefit the poor but leads away from a completely communal interpretation of the law, which would require all property to be given to the Church.

This clarification is further supported by the next item of instruction the Lord provides in the revelation: directives for the priesthood leaders administering the law. Priesthood leaders must provide a stewardship that allows participants to be stewards over their "own property, or that which he has received by consecration, as much as is sufficient for himself and family" (verse 32). Additional revelations confirmed that while unity was a primary goal of the law, equality was a relative term. After receiving the Lord's counsel in the earliest copies of the revelation, Church leaders provided stewardships not only according to the needs and wants of an individual or family.

When the revelation was first published in the 1835 edition of the Doctrine and Covenants, the Prophet was inspired to add the phrase "according to his circumstances."[20] He also added provisions that clarified that if an individual chose to no longer participate in the law, they retained their stewardship but could not reclaim what was consecrated (see Doctrine and Covenants 42:37; 51:5). Private ownership of property and voluntary participation served as key principles of the law from the start. Joseph Smith and other Church leaders wrote in an 1833 letter, "Every man must be his own judge how much he should receive and how much he should suffer to remain in the hands of the Bishop. . . . The matter of consecration must be done by mutual consent of both parties."[21]

> 34 Therefore, the residue shall be kept in my storehouse, to administer to the poor and the needy, as shall be appointed by the high council of the church, and the bishop and his council;
>
> 35 And for the purpose of purchasing lands for the public benefit of the church, and building houses of worship, and building up of the New Jerusalem which is hereafter to be revealed—
>
> 36 That my covenant people may be gathered in one in that day when I shall come to my temple. And this I do for the salvation of my people.
>
> 37 And it shall come to pass, that he that sinneth and repenteth not shall be cast out of the church, and shall not receive again

that which he has consecrated unto the poor and the needy of my church, or in other words, unto me—

38 For inasmuch as ye do it unto the least of these, ye do it unto me.

Another key component of the law consisted of the use of surpluses to provide for "a storehouse, to administer to the poor and the needy" and also for purchasing land, "building houses of worship," and "building up of the New Jerusalem" (verses 34–35). Other revelations instruct that the storehouse be directed under the hands of a bishop or Church agents "appointed by the voice of the church" (Doctrine and Covenants 51:12). The storehouse was "common property of the whole church," with every individual improving on their "talents"—a word denoting both the New Testament currency and the gifts and abilities given by the Lord (see Doctrine and Covenants 82:18). An undergirding motivation for the law was the need for the Saints to sacrifice in order to build a faithful community with the New Jerusalem on their spiritual horizons.[22]

While today the Church operates a number of bishops' storehouses around the world that are intended to help provide for the poor and needy, the resources available through consecration are much larger than can be contained in a few buildings. President Thomas S. Monson taught, "The Lord's storehouse includes the time, talents, skills, compassion, consecrated material, and financial means of faithful Church members. These resources are available to the bishop in assisting those in need."[23]

39 For it shall come to pass, that which I spake by the mouths of my prophets shall be fulfilled; for I will consecrate of the riches of those who embrace my gospel among the Gentiles unto the poor of my people who are of the house of Israel.

40 And again, thou shalt not be proud in thy heart; let all thy garments be plain, and their beauty the beauty of the work of thine own hands;

41 And let all things be done in cleanliness before me.

42 Thou shalt not be idle; for he that is idle shall not eat the bread nor wear the garments of the laborer.

The Lord commanded the Saints to avoid pride, to be modest in dress, and to be clean (see verses 40–41). The revelation also commanded the

Saints to avoid idleness, warning that "he that is idle shall not eat the bread nor wear the garments of the laborer" (verse 42). By no means do these statements represent a comprehensive treatment of all of the Lord's commandments to the early Saints concerning consecration. Our aim here is simply to provide a summary of the key principles of the law.

These principles have remained consistent throughout the history of the Church. Since 1831 successive generations of Church leadership have applied them in a wide variety of circumstances. This adaptation is logical given the varied situations in which the Saints have found themselves, from times when the entire Church membership consisted of a handful of people to today when millions of Saints live in diverse places around the globe. But in all circumstances, the basic concepts and principles the Lord revealed in 1831 remain the same. President J. Reuben Clark succinctly captured the essence of consecration when he taught, "The basic principle of all the revelations on [the law of consecration] is that everything we have belongs to the Lord; therefore, the Lord may call upon us for any and all of the property which we have, because it belongs to him. This, I repeat, is the basic principle."[24]

43 And whosoever among you are sick, and have not faith to be healed, but believe, shall be nourished with all tenderness, with herbs and mild food, and that not by the hand of an enemy.

44 And the elders of the church, two or more, shall be called, and shall pray for and lay their hands upon them in my name; and if they die they shall die unto me, and if they live they shall live unto me.

45 Thou shalt live together in love, insomuch that thou shalt weep for the loss of them that die, and more especially for those that have not hope of a glorious resurrection.

46 And it shall come to pass that those that die in me shall not taste of death, for it shall be sweet unto them;

47 And they that die not in me, wo unto them, for their death is bitter.

48 And again, it shall come to pass that he that hath faith in me to be healed, and is not appointed unto death, shall be healed.

49 He who hath faith to see shall see.

50 He who hath faith to hear shall hear.

51 The lame who hath faith to leap shall leap.

52 And they who have not faith to do these things, but believe in me, have power to become my sons; and inasmuch as they break not my laws thou shalt bear their infirmities.

Verses 43–52 could be titled the Law of Sickness and Healing. Miracles of healing are often included in the scriptures as signs manifest among the followers of Jesus Christ (see Matthew 10:1; 3 Nephi 17:9). More complicated are situations in which faith is manifest and people are not healed. The Lord specifies that those with faith can be healed, as long as they are not "appointed unto death" (verse 48). There are instances in which the worthiness and faith of all involved are sufficient, but it is simply time for the person to move on to the next life.

President Dieter F. Uchtdorf counseled concerning the power and limits of faith: "Faith is powerful, and often it does result in miracles. But no matter how much faith we have, there are two things faith cannot do. For one, it cannot violate another person's agency. . . . God will invite, persuade. God will reach out tirelessly with love and inspiration and encouragement. But God will never compel—that would undermine His great plan for our eternal growth." Pertaining to those who may be appointed to die, he further taught, "The second thing faith cannot do is force our will upon God. We cannot force God to comply with our desires—no matter how right we think we are or how sincerely we pray."[25]

53 Thou shalt stand in the place of thy stewardship.

54 Thou shalt not take thy brother's garment; thou shalt pay for that which thou shalt receive of thy brother.

55 And if thou obtainest more than that which would be for thy support, thou shalt give it into my storehouse, that all things may be done according to that which I have said.

56 Thou shalt ask, and my scriptures shall be given as I have appointed, and they shall be preserved in safety;

57 And it is expedient that thou shouldst hold thy peace concerning them, and not teach them until ye have received them in full.

58 And I give unto you a commandment that then ye shall teach them unto all men; for they shall be taught unto all nations, kindreds, tongues and people.

59 Thou shalt take the things which thou hast received, which have been given unto thee in my scriptures for a law, to be my law to govern my church;

60 And he that doeth according to these things shall be saved, and he that doeth them not shall be damned if he so continue.

Do Latter-day Saints still live the law of consecration? Commitment to the law remains one of the covenants made as part of the temple ordinances. While the law of tithing was revealed in 1838 and became an important element of Church practice, it did not replace or cause a repeal of the law of consecration. Consecration was always a more holistic law encompassing all areas of life, not just finance. President Hinckley said bluntly, "The law of sacrifice and the law of consecration were not done away with and are still in effect."[26]

Though the titles and initiatives of consecration have changed, the principles remain consistent. President Henry B. Eyring taught:

[The Lord] has invited His children to consecrate their time, their means, and themselves to join with Him in serving others. His way of helping has at times been called living the law of consecration. In another period His way was called the united order. In our time it is called the Church welfare program. The names and the details of operation are changed to fit the needs and conditions of people. But always the Lord's way to help those in temporal need requires people who out of love have consecrated themselves and what they have to God and to His work.[27]

One illustration of the power and limits of faith in matters of healing is found in Jesse Knight's story. Jesse Knight was the scion of one of the most famous families in Church history, the son of Newel and Lydia Knight, who were early stalwarts in the Church. Despite his illustrious heritage, as a young man living in the Utah Territory, Jesse found himself estranged from the Church. He was uninterested in actively serving in it, and he was seemingly destined to lead a life outside the faith. Jesse's religious awakening came when his youngest daughter, Jennie, became deathly ill. The water on Jesse's ranch had been contaminated by a dead rat. Jennie, who was only two years old, ran such a high fever that doctors told the Knights she would soon pass away.

When his wife, Amanda, decided to call the local elders from the Church, Jesse stopped her, saying, "No, it would be hypocritical, now that the doctors have given her up, for me to resort to such a thing," adding, "I have no faith in the Church." Amanda replied, "I have, and think my feelings should have consideration at such a serious moment." Jesse backed down and the elders soon arrived. After they gave Jennie a blessing, she immediately rose up from her bed and commented on the flowers placed in the window.

Jennie made a full recovery, but another of the Knights' children, eighteen-year-old Minnie, soon became very ill. Minnie told her parents that when Jennie became ill, she had prayed and asked God to take *her* life and spare her sister's. She believed she would die thirty days from the time she became sick and, true to her prompting, passed away thirty days later. She was the only child of the Knights who had been baptized.

Jesse was twisted in knots by the miraculous healing of one of his daughters followed so soon by the loss of another. He remembered that when Minnie was a baby, she had become deathly ill with diphtheria. At the time, Jesse had promised God that if his daughter was spared, he would return to Church and serve faithfully. She was healed at that time, but in the following years he did not keep his promise. Reflecting on her death, he wrote, "How keenly I felt the justice of her being taken from us!" He pleaded with God for forgiveness, later writing, "My prayer was answered and I received a testimony." Jesse was left to acknowledge that the faith of Amanda to call the elders, and the specific prayer of faith offered by Minnie, produced a desirable outcome. Yet Minnie, seemingly appointed to death, was not saved. The entire family received a difficult lesson on the nature of faith and healing. From that time forward, Jesse lived as a committed Latter-day Saint, as did his family. Another of his daughters, Inez, even became one of the Church's first two female missionaries.[28]

> 61 If thou shalt ask, thou shalt receive revelation upon revelation, knowledge upon knowledge, that thou mayest know the mysteries and peaceable things—that which bringeth joy, that which bringeth life eternal.

> 62 Thou shalt ask, and it shall be revealed unto you in mine own due time where the New Jerusalem shall be built.

63 And behold, it shall come to pass that my servants shall be sent forth to the east and to the west, to the north and to the south.

64 And even now, let him that goeth to the east teach them that shall be converted to flee to the west, and this in consequence of that which is coming on the earth, and of secret combinations.

65 Behold, thou shalt observe all these things, and great shall be thy reward; for unto you it is given to know the mysteries of the kingdom, but unto the world it is not given to know them.

66 Ye shall observe the laws which ye have received and be faithful.

67 And ye shall hereafter receive church covenants, such as shall be sufficient to establish you, both here and in the New Jerusalem.

68 Therefore, he that lacketh wisdom, let him ask of me, and I will give him liberally and upbraid him not.

69 Lift up your hearts and rejoice, for unto you the kingdom, or in other words, the keys of the church have been given. Even so. Amen.

The Lord promises Joseph and the Saints further revelation that they may know the "mysteries and peaceable things" of the kingdom (verse 61). He also promises to make covenants that will allow the Saints to be established in Ohio and in the New Jerusalem. For the next seven years, the Church was administered through two primary centers: Kirtland, Ohio, and different points in Missouri. During this time the majority of the revelations found in the Doctrine and Covenants were received; these revelations comprise sections 41 through 123. As the Lord promised, these revelations unfolded the basic mysteries and knowledge necessary to operate the Church. More revelations came later during the Nauvoo period and during the leadership of the subsequent presidents of the Church, but the Ohio and Missouri revelations provide the foundation upon which the later Church was built.

Among the most vital of these revelations was the restoration of priesthood keys given to restore the Church and kingdom of God, which are here defined as the same thing (see verse 69). Joseph Smith taught that "the fundamental principles, government, and doctrine of the church are vested in the keys of the kingdom."[29]

> 70 The priests and teachers shall have their stewardships, even as the members.
>
> 71 And the elders or high priests who are appointed to assist the bishop as counselors in all things, are to have their families supported out of the property which is consecrated to the bishop, for the good of the poor, and for other purposes, as before mentioned;
>
> 72 Or they are to receive a just remuneration for all their services, either a stewardship or otherwise, as may be thought best or decided by the counselors and bishop.
>
> 73 And the bishop, also, shall receive his support, or a just remuneration for all his services in the church.

This passage specifies that bishops would receive assistance from counselors called from among the members of the Church. While Bishop Partridge and his counselors were to be supported through consecration, today most Church officers receive no paid compensation for their labor. While there have been differences in the way the Church has been administered over time, throughout most of its history the Church has not had a professional ministry. These verses do open the door for a small number of employees to receive payment from the Church, but these employees hold no ecclesiastical position based on their employment.

It is true that those called to full-time service in the Church, such as the General Officers, receive a stipend for support. However, this stipend comes from the private investments of the Church and not from the offerings of members. President Hinckley explained, "The living allowances given the General Authorities, which are very modest in comparison with executive compensation in industry and the professions, come from this business income and not from the tithing of the people."[30] Likewise, the *Encyclopedia of Mormonism*, published in cooperation with the Church, clarifies that "unlike local leaders, who maintain their normal vocations while serving in Church assignments, General Authorities set aside their careers to devote their full time to the ministry of their office. The living allowance given General Authorities rarely if ever equals the earnings they sacrifice to serve full-time in the Church."[31]

In a statement made about bishoprics, but which applies equally to all who serve in the Church, President Boyd K. Packer taught, "Neither the bishop nor his counselors are paid for what they do. They too pay their tithes and offerings, and they devote endless hours to their calling. They are paid only in blessings, as are those who serve with them."[32]

74 Behold, verily I say unto you, that whatever persons among you, having put away their companions for the cause of fornication, or in other words, if they shall testify before you in all lowliness of heart that this is the case, ye shall not cast them out from among you;

75 But if ye shall find that any persons have left their companions for the sake of adultery, and they themselves are the offenders, and their companions are living, they shall be cast out from among you.

76 And again, I say unto you, that ye shall be watchful and careful, with all inquiry, that ye receive none such among you if they are married;

77 And if they are not married, they shall repent of all their sins or ye shall not receive them.

78 And again, every person who belongeth to this church of Christ, shall observe to keep all the commandments and covenants of the church.

79 And it shall come to pass, that if any persons among you shall kill they shall be delivered up and dealt with according to the laws of the land; for remember that he hath no forgiveness; and it shall be proved according to the laws of the land.

80 And if any man or woman shall commit adultery, he or she shall be tried before two elders of the church, or more, and every word shall be established against him or her by two witnesses of the church, and not of the enemy; but if there are more than two witnesses it is better.

81 But he or she shall be condemned by the mouth of two witnesses; and the elders shall lay the case before the church, and the church shall lift up their hands against him or her, that they may be dealt with according to the law of God.

82 And if it can be, it is necessary that the bishop be present also.

83 And thus ye shall do in all cases which shall come before you.

84 And if a man or woman shall rob, he or she shall be delivered up unto the law of the land.

85 And if he or she shall steal, he or she shall be delivered up unto the law of the land.

86 And if he or she shall lie, he or she shall be delivered up unto the law of the land.

87 And if he or she do any manner of iniquity, he or she shall be delivered up unto the law, even that of God.

88 And if thy brother or sister offend thee, thou shalt take him or her between him or her and thee alone; and if he or she confess thou shalt be reconciled.

89 And if he or she confess not thou shalt deliver him or her up unto the church, not to the members, but to the elders. And it shall be done in a meeting, and that not before the world.

90 And if thy brother or sister offend many, he or she shall be chastened before many.

91 And if any one offend openly, he or she shall be rebuked openly, that he or she may be ashamed. And if he or she confess not, he or she shall be delivered up unto the law of God.

92 If any shall offend in secret, he or she shall be rebuked in secret, that he or she may have opportunity to confess in secret to him or her whom he or she has offended, and to God, that the church may not speak reproachfully of him or her.

93 And thus shall ye conduct in all things.

The final part of the revelation, received a few weeks later on February 23, 1831, deals with how various offenses among Church members should be handled. Offenses such as stealing and lying are delivered to the civil authorities of the land. Other offenses, such as immorality, improper behavior, and apostasy, constitute an offense against the laws of the Church and are handled by Church leaders. President James E. Faust explained:

Those who have keys, which include the judicial or disciplinary authority, have the responsibility for keeping the Church cleansed from all iniquity (see Doctrine and Covenants 20:54; Doctrine and Covenants 43:11). Bishops, stake presidents, mission presidents, and others who have the responsibility of keeping the Church pure must perform this labor in a spirit of love and kindness. It should not be done in a spirit of punishment, but rather of helping. However, it is of no kindness to a brother or sister in transgression for their presiding officers to look the other way.[33]

Doctrine and Covenants 42 includes the first introduction of Church membership councils designed to assist individuals who have been involved in the most serious sins. These meetings have at varying times gone by different names, but they have always had the same basic purpose. The 2020 Church handbook explains, "Most repentance takes place between an individual, God, and those who have been affected by a person's sins. However, sometimes a bishop or stake president needs to help Church members in their efforts to repent. . . . When assisting members with repentance, bishops and stake presidents are loving and caring. They follow the example of the Savior, who lifted individuals and helped them turn away from sin and turn toward God (see Matthew 9:10–13; John 8:3–11)."[34]

End Notes

1. Revelation, 9 February 1831 [D&C 42:1–72], 1, josephsmithpapers.org.
2. Letter to Martin Harris, 22 February 1831, 1, josephsmithpapers.org.
3. Revelation Book 1, 62, josephsmithpapers.org.
4. Revelation, 9 February 1831, as Recorded in Gilbert, Notebook [D&C 42:1–72], 22, josephsmithpapers.org.
5. Revelation Book 1, 66–67, josephsmithpapers.org.
6. Revelation, 23 February 1831 [D&C 42:74–93], 6, josephsmithpapers.org.
7. Revelation Book 1, 8, josephsmithpapers.org.
8. See Revelation, 23 February 1831 [D&C 42:74–93], josephsmithpapers.org.
9. John Whitmer, History, 1831–circa 1847, 11, footnote 25, josephsmithpapers.org.
10. *General Handbook: Serving in The Church of Jesus Christ of Latter-day Saints*, 1.2.2, Gospel Library. See also "Historical Introduction," Revelation, 9 February 1831 [D&C 42:1–72]; "Historical Introduction," Revelation, 23 February 1831 [D&C 42:74–93], josephsmithpapers.org.
11. D. Todd Christofferson, "The Blessings of Scripture," *Ensign* or *Liahona*, May 2010, 34.
12. Joseph Smith, in History, 1838–1856, volume E-1 [1 July 1843–30 April 1844], 1922, josephsmithpapers.org.
13. Discourse, 16 May 1841, as Reported by *Times and Seasons*, 430, josephsmithpapers.org.
14. Josiah Jones, "History of the Mormonites," *The Evangelist* 9 (1 June 1831): 132.
15. John Whitmer, History, 1831–circa 1847, 11, josephsmithpapers.org.
16. *An American Dictionary of the English Language*, s.v. "consecration," accessed February 13, 2024, https://webstersdictionary1828.com/Dictionary/consecration.
17. See Casey Paul Griffiths, "A Covenant and a Deed Which Cannot Be Broken," in *Foundations Of The Restoration: Fulfillment Of Covenant Purposes* (Provo, UT: Religious Studies Center, 2016).
18. Revelation, 9 February 1831 [D&C 42:1–72], 3, josephsmithpapers.org.
19. See Doctrine and Covenants, 1835, 122, josephsmithpapers.org.
20. Doctrine and Covenants, 1835, 122, josephsmithpapers.org.
21. Letter to Church leaders in Jackson County, Missouri, 25 June 1833, 2, josephsmithpapers.org.
22. See Craig James Ostler, "Consecration," in *Doctrine and Covenants Reference Companion* (Salt Lake City, UT: Deseret Book, 2015), 108.
23. Thomas S. Monson, "Guiding Principles of Personal and Family Welfare," *Ensign*, Sept. 1986, 5.
24. J. Reuben Clark, in Conference Report, Oct. 1942, 55.

25. Dieter F. Uchtdorf, "Fourth Floor, Last Door," *Ensign* or *Liahona*, Nov. 2016, 16–17.

26. *Teachings of Presidents of the Church: Gordon B. Hinckley* (1997), 639.

27. Henry B. Eyring, "Opportunities to Do Good," *Ensign* or *Liahona*, May 2011, 22.

28. See J. Michael Hunter, "Jesse Knight and His Humbug Mine," *Pioneer* 51, no. 2 (2004): 9.

29. Joseph Smith, in History, 1838–1856, volume A-1 [23 December 1805–30 August 1834], 285, josephsmithpapers.org.

30. Gordon B. Hinckley, "Questions and Answers," *Ensign*, Nov. 1985, 50.

31. Marvin K. Gardner, "General Authorities," *Encyclopedia of Mormonism* (New York: Macmillan Publishing Company, 1992).

32. Boyd K. Packer, "The Bishop and His Counselors," *Ensign*, May 1999, 57.

33. James E. Faust, "Keeping Covenants and Honoring the Priesthood," *Ensign*, Nov. 1993, 37.

34. *General Handbook: Serving in The Church of Jesus Christ of Latter-day Saints*, 32.0, Gospel Library.

Doctrine and Covenants Section 43

Come In at the Gate

Historical Context

JOSEPH SMITH RECEIVED THE REVELATION IN SECTION 43 SHORTLY AFTER his arrival in Ohio. The need for guidance seems to have arisen from a challenge to Joseph's role as revelator for the entire Church. Similar to the controversy a few months earlier involving Hiram Page and his seer stone (see Doctrine and Covenants 28), the question arose over who has the right to receive revelation on behalf of the Church. Church Historian John Whitmer later wrote of the incident, "About these days there was a woman by the name of Hubble who professed to be a prophetess of the Lord, and professed to have many revelations and knew that the Book of Mormon was true; and that she should become a teacher in the Church of Christ. She appeared very sanctimonious and deceived some, who were not able to detect her in her hypocrisy: others however had a spirit of discernment and her follies and abominations were made manifest. The Lord gave Revelation that the saints might not be deceived."[1]

We do not know the precise identity of the woman involved in the controversy. Whitmer may have been referencing Laura Fuller Hubble, the older sister of Edson Fuller, a man who had joined the Church and been ordained an elder. Another possibility is that he was referring to Louisa Hubbell, a convert from the Disciples of Christ who left the Church and rejoined her prior faith a few months after the revelation was received.[2] Regardless of the identity of the prophetess in question, the incident represented a larger issue among the Saints in Kirtland. The issue centered around their confusion about spiritual manifestations and the nature of personal and ecclesiastical forms of revelation. Joseph Smith saw the need to establish the order of the Church among the new converts in Kirtland. Reflecting on the experience, he later wrote, "A woman came with great pretensions to revealing commandments, laws and other curious matters; and, as every person, (almost) has advocates for both theory and practice, in the various notions and projects of the age, it became necessary to inquire of the Lord."[3]

The dispute was only one of the struggles that the new converts in Kirtland were experiencing. John Whitmer later noted:

> The enemy of all righteous had got hold of some of those who professed to be his followers, because they had not sufficient knowledge to detect him in all his devices. He took a notion to blind their minds of some of the weaker ones, and made them think that an angel of God appeared to them, and showed them writings on the outside cover of the Bible, and on parchment, which flew through the air, and on the back of their hands, and many such foolish and vain things, others lost their strength, and some slid on the floor, and such like maneuvers, which proved greatly to the injury of the cause.[4]

During this time Joseph received several revelations that were intended to quell the controversies among the Saints and to create a house of order for the new converts. This revelation, and several others given soon after (see Doctrine and Covenants 46, 50, 52), in particular show the gentle reasoning the Lord used to help His disciples find their way amid the challenges they faced. This was a time of stretching and growth for the Saints. While noting the challenges among them, John Whitmer also recognized the growing progress of the work, recording, "The Lord also worked and many embraced the work, and the honest in heart stood firm and immovable."[5]

$\mathcal{V}$erse-by-$\mathcal{V}$erse $\mathcal{C}$ommentary

1 O hearken, ye elders of my church, and give ear to the words which I shall speak unto you.

2 For behold, verily, verily, I say unto you, that ye have received a commandment for a law unto my church, through him whom I have appointed unto you to receive commandments and revelations from my hand.

3 And this ye shall know assuredly—that there is none other appointed unto you to receive commandments and revelations until he be taken, if he abide in me.

4 But verily, verily, I say unto you, that none else shall be appointed unto this gift except it be through him; for if it be taken from him he shall not have power except to appoint another in his stead.

5 And this shall be a law unto you, that ye receive not the teachings of any that shall come before you as revelations or commandments;

6 And this I give unto you that you may not be deceived, that you may know they are not of me.

7 For verily I say unto you, that he that is ordained of me shall come in at the gate and be ordained as I have told you before, to teach those revelations which you have received and shall receive through him whom I have appointed.

In a Church where every member has the promise of revelation, there must be rules and standards about how this guidance is received. Authoritative revelation must come within the boundaries of stewardship, and once again the Lord outlines these principles, this time for the new converts of the Church in Ohio.

In 1833 a situation similar to the controversy with "Mrs. Hubble" arose when John S. Carter, an elder of the Church in the eastern United States, wrote to Joseph Smith about disunity among the Saints in his area. He wondered specifically about a woman named Jane McManagal Sherwood, a convert in Benson, Vermont, who claimed she had received "visions of the Lord."[6] In response to this situation, Joseph Smith replied in a letter. The

Prophet instructed, "It is contrary to the economy of God for any member of the Church or anyone to receive instruction for those in authority higher than themselves, therefore you will see the impropriety of giving heed to them, but if any have a vision or a visitation from an heavenly messenger it must be for their own benefit and instruction, for the fundamental principles, government, and doctrine of the church is invested in the keys of the kingdom."[7]

As it was in the days of Joseph Smith, so it is in our time. Every worthy member of the Church is entitled to receive revelation, but it must come within the proper stewardship and from those with the appropriate authority.

> 8 And now, behold, I give unto you a commandment, that when ye are assembled together ye shall instruct and edify each other, that ye may know how to act and direct my church, how to act upon the points of my law and commandments, which I have given.
>
> 9 And thus ye shall become instructed in the law of my church, and be sanctified by that which ye have received, and ye shall bind yourselves to act in all holiness before me—
>
> 10 That inasmuch as ye do this, glory shall be added to the kingdom which ye have received. Inasmuch as ye do it not, it shall be taken, even that which ye have received.
>
> 11 Purge ye out the iniquity which is among you; sanctify yourselves before me;
>
> 12 And if ye desire the glories of the kingdom, appoint ye my servant Joseph Smith, Jun., and uphold him before me by the prayer of faith.
>
> 13 And again, I say unto you, that if ye desire the mysteries of the kingdom, provide for him food and raiment, and whatsoever thing he needeth to accomplish the work wherewith I have commanded him;
>
> 14 And if ye do it not he shall remain unto them that have received him, that I may reserve unto myself a pure people before me.

The Book of Mormon provides specific details about how the ancient Saints worshipped together: "The church did meet together oft, to fast and to pray, and to speak one with another concerning the welfare of their souls. And they did meet together oft to partake of bread and wine, in remembrance of the Lord Jesus" (Moroni 6:5–6). Likewise, in these verses the Lord commands the Church to edify and instruct each other during the time they are assembled together.

While a spiritual connection to God is cultivated on an individual level, there are also great advantages to meeting regularly with other believers. Elder Christofferson taught, "In the Church we not only learn divine doctrine; we also experience its application. As the body of Christ, the members of the Church minister to one another in the reality of day-to-day life. All of us are imperfect; we may offend and be offended. We often test one another with our personal idiosyncrasies. In the body of Christ, we have to go beyond concepts and exalted words and have a real 'hands-on' experience as we learn to 'live together in love.'"[8]

While our personal studies and devotion draw us closer to God, being involved in the communities formed by Church members gives us great opportunities to act on the principles we are taught and to apply the principles of the gospel as we interact with our fellow Saints.

> 15 Again I say, hearken ye elders of my church, whom I have appointed: Ye are not sent forth to be taught, but to teach the children of men the things which I have put into your hands by the power of my Spirit;
>
> 16 And ye are to be taught from on high. Sanctify yourselves and ye shall be endowed with power, that ye may give even as I have spoken.
>
> 17 Hearken ye, for, behold, the great day of the Lord is nigh at hand.
>
> 18 For the day cometh that the Lord shall utter his voice out of heaven; the heavens shall shake and the earth shall tremble, and the trump of God shall sound both long and loud, and shall say to the sleeping nations: Ye saints arise and live; ye sinners stay and sleep until I shall call again.
>
> 19 Wherefore gird up your loins lest ye be found among the wicked.

20 Lift up your voices and spare not. Call upon the nations to repent, both old and young, both bond and free, saying: Prepare yourselves for the great day of the Lord;

21 For if I, who am a man, do lift up my voice and call upon you to repent, and ye hate me, what will ye say when the day cometh when the thunders shall utter their voices from the ends of the earth, speaking to the ears of all that live, saying—Repent, and prepare for the great day of the Lord?

22 Yea, and again, when the lightnings shall streak forth from the east unto the west, and shall utter forth their voices unto all that live, and make the ears of all tingle that hear, saying these words—Repent ye, for the great day of the Lord is come?

While the Church values and upholds the importance of learning, the Lord also explains to the elders that they are sent forth to teach and not to be taught. Those with a charge to teach the gospel must ensure that their message is shared. They cannot afford to be caught up in arguments or debate. While those who teach are able to learn much about the faith and belief of the people they serve among, they also have a solemn obligation to lift up their voices and share the message of the Restoration of the gospel of Jesus Christ in the latter days. Elder Anthon H. Lund taught:

We have only one object in view in going out amongst the nations, and that is to follow the Master's instructions—to go out and teach men. That is our work. We do not go out to win battles as debaters; but we go out to teach men that which we have received, which we know is true. If men are not willing to receive it, that is their own concern, not ours. . . . The Elders do their duty, and leave the result to the Lord. Those who seek to debate with our Elders and thirst for the honor of beating them in argument, do not want to be taught, they simply want contention.[9]

23 And again, the Lord shall utter his voice out of heaven, saying: Hearken, O ye nations of the earth, and hear the words of that God who made you.

24 O, ye nations of the earth, how often would I have gathered you together as a hen gathereth her chickens under her wings, but ye would not!

25 How oft have I called upon you by the mouth of my servants, and by the ministering of angels, and by mine own voice, and by the voice of thunderings, and by the voice of lightnings, and by the voice of tempests, and by the voice of earthquakes, and great hailstorms, and by the voice of famines and pestilences of every kind, and by the great sound of a trump, and by the voice of judgment, and by the voice of mercy all the day long, and by the voice of glory and honor and the riches of eternal life, and would have saved you with an everlasting salvation, but ye would not!

26 Behold, the day has come, when the cup of the wrath of mine indignation is full.

27 Behold, verily I say unto you, that these are the words of the Lord your God.

28 Wherefore, labor ye, labor ye in my vineyard for the last time—for the last time call upon the inhabitants of the earth.

An essential part of understanding the Church's missionary efforts comes from understanding the Lord's commandments to warn the people. As explained in these verses, the Lord calls the people of the world to repentance through the voice of His servants, through ministering angels, and through the natural calamities which will exist in the last days. In the scriptures, natural disasters are often seen as manifestations of God's punishment for wickedness. Such events can also be seen as a way of opening doors for the gospel, softening hearts, and bringing people to the Savior.

In 2005 Hurricane Katrina destroyed large parts of the city of New Orleans and ravaged the regions around the Gulf of Mexico in the United States. Speaking of the damage, President Hinckley noted, "Many have lost all they had. The damage has been astronomical. Literally millions have suffered. Fear and worry have gripped the hearts of many. Lives have been lost." Listing the tragedy of the lives lost and property damaged in the hurricane, President Hinckley then noted:

With all of this, there has been a great outpouring of help. Hearts have been softened. Homes have been opened. Critics love to talk about the failures of Christianity. Any such should take a look at what the churches have done in these circumstances. Those of many denominations have accomplished wonders. And far from the least among these has been our own Church. Great numbers of our men have traveled considerable

39

distances, bringing with them tools and tents and radiant hope. Men of the priesthood have given thousands upon thousands of hours in the work of rehabilitation. There have been three and four thousand at a time. There are some there tonight. We cannot say enough of thanks to them. Please know of our gratitude, of our love, and of our prayers in your behalf.[10]

Disputing any notion of the hurricane damage being a punishment from God, President Hinckley also added

Now, I do not say, and I repeat emphatically that I do not say or infer, that what has happened is the punishment of the Lord. Many good people, including some of our faithful Latter-day Saints, are among those who have suffered. Having said this, I do not hesitate to say that this old world is no stranger to calamities and catastrophes. Those of us who read and believe the scriptures are aware of the warnings of prophets concerning catastrophes that have come to pass and are yet to come to pass.[11]

The increasing calamities of the last days can be seen not simply as divine retribution but as a way to open doors and provide the men and women called of God with opportunities to spread the work of God through humanitarian service.

29 For in mine own due time will I come upon the earth in judgment, and my people shall be redeemed and shall reign with me on earth.

30 For the great Millennium, of which I have spoken by the mouth of my servants, shall come.

31 For Satan shall be bound, and when he is loosed again he shall only reign for a little season, and then cometh the end of the earth.

32 And he that liveth in righteousness shall be changed in the twinkling of an eye, and the earth shall pass away so as by fire.

33 And the wicked shall go away into unquenchable fire, and their end no man knoweth on earth, nor ever shall know, until they come before me in judgment.

34 Hearken ye to these words. Behold, I am Jesus Christ, the Savior of the world. Treasure these things up in your hearts, and let the solemnities of eternity rest upon your minds.

35 Be sober. Keep all my commandments. Even so. Amen.

At the end of the revelation, the Savior speaks of the Millennium, or the thousand years of peace following the Savior's return to the earth (see Isaiah 2:4; Revelation 20:4; Doctrine and Covenants 29:11). It has long been an article of faith for the Latter-day Saints that "Christ will reign personally upon the earth" (Articles of Faith 1:10). While peace in Christ can be achieved at any time or place, our belief in the return and reign of Christ is not figurative but literal. An editorial published in the Church periodical *Times and Seasons* in July 1842 declared:

> It has been the design of Jehovah, from the commencement of the World, and is his purpose now, to regulate the affairs of the World in his own time; to stand as head of the universe and take the reins of government into his own hand. When that is done judgement will be administered in righteousness: anarchy and confusion will be destroyed, and "nations will learn war no more." It is for want of this great governing principle that all this confusion has existed: "for it is not in man that walketh to direct his steps;" this we have fully shewn.[12]

End Notes

1. John Whitmer, History, 1831–circa 1847, 18, josephsmithpapers.org.

2. See Mark Staker, *Hearken, O Ye People: The Historical Setting of Joseph Smith's Ohio Revelations* (Sandy, UT: Greg Kofford Books, 2010), 79–80, 111–114.

3. Joseph Smith, in History, 1838–1856, volume A-1 [23 December 1805–30 August 1834], 101, josephsmithpapers.org.

4. History, 1838–1856, volume A-1 [23 December 1805–30 August 1834], 101, josephsmithpapers.org.

5. John Whitmer, History, 1831–circa 1847, 10, josephsmithpapers.org. See also "Historical Introduction," Revelation, February 1831–A [D&C 43], josephsmithpapers.org.

6. Letter to John S. Carter, 13 April 1833, 29, footnote 2, josephsmithpapers.org.

7. Letter to John S. Carter, 13 April 1833, 30, josephsmithpapers.org.

8. D. Todd Christofferson, "Why the Church," *Ensign* or *Liahona*, Nov. 2015, 109.

9. Anthon H. Lund, in Conference Report, Oct. 1902, 80–81.

10. Gordon B. Hinckley, "If Ye Are Prepared Ye Shall Not Fear," *Ensign* or *Liahona*, Nov. 2005, 60.

11. Gordon B. Hinckley, "If Ye Are Prepared Ye Shall Not Fear," 60–61.

12. *Times and Seasons*, 15 July 1842, 856, josephsmithpapers.org.

$\mathcal{D}$octrine and $\mathcal{C}$ovenants
Section 44
Visit the Poor and the Needy

$\mathcal{H}$istorical $\mathcal{C}$ontext

THE REVELATION IN SECTION 44 WAS AMONG THE OUTPOURING OF INSTRUC-
tions Joseph Smith received when he first arrived in Ohio. We do not know
the exact date this revelation was received, but its placement among the
others given around this time suggests that it came late in February 1831.
The revelation calls for a gathering of elders to assemble themselves together.
This commandment may have been fulfilled in a meeting held on April 9,
1831, but it was more likely in a conference held later that year on June 6.
In his later history Joseph Smith tied this revelation directly to the meeting
held on June 6, 1831, where the Prophet and others were ordained to the
high priesthood.[1]

The revelation was given during an exciting and challenging time for
the Church. Around this same time, Joseph wrote to Martin Harris, asking him to "inform the Elders which are there that all of them who can be

spared will come here without delay, if possible . . . by Commandment of the Lord as he has a great work for them all in this our inheritance."[2] A few days later Joseph wrote to his brother Hyrum, saying, "I have been engaged in regulating the Churches here as the disciples are numerous and the devil had made many attempts to overthrow them. It has been a serious job, but the Lord is with us, and we have overcome, and have all things regular. The work is breaking forth on the right hand and on the left and there is a great Call for Elders in this place."[3]

Verse-by-Verse Commentary

1 Behold, thus saith the Lord unto you my servants, it is expedient in me that the elders of my church should be called together, from the east and from the west, and from the north and from the south, by letter or some other way.

2 And it shall come to pass, that inasmuch as they are faithful, and exercise faith in me, I will pour out my Spirit upon them in the day that they assemble themselves together.

3 And it shall come to pass that they shall go forth into the regions round about, and preach repentance unto the people.

4 And many shall be converted, insomuch that ye shall obtain power to organize yourselves according to the laws of man;

5 That your enemies may not have power over you; that you may be preserved in all things; that you may be enabled to keep my laws; that every bond may be broken wherewith the enemy seeketh to destroy my people.

6 Behold, I say unto you, that ye must visit the poor and the needy and administer to their relief, that they may be kept until all things may be done according to my law which ye have received. Amen.

Among the charges given to the elders of the Church is an obligation to visit and administer relief to "the poor and the needy," a category broad enough to include every member of the Church and their neighbors. In the

Church in our time, the charge to minister is shared by both the elders and the sisters.

Sister Jean B. Bingham, serving as the General Relief Society President, spoke of the Lord's charge to visit and minister to those in need. She said, "After all is said and done, true ministering is accomplished one by one with love as the motivation. The value and merit and wonder of sincere ministering is that it truly changes lives! When our hearts are open and willing to love and include, encourage and comfort, the power of our ministering will be irresistible. With love as the motivation, miracles will happen, and we will find ways to bring our 'missing' sisters and brothers into the all-inclusive embrace of the gospel of Jesus Christ."[4]

At the same conference, President Jeffrey R. Holland outlined the purpose of visiting those in need: "In spite of what we all feel are our limitations and inadequacies—and we all have challenges—nevertheless, may we labor side by side with the Lord of the vineyard, giving the God and Father of us all a helping hand with His staggering task of answering prayers, providing comfort, drying tears, and strengthening feeble knees. If we will do that, we will be more like the true disciples of Christ we are meant to be."[5] Regardless of whether the program is called home or visiting teaching, ministering, or any other title, the principle of visiting and assisting those in need will always be central to the work of the Lord's Church.

End Notes

1. See History, 1838–1856, volume A-1 [23 December 1805–30 August 1834], 103, josephsmithpapers.org.

2. Letter to Martin Harris, 22 February 1831, 1, josephsmithpapers.org.

3. Letter to Hyrum Smith, 3–4 March 1831, 1, josephsmithpapers.org. See also "Historical Introduction," Revelation, February 1831–B [D&C 44], josephsmithpapers.org.

4. Jean B. Bingham, "Ministering as the Savior Does," *Ensign* or *Liahona*, May 2018, 106.

5. Jeffrey R. Holland, "Be With and Strengthen Them," *Ensign* or *Liahona*, May 2018, 103.

$\mathcal{D}$octrine and $\mathcal{C}$ovenants
Section 45
The Signs of My Coming

$\mathcal{H}$istorical $\mathcal{C}$ontext

DOCTRINE AND COVENANTS 45 WAS RECEIVED ON MARCH 7, 1831, DURING a time when the Saints were experiencing increasing opposition. Joseph Smith later recorded in his history, "At this age of the church many false reports, lies, and foolish stories were published in the newspapers, and circulated in every direction, to prevent people from investigating the work, or embracing the faith. A great earthquake in China, which destroyed from one to two hundred thousand inhabitants, was burlesqued in some papers, as 'Mormonism in China.'"[1]

Doctrine and Covenants 45 was received on March 7, 1831, during a time when Joseph was deeply engaged in his project to produce a new translation of the Bible. Working alongside different scribes, Joseph began translating the Old Testament in June 1830. In the revelation in section 45, the Lord directs Joseph to shift his focus and begin the translation of the New

Testament. This direction is fitting because parts of the revelation closely parallel the discourse the Savior gave to his disciples on the Mount of Olives shortly before His death, found in Matthew 24. The Lord Himself makes this connection when He says He "will show it plainly as I showed it unto my disciples as I stood before them in the flesh, and spake unto them concerning the signs of my coming, in the day when I shall come in my glory in the clouds of heaven" (Doctrine and Covenants 45:16).

Disciples of Christ in all ages have held a special fascination with the latter days and the coming of the Savior in glory. The Doctrine and Covenants is unique among texts that contain the signs of the times because it tells of the wonders and destructions near the time of the Second Coming not only in the regions surrounding Jerusalem but also in the Western Hemisphere, where these modern disciples lived. The last part of the revelation in particular urges the Saints to gather and build the New Jerusalem as a place of safety for all people during the time leading up to Jesus Christ's return. Considering the value of this information, it is no wonder that Joseph recorded, "But to the joy of the saints who had to struggle against everything that prejudice and wickedness could invent, I received the following."[2]

Verse-by-Verse Commentary

1 Hearken, O ye people of my church, to whom the kingdom has been given; hearken ye and give ear to him who laid the foundation of the earth, who made the heavens and all the hosts thereof, and by whom all things were made which live, and move, and have a being.

2 And again I say, hearken unto my voice, lest death shall overtake you; in an hour when ye think not the summer shall be past, and the harvest ended, and your souls not saved.

3 Listen to him who is the advocate with the Father, who is pleading your cause before him—

4 Saying: Father, behold the sufferings and death of him who did no sin, in whom thou wast well pleased; behold the blood of thy Son which was shed, the blood of him whom thou gavest that thyself might be glorified;

5 Wherefore, Father, spare these my brethren that believe on my name, that they may come unto me and have everlasting life.

Doctrine and Covenants 45 is among the most comprehensive revelations concerning the signs of the times and the end of the world. However, before the Savior begins to give this crucial information, He points His disciples toward an even more important event than the Second Coming. President Marion G. Romney taught, "The atonement of the Master is the central point of world history. Without it, the whole purpose for the creation of earth and our living upon it would fail."[3] The great and terrible events surrounding the Savior's coming in glory have no meaning unless His first coming is fully understood and appreciated.

It is natural for us to want to fixate on the conditions of the last days and to consider the best way to navigate the challenges we will face. But the tumult and upheaval of the time preceding the Second Coming are best overcome by appreciation and acceptance of the atoning Christ. Knowing the Savior and His gospel can allow us to have peace in our hearts and a hope for a better world, even if the world around us seems to be falling into disarray.

6 Hearken, O ye people of my church, and ye elders listen together, and hear my voice while it is called today, and harden not your hearts;

7 For verily I say unto you that I am Alpha and Omega, the beginning and the end, the light and the life of the world—a light that shineth in darkness and the darkness comprehendeth it not.

8 I came unto mine own, and mine own received me not; but unto as many as received me gave I power to do many miracles, and to become the sons of God; and even unto them that believed on my name gave I power to obtain eternal life.

9 And even so I have sent mine everlasting covenant into the world, to be a light to the world, and to be a standard for my people, and for the Gentiles to seek to it, and to be a messenger before my face to prepare the way before me.

10 Wherefore, come ye unto it, and with him that cometh I will reason as with men in days of old, and I will show unto you my strong reasoning.

The Lord speaks of His everlasting covenant as a messenger He sends forth to prepare people for His return and the standard to which the righteous shall rally in the latter days. Much of verse 9, in fact, is a paraphrase of His own words in Isaiah 49:22 where He speaks of the day when "I will lift up mine hand to the Gentiles, and set up my standard to the people." That day is now, the Lord is saying, and the standard to which the Gentiles should gather is the Lord's everlasting covenant (which He defined earlier in Doctrine and Covenants 39:11 as "the fulness of my gospel"). As men and women from the nations of the world "come . . . unto it" (verse 9), they too will receive power from the Lord to "become the sons of God" and "to obtain eternal life" (verse 8), as happened to the faithful who received Christ during His first coming.

The role the Church of Christ plays in the salvation of God's children in the latter days is to invite mankind to come unto Christ through His everlasting covenant. Church members and leaders are to be those holding up Christ's everlasting covenant as a light to the world and a rallying point for God's people, beckoning all truth seekers the world over to come unto it and thereby receive Christ (see Doctrine and Covenants 39:2–6, 11 for added clarity on this point). Hence, as the custodians of the everlasting covenant, they are to hear Christ's voice and to harden not their hearts (see verse 6).

> 11 Wherefore, hearken ye together and let me show unto you even my wisdom—the wisdom of him whom ye say is the God of Enoch, and his brethren,
>
> 12 Who were separated from the earth, and were received unto myself—a city reserved until a day of righteousness shall come—a day which was sought for by all holy men, and they found it not because of wickedness and abominations;
>
> 13 And confessed they were strangers and pilgrims on the earth;
>
> 14 But obtained a promise that they should find it and see it in their flesh.
>
> 15 Wherefore, hearken and I will reason with you, and I will speak unto you and prophesy, as unto men in days of old.

The revelations that flesh out the story of Enoch and the City of Zion (see Moses 6–7) were revealed in December 1830, just three months prior to this revelation. The connection between the Zion built by the ancient Saints and the modern Zion being built up by the Latter-day Saints is a strong theme in the Doctrine and Covenants. Joseph Smith personally identified with Enoch and his work, even using the alias "Enoch" for himself in later revelations when it was necessary to keep the identities of the individuals named private. And only a few months after section 45 was received, Joseph Smith would be commanded to travel to Missouri to identify the location for the modern city of Zion (see Doctrine and Covenants 52:1–2).

In a later revelation, the Lord gave the lyrics of a song that was to be sung by the righteous. The lyrics say that Zion would come to earth again in two ways: "The Lord hath brought down Zion from above [the city of Enoch] and the Lord hath brought up Zion from beneath [the New Jerusalem built by the Saints]" (Doctrine and Covenants 84:100). The two cities, reaching each other as one descends and the other rises, are brought together at the beginning of Christ's reign on the earth.

The invocation of Enoch in these verses is significant as it invites the reader to mentally upload the Enochian Covenant as important context to what the Lord is about to explain in this section. Three months earlier Joseph had learned (and recorded in Moses 7) of a covenant God made to Enoch wherein He personally promised him that He would (1) call upon the descendants of Noah (which is all mankind) (2) in the latter-days (3) by way of flooding the earth with righteousness and truth (which are essentially the truths and ordinances of the gospel). This He would do in order to gather out an elect people to a Zion built upon the earth to prepare for Christ's return. And when Christ returns, He promised that He will bring with Him those in the heavenly Zion above (Enoch's people) to unite with the earthly Zion below, when this earth will finally rest from wickedness and enjoy a one-thousand-year period where only righteous people will live upon its surface (see Moses 7:49–67).

The Lord invokes all of this in verse 12 when He speaks of the promised "day of righteousness" for which Enoch's city was reserved to return. This promised day of rest and peace was "a day which was sought for by all holy men" down through the ages of time, but "they found it not because of wickedness and abominations" that prevailed on earth during their days. Nevertheless, as the Lord explains here in verse 14, "they obtained a promise that they should find it and see it in their flesh." Such was the case with father Abraham (see Joseph Smith Translation, Genesis 15:9–12 [in Genesis 15:6, footnote *a*]), for instance, and with righteous members of the house of Israel (see Ezekiel 37), as well as with many of Jesus's disciples during His mortal ministry, about whom He goes on to speak in the next verses.

51

16 And I will show it plainly as I showed it unto my disciples as I stood before them in the flesh, and spake unto them, saying: As ye have asked of me concerning the signs of my coming, in the day when I shall come in my glory in the clouds of heaven, to fulfil the promises that I have made unto your fathers,

17 For as ye have looked upon the long absence of your spirits from your bodies to be a bondage, I will show unto you how the day of redemption shall come, and also the restoration of the scattered Israel.

In these important verses, Jesus declares to His disciples that the purpose of His Second Coming is "to fulfil the promises that I have made unto your fathers" (such as Enoch mentioned above) concerning "the day of redemption"—a reference to the millennial era when scattered Israel will be fully restored and righteousness alone will reign upon the earth.

The context of the Savior's remarks in these verses and those that follow is during the last week of His life when He took his disciples to the Mount of Olives to speak with them privately. As the disciples gathered, they asked Jesus about His prophecy that the temple in Jerusalem would be destroyed. "Tell us, when shall these things be?" they petitioned the Lord. "And what shall be the sign of thy coming, and of the end of the world?" (Matthew 24:1–3). The following discussion, commonly called the Olivet Discourse because of the location where it was given, is included in different forms in the gospels written by Matthew, Mark, and Luke (see Matthew 24–25; Mark 13; Luke 21). Doctrine and Covenants 45 includes an additional version of that discussion that offers added insights to the gospel accounts.

Later in this section, in verses 60–62, Joseph is instructed to begin translating the New Testament. Sometime later in this same year, 1831, Joseph Smith translated the text of Matthew 23:39–Matthew 24, producing the text now known as Joseph Smith—Matthew in the Pearl of Great Price. Both Doctrine and Covenants 45 and the inspired translation of the Olivet Discourse found in Joseph Smith—Matthew greatly add to our understanding of the signs of the last days, with each text contributing to our knowledge in distinct ways.

18 And now ye behold this temple which is in Jerusalem, which ye call the house of God, and your enemies say that this house shall never fall.

19 But, verily I say unto you, that desolation shall come upon this generation as a thief in the night, and this people shall be destroyed and scattered among all nations.

20 And this temple which ye now see shall be thrown down that there shall not be left one stone upon another.

21 And it shall come to pass, that this generation of Jews shall not pass away until every desolation which I have told you concerning them shall come to pass.

22 Ye say that ye know that the end of the world cometh; ye say also that ye know that the heavens and the earth shall pass away;

23 And in this ye say truly, for so it is; but these things which I have told you shall not pass away until all shall be fulfilled.

One of the primary contributions of Joseph Smith—Matthew is that it clarifies that in the Olivet Discourse, the Savior was speaking about two different time periods: (1) the destruction and diaspora of the Jewish people around AD 70, and (2) the last days and the signs that will appear then. While the version found in Matthew 24 intertwines these two events, Joseph Smith—Matthew separates them and clarifies which events belong to each era. The destruction of Jerusalem is covered in Joseph Smith—Matthew 1:5–21, while the signs linked to the Second Coming are found in Joseph Smith—Matthew 1:22–55.

As an additional version of the Olivet Discourse, Doctrine and Covenants 45 likewise starts with a repetition of the Savior's prophecy about the destruction of Jerusalem (see verses 18–23) and then moves on to the signs of the last days (see verses 24–59). In the Joseph Smith—Matthew version of this prophecy, Jesus refers to the events described here in verses 18–23 as "the abomination of desolation, spoken of by Daniel the prophet" (Joseph Smith—Matthew 1:12). In AD 70 a Roman army led by Titus swept into Palestine and laid siege to Jerusalem. During this conflict, the temple in Jerusalem was destroyed and left in ruin. As one Jewish historian noted, the destruction of Jerusalem in this time "marked a transition period between the independence of Israel as a people living in its own political and social framework, and the period of exile when the nation was dispersed as a minority, large or small, without any center of national leadership and without any active political initiative."[4]

24 And this I have told you concerning Jerusalem; and when that day shall come, shall a remnant be scattered among all nations;

25 But they shall be gathered again; but they shall remain until the times of the Gentiles be fulfilled.

26 And in that day shall be heard of wars and rumors of wars, and the whole earth shall be in commotion, and men's hearts shall fail them, and they shall say that Christ delayeth his coming until the end of the earth.

27 And the love of men shall wax cold, and iniquity shall abound.

28 And when the times of the Gentiles is come in, a light shall break forth among them that sit in darkness, and it shall be the fulness of my gospel;

29 But they receive it not; for they perceive not the light, and they turn their hearts from me because of the precepts of men.

30 And in that generation shall the times of the Gentiles be fulfilled.

31 And there shall be men standing in that generation, that shall not pass until they shall see an overflowing scourge; for a desolating sickness shall cover the land.

32 But my disciples shall stand in holy places, and shall not be moved; but among the wicked, men shall lift up their voices and curse God and die.

33 And there shall be earthquakes also in divers places, and many desolations; yet men will harden their hearts against me, and they will take up the sword, one against another, and they will kill one another.

34 And now, when I the Lord had spoken these words unto my disciples, they were troubled.

35 And I said unto them: Be not troubled, for, when all these things shall come to pass, ye may know that the promises which have been made unto you shall be fulfilled.

36 And when the light shall begin to break forth, it shall be with them like unto a parable which I will show you—

37 Ye look and behold the fig trees, and ye see them with your eyes, and ye say when they begin to shoot forth, and their leaves are yet tender, that summer is now nigh at hand;

38 Even so it shall be in that day when they shall see all these things, then shall they know that the hour is nigh.

Doctrine and Covenants 45:24 marks the transition between the Savior's description of Jerusalem's destruction in His time and the signs of the last days in our time. There is a long tradition of speculation about the Second Coming among Latter-day Saints and Christians of other denominations. While the scriptures contain vast amounts of information about the last days, people often become obsessed with the end times and rely on questionable sources for their information. In 1973 President Harold B. Lee gave the following counsel: "There are among us many loose writings predicting the calamities which are about to overtake us. Some of these have been publicized as though they were necessary to wake up the world to the horrors about to overtake us. Many of these are from sources upon which there cannot be unquestioned reliance. . . . We need no such publications to be forewarned, if we were only conversant with what the scriptures have already spoken to us in plainness."[5]

President Lee then provided his own inspired list of readings to know the signs of the Second Coming:

Let me give you the sure word of prophecy on which you should rely for your guide instead of these strange sources which may have great political implications. Read the 24th chapter of Matthew—particularly that inspired version as contained in the Pearl of Great Price. (JS—M 1.) Then read the 45th section of the Doctrine and Covenants where the Lord, not man, has documented the signs of the times. Now turn to section 101 and section 133 of the Doctrine and Covenants and hear the step-by-step recounting of events leading up to the coming of the Savior. Finally, turn to the promises the Lord makes to those who keep the commandments when these judgments descend upon the wicked, as set forth in the Doctrine and Covenants, section 38.

Brethren, these are some of the writings with which you should concern yourselves, rather than commentaries that may come from those whose information may not be the most reliable and whose motives may be subject to question.[6]

When the signs in verses 24–33 occur, grim though some of them may be, Christ's disciples are not to be troubled; rather, they are to take heart knowing that these signs indicate "that the promises which have been made unto you shall be fulfilled" (verse 35). With the passing of each of these signs, disciples of Jesus Christ are to recognize that we are steadily approaching the millennial "day of righteousness" spoken of in verse 12 and the promised "day of redemption" spoken of in verse 17, as surely as summer follows the budding of spring leaves on fig trees in Jerusalem.

> 39 And it shall come to pass that he that feareth me shall be looking forth for the great day of the Lord to come, even for the signs of the coming of the Son of Man.
>
> 40 And they shall see signs and wonders, for they shall be shown forth in the heavens above, and in the earth beneath.
>
> 41 And they shall behold blood, and fire, and vapors of smoke.
>
> 42 And before the day of the Lord shall come, the sun shall be darkened, and the moon be turned into blood, and the stars fall from heaven.
>
> 43 And the remnant shall be gathered unto this place;
>
> 44 And then they shall look for me, and, behold, I will come; and they shall see me in the clouds of heaven, clothed with power and great glory; with all the holy angels; and he that watches not for me shall be cut off.
>
> 45 But before the arm of the Lord shall fall, an angel shall sound his trump, and the saints that have slept shall come forth to meet me in the cloud.
>
> 46 Wherefore, if ye have slept in peace blessed are you; for as you now behold me and know that I am, even so shall ye come unto me and your souls shall live, and your redemption shall be perfected; and the saints shall come forth from the four quarters of the earth.
>
> 47 Then shall the arm of the Lord fall upon the nations.

Many of the signs the Savior speaks of in this passage have undoubtedly already begun. However, members of the Church must be careful in the way we interpret the signs and their fulfillment. Signs can be fulfilled in surprising ways, and rather than following private interpretations, we need to look to the authorized servants whom God has called to offer their interpretations of the signs. In an 1843 discourse, Joseph Smith taught:

> Christ says no man knoweth the day or the hour when the Son of man cometh. . . . Did Christ speak this as a general principle throughout all generations? Oh no, he spake in the present tense; no man that was then living upon the footstool of God knew the day or the hour. But he did not say that there was no man throughout all generations that should not know the day or the hour. No, for this would be in flat contradiction with other scripture, for the prophet says that God will do nothing but what he will reveal unto his Servants the prophets (Amos 3:7). Consequently, if it is not made known to the Prophets it will not come to pass.[7]

48 And then shall the Lord set his foot upon this mount, and it shall cleave in twain, and the earth shall tremble, and reel to and fro, and the heavens also shall shake.

49 And the Lord shall utter his voice, and all the ends of the earth shall hear it; and the nations of the earth shall mourn, and they that have laughed shall see their folly.

50 And calamity shall cover the mocker, and the scorner shall be consumed; and they that have watched for iniquity shall be hewn down and cast into the fire.

51 And then shall the Jews look upon me and say: What are these wounds in thine hands and in thy feet?

52 Then shall they know that I am the Lord; for I will say unto them: These wounds are the wounds with which I was wounded in the house of my friends. I am he who was lifted up. I am Jesus that was crucified. I am the Son of God.

53 And then shall they weep because of their iniquities; then shall they lament because they persecuted their king.

One addition Doctrine and Covenants 45 makes to the Olivet Discourse is a focus on the prophecies of Zechariah, a prophet from around 520 BC. Zechariah spoke at length about the return of a remnant of the Jewish people to Jerusalem and of their fate in the last days. He prophesied that all nations would gather to battle against Jerusalem and that half the city would be taken into captivity. In this dark moment, he said, "Then shall the Lord go forth, and fight against those nations" (Zechariah 14:4). In section 45 the Savior makes reference to Zechariah's prophecy about when the Lord "shall stand in that day upon the mount of Olives, which is before Jerusalem on the east, and the mount of Olives shall cleave in the midst thereof toward the east and toward the west, and there shall be a very great valley; and half of the mountain shall remove toward the north, and half of it toward the south" (Zechariah 14:4). He also connects this moment to an earlier prophecy by Zechariah in which this remnant of the Jews will meet the Lord and ask, "What are these wounds in thine hands? Then he shall answer, Those with which I was wounded in the house of my friends" (Zechariah 13:6).

> 54 And then shall the heathen nations be redeemed, and they that knew no law shall have part in the first resurrection; and it shall be tolerable for them.
>
> 55 And Satan shall be bound, that he shall have no place in the hearts of the children of men.
>
> 56 And at that day, when I shall come in my glory, shall the parable be fulfilled which I spake concerning the ten virgins.
>
> 57 For they that are wise and have received the truth, and have taken the Holy Spirit for their guide, and have not been deceived—verily I say unto you, they shall not be hewn down and cast into the fire, but shall abide the day.
>
> 58 And the earth shall be given unto them for an inheritance; and they shall multiply and wax strong, and their children shall grow up without sin unto salvation.
>
> 59 For the Lord shall be in their midst, and his glory shall be upon them, and he will be their king and their lawgiver.

After the Savior returns to the earth in glory, the members of the Church will carry out two great labors: temple work and missionary work. In the temples of God, Latter-day Saints will do the work of inviting those who are deceased to receive Christ through His everlasting covenant. President M. Russell Ballard taught, "We're building these temples not only for us in this moment of our history, but we're building temples which will be used during the Millennium when this great work will be carried on in the house of the Lord . . . under the direction and supervision of the Lord Jesus Christ Himself."[8]

Second, missionary work will be carried out throughout the world to invite those who have not yet received Christ through His everlasting covenant to do so. The term "heathen nations" (verse 54) generally refers to those who are neither Christian nor Jewish. While the word *heathen* often carries negative connotations, there is no suggestion that those referred to here are barbarous or uncivilized, just unfamiliar with the teachings of the Bible. These sons and daughters of God are not cast off in His sight. Nephi taught that the Lord "remembereth the heathen, and all are alike unto God" (2 Nephi 26:33). After the Savior's return to earth, righteous individuals of all faiths will remain on the earth.

In 1842 Joseph Smith taught:

> To say that the heathen would be damned because they did not believe the gospel would be preposterous; and to say that the Jews would all be damned that do not believe in Jesus, would be equally absurd; for, "how can they believe on him of whom they have not heard; and how can they hear without a preacher; and how can he preach except he be sent;" consequently neither Jew, nor heathen, can be culpable for rejecting the conflicting opinions of sectarianism, nor for rejecting any testimony but that which is sent of God, for as the preacher cannot preach except he be sent, so the hearer cannot believe without he hearing a sent preacher; and cannot be condemned for what he has not heard; and being without law will have to be judged without law.[9]

To the faithful Jews, Gentiles, and heathen in this day of promise, "the earth shall be given . . . for an inheritance," they will continue in glorious family life as "their children . . . grow up without sin unto salvation," and they will rest secure as "the Lord shall be in their midst, and his glory shall be upon then, and he will be their king and lawgiver" (verses 58–59).

President Brigham Young summarized the conditions of this time of peace when he declared that "the Millennium consists in this—every heart in the Church and Kingdom of God being united in one; the Kingdom increasing to the overcoming of everything opposed to the economy of heaven, and Satan being bound, and having a seal set upon him. All things else will be as they are now, we shall eat, drink, and wear clothing."[10]

> 60 And now, behold, I say unto you, it shall not be given unto you to know any further concerning this chapter, until the New Testament be translated, and in it all these things shall be made known;

61 Wherefore I give unto you that ye may now translate it, that ye may be prepared for the things to come.

62 For verily I say unto you, that great things await you;

The day after Doctrine and Covenants 45 was revealed, March 8, 1831, Joseph Smith and his scribes began translating the New Testament. In the months following, the Prophet's study of the New Testament was particularly fruitful and led to some of the most important revelations given to Joseph Smith. These sections included Doctrine and Covenants 74, which clarified questions about infant baptism; section 76, which outlined the different degrees of glory in the next world; and section 77, which answers crucial questions about the book of Revelation. In addition, Doctrine and Covenants 86, 88, and 93 are all linked closely to the Prophet's translation of the New Testament.

Upon completing his work on the New Testament, Joseph returned to the Old Testament. He noted in the Old Testament manuscripts that the project was completed on July 2, 1833.[11] The impact of Joseph Smith's Bible translation project as a springboard to further revelations can hardly be overstated. Joseph received a large majority of the Doctrine and Covenants, roughly every revelation from section 29 to section 96, during the time he was translating the Bible. The study of the scriptures brought revelation for Joseph Smith, as it does for men and women in any time.

In one sense, it could be said that Joseph Smith never fully completed his translation of the Bible. He kept working on it right up until the end of his life. For him, translation meant a deep engagement with the sacred texts, a practice that continued to the end of his life. After Joseph's death, Brigham Young remarked that "he should not be stumbled if the prophet should translate the bible forty thousand times over and yet it should be different in some places every time, because when God speak[s], he always speaks according to the capacity of the people."[12]

63 Ye hear of wars in foreign lands; but, behold, I say unto you, they are nigh, even at your doors, and not many years hence ye shall hear of wars in your own lands.

64 Wherefore I, the Lord, have said, gather ye out from the eastern lands, assemble ye yourselves together ye elders of my church; go ye forth into the western countries, call upon the

inhabitants to repent, and inasmuch as they do repent, build up churches unto me.

65 And with one heart and with one mind, gather up your riches that ye may purchase an inheritance which shall hereafter be appointed unto you.

Another contribution of Doctrine and Covenants 45 is to provide information about the conditions of the last days in the Western Hemisphere. Most prophecies of the last days focus on the regions surrounding Jerusalem. In these verses the Lord warns the Saints to gather from the eastern lands and warns of wars happening in the regions close to their own location. Two years after this revelation was given, Joseph Smith declared, "I am prepared to say by the authority of Jesus Christ, that not many years shall pass, away before the United States shall present such a scene of bloodshed as has not a parallel in the history of our nation."[13]

This prophecy found partial fulfillment in the American Civil War (1861–1865), which remains the deadliest war in American history. By one estimate, the war took the lives of 10 percent of Northern men between the ages of 20 and 45, and 30 percent of all Southern white men between the ages of 18 and 40.[14] But the American Civil War was not the only calamity spoken of in Joseph Smith's prophecies. The Prophet also declared that "pestilence, hail, famine, and earthquake will sweep the wicked of this generation from off the face of the land, to open and prepare the way for the return of the lost tribes of Israel."[15] Further, Joseph Smith received another revelation explaining that "the days will come when war will be poured out upon all nations" (Doctrine and Covenants 87:2) but counseling the Saints to "stand ye in holy places and be not moved until the day of the Lord come" (Doctrine and Covenants 87:8).

66 And it shall be called the New Jerusalem, a land of peace, a city of refuge, a place of safety for the saints of the Most High God;

67 And the glory of the Lord shall be there, and the terror of the Lord also shall be there, insomuch that the wicked will not come unto it, and it shall be called Zion.

68 And it shall come to pass among the wicked, that every man that will not take his sword against his neighbor must needs flee unto Zion for safety.

69 And there shall be gathered unto it out of every nation under heaven; and it shall be the only people that shall not be at war one with another.

70 And it shall be said among the wicked: Let us not go up to battle against Zion, for the inhabitants of Zion are terrible; wherefore we cannot stand.

71 And it shall come to pass that the righteous shall be gathered out from among all nations, and shall come to Zion, singing with songs of everlasting joy.

72 And now I say unto you, keep these things from going abroad unto the world until it is expedient in me, that ye may accomplish this work in the eyes of the people, and in the eyes of your enemies, that they may not know your works until ye have accomplished the thing which I have commanded you;

73 That when they shall know it, that they may consider these things.

74 For when the Lord shall appear he shall be terrible unto them, that fear may seize upon them, and they shall stand afar off and tremble.

75 And all nations shall be afraid because of the terror of the Lord, and the power of his might. Even so. Amen.

In the midst of a world descending into deepening chaos, the New Jerusalem will be built as a place of refuge and safety for the Saints and for those who choose to gather with them. Inhabitants of every nation will flee unto Zion seeking escape from the worsening conditions of the world. These verses serve as a reminder that Latter-day Saints must do more than simply wait for the Savior to descend and cure the ills of the world. We build Zion as we create places of safety for all people around us. Refuge will be found not only in the New Jerusalem but in the stakes of Zion built around the world (see Doctrine and Covenants 115:5–6).

In an 1839 discourse, Joseph Smith taught, "Some may have cried peace, but the Saints and the world will have little peace from henceforth. Let this not hinder us from going to the Stake[s]; for God has told us to flee not or we shall be scattered, one here another there." He continued:

We ought to have the building up of Zion as our greatest object. When wars come, we shall have to flee to Zion, the cry is to make haste. The last revelation says ye shall not have time to have gone over the earth until these things come. It will come as did the cholera, war and fires, burning, earthquakes, one pestilence after another, until the Ancient of Days come, then judgment will be given to the Saints. . . . There your children shall <be> blessed and you in the midst of friends where you may be blessed. The Gospel net gathers in [people] of every kind."[16]

End Notes

1. Joseph Smith, in History, 1838–1856, volume A-1 [23 December 1805–30 August 1834], 104, josephsmithpapers.org.

2. Joseph Smith, in History, 1838–1856, volume A-1 [23 December 1805–30 August 1834], 104, josephsmithpapers.org. See also "Historical Introduction," Revelation, circa 7 March 1831 [D&C 45], josephsmithpapers.org.

3. Marion G. Romney, in Conference Report, Oct. 1953, 34.

4. *The Illustrated History of the Jews* (New York: Harper & Row, 1963), 138.

5. Harold B. Lee, "Admonitions for the Priesthood of God," *Ensign*, Jan. 1973, 106.

6. Harold B. Lee, "Admonitions for the Priesthood of God," 106.

7. Discourse, 6 April 1843–B, as Reported by James Burgess, 2, josephsmithpapers.org.

8. Rachel Sterzer, "Today's Temples Will Be Used in the Millennium," *Church News,* June 8, 2017.

9. *Times and Seasons,* 15 April 1842, 760, josephsmithpapers.org.

10. *Teachings of Presidents of the Church: Brigham Young* (1997), 333.

11. See Old Testament Revision 2, 119, josephsmithpapers.org.

12. Council of Fifty, Minutes, March 1844–January 1846; Volume 1, 10 March 1844–1 March 1845, 172, josephsmithpapers.org.

13. Joseph Smith, in History, 1838–1856, volume A-1 [23 December 1805–30 August 1834], 262, josephsmithpapers.org.

14. See John Huddleston, *Killing Ground: The Civil War and the Changing American Landscape (Creating the North American Landscape)* (Baltimore, MD: Johns Hopkins University Press, 2002), 3.

15. Joseph Smith, in History, 1838–1856, volume A-1 [23 December 1805–30 August 1834], 262, josephsmithpapers.org.

16. Discourse, between circa 26 June and circa 4 August 1839–A, as Reported by William Clayton, 20–21, josephsmithpapers.org.

$\mathcal{D}$octrine and $\mathcal{C}$ovenants
Section 46
All These Gifts Come from God

$\mathcal{H}$istorical $\mathcal{C}$ontext

THE REVELATION IN SECTION 46 WAS RECEIVED THE DAY AFTER JOSEPH Smith received Doctrine and Covenants 45. According to Church Historian John Whitmer, the revelation came in response to a question about whether nonbelievers should be allowed to meet with Church members. He later wrote, "In the beginning of the church, while yet in her infancy, the disciples used to exclude unbelievers, which caused some to marvel, and converse about this matter because of the things that were written in the Book of Mormon."[1] It is likely that the members were discussing a passage found in the book of Moroni, which reads, "And they were strict to observe that there should be no iniquity among them; and whoso was found to commit iniquity, and three witnesses of the church did condemn them before the elders, and if they repented not, and confessed not, their names were blotted out, and they were not numbered among the people of Christ" (Moroni 6:7).

During this time, Joseph Smith was working to stem some unusual spiritual manifestations among the Saints. For example, in a letter written to his brother Hyrum only a few days before this revelation was given, Joseph wrote, "This morning after being called out of my bed in the night to go a small distance I went and had an awful struggle with Satan, but being armed with the power of God he was cast out." Joseph may have been referring to a member of the Kirtland community who had been affected by a demonic possession because he added, "The woman is Clothed in her right mind; the Lord worketh wonders in this land."[2]

Regarding the question of Church members meeting with nonbelievers, John Whitmer wrote that "the Lord deigned to speak on this subject, that his people might come to understanding, and said that he had always given to his Elders to conduct all meetings as they were led by the spirit."[3] In the revelation, the Lord explained that Church members were not to cast anyone out of sacrament or confirmation meetings (see Doctrine and Covenants 46:3–4). The revelation warns against those who had been "seduced by evil spirits, or doctrines of devils, or the commandments of men" (Doctrine and Covenants 46:7). The Lord also provided information about spiritual gifts available to members of the Church and explained some of the guidelines for how the gifts are given and used.[4]

Verse-by-Verse Commentary

1 Hearken, O ye people of my church; for verily I say unto you that these things were spoken unto you for your profit and learning.

2 But notwithstanding those things which are written, it always has been given to the elders of my church from the beginning, and ever shall be, to conduct all meetings as they are directed and guided by the Holy Spirit.

3 Nevertheless ye are commanded never to cast any one out from your public meetings, which are held before the world.

4 Ye are also commanded not to cast any one who belongeth to the church out of your sacrament meetings; nevertheless, if any

have trespassed, let him not partake until he makes reconciliation.

5 And again I say unto you, ye shall not cast any out of your sacrament meetings who are earnestly seeking the kingdom—I speak this concerning those who are not of the church.

6 And again I say unto you, concerning your confirmation meetings, that if there be any that are not of the church, that are earnestly seeking after the kingdom, ye shall not cast them out.

In answer to the question of who is allowed to attend church meetings, the Lord instructs the Saints to be as inclusive as possible in their public meetings. Confirmation meetings were open to all who were "earnestly seeking the kingdom" (Doctrine and Covenants 46:5). In all of the Church's public meetings, leaders are expected to follow the promptings of the Spirit and to look after the needs of the members of the Church.

In the modern Church, ordinances such as the sacrament and confirmations can take place in the same meeting. Attendees who are not members of the Church are allowed to choose whether they participate in ordinances such as the sacrament. In a meeting instructing Church leaders, President Russell M. Nelson taught, "Because we invite all to come unto Christ, friends and neighbors are always welcome but not expected to take the sacrament. However, it is not forbidden. They choose for themselves. We hope that newcomers among us will always be made to feel wanted and comfortable. Little children, as sinless beneficiaries of the Lord's Atonement, may partake of the sacrament as they prepare for covenants that they will make later in life."[5]

7 But ye are commanded in all things to ask of God, who giveth liberally; and that which the Spirit testifies unto you even so I would that ye should do in all holiness of heart, walking uprightly before me, considering the end of your salvation, doing all things with prayer and thanksgiving, that ye may not be seduced by evil spirits, or doctrines of devils, or the commandments of men; for some are of men, and others of devils.

8 Wherefore, beware lest ye are deceived; and that ye may not be deceived seek ye earnestly the best gifts, always remembering for what they are given;

9 For verily I say unto you, they are given for the benefit of those who love me and keep all my commandments, and him that seeketh so to do; that all may be benefited that seek or that ask of me, that ask and not for a sign that they may consume it upon their lusts.

Because the new converts in Kirtland held an unusual regard for spiritual gifts, the Lord takes time in these verses to explain several principles of spiritual gifts. The first counsel He gives the Saints is to earnestly seek the best gifts. The spiritual gifts a person receives in this life are not set in stone. It is true that premortal experiences may predispose a person to one or more gifts of the Spirit. It is also true that sin and transgression may cause a person to lose a spiritual gift. The Lord emphasizes here that men and women have the power to seek gifts that will help them build the kingdom and progress toward eternal life.

What kind of gifts should a person seek? President George Q. Cannon provided this counsel:

If any of us are imperfect, it is our duty to pray for the gift that will make them perfect. Have I imperfections? I am full of them. What is my duty? To pray to God to give me the gifts that will correct these imperfections. If I am an angry man, it is my duty to pray for charity, which suffereth long and is kind. . . . No man ought to say, "Oh, I cannot help this; it is my nature." He is not justified in it, for the reason that God has promised to give strength [is] to correct these things, and to give gifts that will eradicate them. . . . For this purpose he gives these gifts, and bestows them upon [those] who seek after them, in order that they may be a perfect people upon the face of the earth, notwithstanding their many weaknesses.[6]

10 And again, verily I say unto you, I would that ye should always remember, and always retain in your minds what those gifts are, that are given unto the church.

11 For all have not every gift given unto them; for there are many gifts, and to every man is given a gift by the Spirit of God.

12 To some is given one, and to some is given another, that all may be profited thereby.

Latter-day Saints believe that the same miraculous gifts and manifestations present in the ancient Church exist in the modern Church today. The

Prophet Joseph Smith taught, "We believe in the gift of the Holy Ghost being enjoyed now, as much as it was in the apostles days;—we believe that it is necessary to make and to organize the priesthood; that no man can be called to fill any office in the ministry without it; we also believe in prophesy, in tongues, in visions, and in revelations, in gifts, and in healings; and that these things cannot be enjoyed without the gift of the Holy Ghost." At the same time, the Prophet cautioned, "We believe in it in all its fulness, and power, and greatness, and glory: but whilst we do this we believe in it rationally, reasonably, consistently, and scripturally, and not according to the wild vagaries, foolish, notions and traditions of men."[7]

One of the rules the Lord provides for spiritual gifts is that every man and woman in the Church is given at least one spiritual gift, but not all members possess all the gifts. The Lord asks that the Saints work together, drawing upon their unique gifts, to help others and to move the Lord's work forward. Working with others brings forth the fruits of the Spirit. President Eyring explained, "Vibrant faith in God comes best from serving Him regularly. Not all of us have received callings to offices in the Church. Some of you may not yet be called to something in a formal way, yet every member has a multitude of opportunities to serve God."[8]

> 13 To some it is given by the Holy Ghost to know that Jesus Christ is the Son of God, and that he was crucified for the sins of the world.

A testimony of Jesus Christ is the most vital of spiritual gifts. Joseph Smith taught, "We believe that no man can know that Jesus is the Christ, but by the Holy Ghost."[9] Note that the phrasing used here is not "that a person may *believe*" but "that a person may *know*" by the power of the Holy Ghost that Jesus is the Christ. Testimonies can come through logic, evidence, and study. But to gain true power, each of these methods must be supplemented by the witness of the Holy Ghost.

President George Albert Smith taught, "We have another testimony, another evidence that is even more perfect and more convincing than the others, because it is a testimony that comes to the individual when he has complied with the requirements of our Father in Heaven. It is a testimony that is burned into our souls by the power of the Holy Ghost, when we have performed the work that the Lord has said must be performed if we would know that the doctrine be of God or whether it be of man."[10]

14 To others it is given to believe on their words, that they also might have eternal life if they continue faithful.

Elder Joseph F. Merrill, a scientist by profession, saw the process of gaining faith not just as mystical development but also as demonstrable process, much like the rules of science. He taught:

> Faith is one of those spiritual gifts that I believe is based on laws. We learn, from the teachings of the Prophet Joseph, that if we get any blessing from heaven, it is because we fulfill the conditions upon which that blessing is based, and that is a truth that not only comes from the mouth of our Prophet, it is also a truth that has been established by scientific research. Every investigator in the field of material science knows that when he fulfills the conditions he can predict the results, and if the conditions vary, then the results will vary, and when the conditions are completely fulfilled the results will be realized completely. So faith is one of those gifts we acquire, that we may cultivate only if we fulfill the conditions upon which faith is based.[11]

15 And again, to some it is given by the Holy Ghost to know the differences of administration, as it will be pleasing unto the same Lord, according as the Lord will, suiting his mercies according to the conditions of the children of men.

Hyrum M. Smith and Janne M. Sjodahl, early commentators on the revelations, noted that the phrase "differences of administration" has a connection to a phrase Paul used in his discussion of the "different divisions or courses of service the priests and Levites engaged in the temple service" (1 Corinthians 12:5). Because of this connection, Smith and Sjodahl believed that the gift described in verse 15 pertains specifically to an understanding of how priesthood holders should be directed in their duties and responsibilities.[12]

More recently, Church leaders have taken notice of the accompanying phrase—that the Lord will "[suit] his mercies according the conditions of the children of men" (verse 15). Only the Savior understands perfectly the conditions in which individuals find themselves, and He suits the mercies to provide everyone with the gifts they need to handle their own personal challenges. Elder Bednar noted, "Through personal study, observation, pondering, and prayer, I believe I have come to better understand that the Lord's tender mercies are the very personal and individualized blessings, strength, protection, assurances, guidance, loving-kindnesses, consolation, support, and spiritual gifts which we receive from and because of and through the Lord Jesus Christ."[13]

> 16 And again, it is given by the Holy Ghost to some to know the diversities of operations, whether they be of God, that the manifestations of the Spirit may be given to every man to profit withal.

The phrase "diversities of operations" is also found in 1 Corinthians 12:5. In alternate translations of the Greek, the phrase has been written as "differences of ministries" (New King James Version) or "different kinds of service" (New International Version). In the larger context of Paul's sermon on the body of Christ, the Lord appears to be noting that there are different kinds of service within the Church and that one of the spiritual gifts is to recognize the value of each type of service. The Apostle Paul notes, "But now are they many members, yet but one body. And the eye cannot say unto the hand, I have no need of thee: nor again the head to the feet, I have no need of you" (1 Corinthians 12:20–21).

President Dallin H. Oaks has noted, "At this conference we have seen the release of some faithful brothers, and we have sustained the callings of others. In this rotation—so familiar in the Church—we do not 'step down' when we are released, and we do not 'step up' when we are called. There is no 'up or down' in the service of the Lord. There is only 'forward or backward,' and that difference depends on how we accept and act upon our releases and our callings."[14]

In 1951 President J. Reuben Clark was released from serving as the First Counselor in the First Presidency and was called instead to serve as the Second Counselor. Leaders in many other organizations would have seen this change as a demotion. However, rising to speak, President Clark noted, "In the service of the Lord, it is not where you serve but how. In The Church of Jesus Christ of Latter-day Saints, one takes the place to which one is duly called, which place one neither seeks nor declines."[15] While all officers of the Church are expected to be worthy of the callings they hold, blessings and righteousness are not measured according to the office held, only by the dedication shown in carrying out the service the Lord asks of a person.

> 17 And again, verily I say unto you, to some is given, by the Spirit of God, the word of wisdom.

18 To another is given the word of knowledge, that all may be taught to be wise and to have knowledge.

Though the phrase "word of wisdom" would eventually be associated with the law of health given to the Lord's Church in the last days, that revelation did not come until nearly two years later, in February 1833. In these verses, the Lord refers to knowledge and wisdom as two separate gifts. President Stephen L. Richards, a counselor in the First Presidency, defined wisdom as "the beneficent application of knowledge in decision." He added:

> I think of wisdom not in the abstract but as functional. Life is largely made up of choices and determinations, and I can think of no wisdom that does not contemplate the good of man and society. . . . I do not believe that wisdom can be exercised in living without a sound fundamental knowledge of truth about life and living. . . . The fundamental knowledge which the Church brings you will bring understanding. Your testimony, your spirit, and your service will direct the application of your knowledge; that is wisdom.[16]

19 And again, to some it is given to have faith to be healed;

20 And to others it is given to have faith to heal.

One of the most prominent gifts of the Spirit demonstrated in the latter-day Church is the gift of healing. Around the time this revelation was received, Joseph Smith exercised the gift of healing. Elsa Johnson, who lived in the town of Hiram, Ohio, about forty miles from Kirtland, traveled with her husband, John Johnson, to where the Prophet was lodging. They were seeking for a way to heal Elsa's arm, which she had not been able to use for some time. Philo Dibble, who was present in Kirtland when the Johnsons met with Joseph, later recalled:

> [Elsa] went to Joseph and requested him to heal her. Joseph asked her if she believed the Lord was able to make him an instrument in healing her arm. She said she believed the Lord was able to heal her arm. Joseph put her off till the next morning, when he met her at Brother [Newel K.] Whitney's house. There were eight persons present, one a Methodist preacher, and one a doctor. Joseph took her by the hand, prayed in silence a moment, pronounced her arm whole, in the name of Jesus Christ, and turned and left the room. The preacher asked her if her arm was whole, and she straightened it out and replied: "It is as good as the other." The question was then asked if it would remain whole. Joseph hearing this,

answered and said, "It is as good as the other, and as liable to accident as the other."[17]

After Elsa's healing, the Johnson family joined the Church, and they allowed Joseph and Emma to stay in their home for several months. During this time, Joseph worked on his translation of the Bible, held the conference determining to print the revelations (see Doctrine and Covenants 1), and received the vision of the different degrees of glory (see Doctrine and Covenants 76). Two of John and Elsa's sons, Luke and Lyman, also served as original members of the Quorum of the Twelve called in 1835.

21 And again, to some is given the working of miracles;

Miracles large and small took place among the early Saints, and they still take place in the Church today. The prophet Moroni chastised those who believe the day of miracles has passed: "O all ye that have imagined up unto yourselves a god who can do no miracles, I would ask of you, have all these things passed, of which I have spoken? Has the end come yet? Behold I say unto you, Nay; and God has not ceased to be a God of miracles" (Mormon 9:15).

Levi Curtis recalled a conversation with William D. Huntington in which William described a time that Joseph Smith exercised the power to raise the dead. Levi wrote that William recalled how he had become deathly ill while living in Joseph Smith's home in Nauvoo:

> He said he had been sick some weeks and kept getting weaker, until he became so helpless that he could not move. Finally, he got so low he could not speak, but had perfect consciousness of all that was passing in the room. He saw friends come to the bedside, look at him a moment and commence weeping, then turn away.
>
> He further stated that he presently felt easy, and observing his situation found that he was in the upper part of the room near the ceiling, and could see the body he had occupied lying on the bed, with weeping friends, standing around as he had witnessed in many cases where people had died under his own observation.
>
> About this time he saw Joseph Smith and two other brethren come into the room. Joseph turned to his wife Emma and asked her to get him a dish of clean water. This she did; and the Prophet with the two brethren accompanying him washed their hands and carefully wiped them. Then they stepped to the bed and laid their hands upon the head of his body, which at that time looked loathsome to him, and as the three stretched

out their hands to place them upon the head, he by some means became aware that he must go back into that body and started to do so. The process of getting in he could not remember; but when Joseph said "amen," he heard and could see and feel with his body. The feeling for a moment was most excruciating, as though his body was pierced in every part with some sharp instruments.

As soon as the brethren had taken their hands from his head he raised up in bed, sitting erect, and in another moment turned his legs off the bed. At this juncture Joseph asked him if he had not better be careful, for he was very weak. He replied, "I never felt better in my life," almost immediately adding, "I want my pants" . . . every looker-on was ready to weep for joy . . . every hand was anxious to supply the wants of a man who, a few moments before was dead, really and truly dead! . . . Joseph listened to the conversation and in his turn remarked that they had just witnessed as great a miracle as Jesus did while on the earth. They had seen the dead brought to life.[18]

22 And to others it is given to prophesy;

The gift of prophesy is to speak in the name of the Lord, declaring things past, present, or future. The gift has been present in both men and women in the Church. As a child, Heber J. Grant witnessed a meeting where his mother, Emmeline B. Wells, Eliza R. Snow, Zina D. Young, and a number of other prominent women in the Church were present. In the meeting, both the gift of tongues and the gift of prophesy were exercised. Heber later wrote:

After the meeting was over Sister Eliza R. Snow, by the gift of tongues, gave a blessing to each and every one of those good sisters, and Sister Zina D. Young gave the interpretation. After blessing those sisters, she turned to the boy playing on the floor and pronounced a blessing upon my head by the gift of tongues, and Zina D. Young gave the interpretation. I of course did not understand one word that Aunt Eliza was saying. I was astonished because she was talking to me and pointing at me. I could not understand a word, and all I got of the interpretation, as a child, was that some day I should be a big man. I thought it meant I would grow tall.[19]

Thanks to Heber's mother, Rachel Ivins Grant, he later found out what Eliza R. Snow had said to him on that occasion. "My mother made a record of that blessing," Heber later recalled. "What was it? It was a prophecy, by the gift of tongues, that her boy should live to be an apostle of the Lord Jesus

Christ; and oftimes she told me that if I would behave myself, that honor would come to me. I always laughed at her and said, 'Every mother believes that her son will become president of the United States, or hold some great office. You ought to get that out of your head, Mother.' I did not believe her until that honor came to me."[20]

23 And to others the discerning of spirits.

This gift refers to the ability to discern whether a spiritual manifestation has come from God or another source. As mentioned earlier, spiritual manifestations were abundant among the Saints at Kirtland, but not all manifestations came from God. The Prophet addressed this question in this revelation and again in another revelation received a few months later (see Doctrine and Covenants 50). Joseph Smith counseled the Saints to "try the spirits" manifested among them to see if they came from God or Satan. In an 1839 discourse reported by William Clayton, Joseph taught, "We may look for angels . . . but we are to try the spirits and prove them. It is often the case that men make a mistake in regard to these things. God has so ordained that when he has communicated no vision to be taken but what you see by the seeing of the eye, or what you hear by the hearing of the ear. When you see a vision, pray for the interpretation, if you get not this shut it up."[21]

24 And again, it is given to some to speak with tongues;

25 And to another is given the interpretation of tongues.

26 And all these gifts come from God, for the benefit of the children of God.

The gift of speaking in tongues was common in the early Church and manifested abundantly among the Saints in Kirtland. Elizabeth Ann Whitney reported that after she received her patriarchal blessing from Joseph Smith Sr., she received an unusual expression of the gifts of the Spirit: singing in tongues. She wrote, "I received the gift of singing inspirationally, and the first Song of Zion ever given in the pure language was sung by me then, and interpreted by Parley P. Pratt, and written down; of which I have preserved the original copy. It describes the manner in which the ancient patriarchs blessed their families, and gives some account of 'Adamoni Ahman.' . . . The Prophet Joseph promised me that I should never lose this gift if I would be wise in using it; and his words have been verified."[22]

Because of its dramatic nature, the gift of tongues is often sought after by believers in Jesus Christ, but the gift comes with some warnings. Paul described speaking in tongues as a lesser gift of the Spirit than the gift of charity, which isn't as conspicuous (see 1 Corinthians 13:8). President Joseph F. Smith warned:

> There is perhaps no gift of the spirit of God more easily imitated by the devil than the gift of tongues. Where two men or women exercise the gift of tongues by the inspiration of the spirit of God, there are a dozen perhaps who do it by the inspiration of the devil. . . . So far as I am concerned, if the Lord will give me ability to teach the people in my native tongue, or in their own language, to the understanding of those who hear me, that will be sufficient gift of tongues to me. Yet if the Lord gives you the gift of tongues, do not despise it, do not reject it.[23]

The Prophet Joseph Smith counseled, "Be not so curious about tongues, do not speak in tongues except there be an interpreter present; the ultimate design of tongues is to speak to foreigners, and if persons are very anxious to display their intelligence, let them speak to such in their own tongues. The gifts of God are all useful in their place, but when they are applied to that which God does not intend, they prove an injury, a snare, and a curse instead of a blessing."[24]

> 27 And unto the bishop of the church, and unto such as God shall appoint and ordain to watch over the church and to be elders unto the church, are to have it given unto them to discern all those gifts lest there shall be any among you professing and yet be not of God.

At the time this revelation was given, there was only one bishop in the Church, Edward Partridge. The system of presiding Church officers—including stake presidents, bishops, Relief Society presidents, and others "such as God shall appoint and ordain to watch over the church" (Doctrine and Covenants 46:27)—was gradually revealed in the years following. The general principle given here is that those appointed as presiding officers in the Church are given the power to discern what gifts come from God. President Packer commented:

> There is a power of discernment granted "unto such as God shall appoint . . . to watch over [his] church." To discern means "to see." President Harold B. Lee told me once of a conversation he had with Elder Charles A. Callis

of the Quorum of the Twelve. Brother Callis had remarked that the gift of discernment was an awesome burden to carry. To see clearly what is ahead and yet find members slow to respond or resistant to counsel or even rejecting the witness of the apostles and prophets brings deep sorrow. Nevertheless, "the responsibility of leading this church" must rest upon us until "you shall appoint others to succeed you."[25]

> 28 And it shall come to pass that he that asketh in Spirit shall receive in Spirit;
>
> 29 That unto some it may be given to have all those gifts, that there may be a head, in order that every member may be profited thereby.
>
> 30 He that asketh in the Spirit asketh according to the will of God; wherefore it is done even as he asketh.
>
> 31 And again, I say unto you, all things must be done in the name of Christ, whatsoever you do in the Spirit;
>
> 32 And ye must give thanks unto God in the Spirit for whatsoever blessing ye are blessed with.
>
> 33 And ye must practice virtue and holiness before me continually. Even so. Amen.

We should not assume that the list the Lord gives in these verses, or the list Moroni gives in the Book of Mormon's concluding chapter, or the list Paul gives in 1 Corinthians 12–13 represent all of the gifts of the Spirit. "Spiritual gifts are endless in number and infinite in variety," taught Elder Bruce R. McConkie. "Those listed in the revealed word are simply illustrations of the boundless outpouring of divine grace God gives those who love and serve him."[26]

Elder Marvin J. Ashton listed a few of the gifts of the Spirit not mentioned in the scripture canon. He said, "Taken at random, let me mention a few gifts that are not always evident or noteworthy but that are very important. Among these may be your gifts—gifts not so evident but nevertheless real and valuable." Elder Ashton took a moment to review some of these less-conspicuous gifts:

The gift of asking; the gift of listening; the gift of hearing and using a still, small voice; the gift of being able to weep; the gift of avoiding contention; the gift of being agreeable; the gift of avoiding vain repetition; the gift of seeking that which is righteous; the gift of not passing judgment; the gift of looking to God for guidance; the gift of being a disciple; the gift of caring for others; the gift of being able to ponder; the gift of offering prayer; the gift of bearing a mighty testimony; and the gift of receiving the Holy Ghost.[27]

While the lists provided in the scriptures provide a useful start in understanding the gifts God offers His children, they are not a comprehensive list of all spiritual gifts. Our own spiritual gifts are discovered through study, revelation, and earnest labors in the service of God.

End Notes

1. John Whitmer, History, 1831–circa 1847, 23, josephsmithpapers.org.

2. Letter to Hyrum Smith, 3–4 March 1831, 2, josephsmithpapers.org.

3. John Whitmer, History, 1831–circa 1847, 23, josephsmithpapers.org.

4. See "Historical Introduction," Revelation, circa 8 March 1831–A [D&C 46], josephsmithpapers.org.

5. Russell M. Nelson, "Worshiping at a Sacrament Meeting," *Ensign,* Aug. 2004, 28.

6. "Discourse by President George Q. Cannon," *Millennial Star* 56 (April 23, 1894): 260–61.

7. *Times and Seasons,* 15 June 1842, 823, josephsmithpapers.org.

8. Henry B. Eyring, "Gifts of the Spirit for Hard Times" (Brigham Young University devotional, Sept. 10, 2006), 4, speeches.byu.edu.

9. *Times and Seasons,* 15 June 1842, 823, josephsmithpapers.org.

10. *Teachings of Presidents of the Church: George Albert Smith* (2011), 28.

11. Joseph F. Merrill, in Conference Report, Oct. 1937, 72.

12. See *Doctrine and Covenants Commentary* (Salt Lake City, UT: Deseret Book, 1951), 274.

13. David A. Bednar, "The Tender Mercies of the Lord," *Ensign* or *Liahona,* May 2005, 99.

14. Dallin H Oaks, "The Keys and Authorities of the Priesthood," *Ensign* or *Liahona,* May 2014, 49.

15. J. Reuben Clark, in Conference Report, Apr. 1951, 154.

16. Stephen L. Richards, in Conference Report, Apr. 1950, 163–164.

17. Philo Dibble, "Recollections of the Prophet Joseph Smith," *Juvenile Instructor* 27, no. 10 (May 15, 1892): 303.

18. Levi Curtis, "Recollections of the Prophet Joseph Smith," *Juvenile Instructor* 27, no. 12 (June 15, 1892): 385–86.

19. Janiece Johnson and Jennifer Reeder, *The Witness of Women: Firsthand Experiences and Testimonies from the Restoration* (Salt Lake City, UT: Deseret Book, 2016), 103–104.

20. Johnson and Reeder, *The Witness of Women,* 103–104.

21. Discourse, between circa 26 June and circa 4 August 1839–A, 23, josephsmithpapers.org.

22. Johnson and Reeder, *The Witness of Women,* 99.

23. Joseph F. Smith, in Conference Report, Apr. 1900, 41.

24. *Times and Seasons,* 15 June 1842, 825–826, josephsmithpapers.org.

25. Boyd K. Packer, "The Twelve Apostles," *Ensign,* Nov. 1996, 7.

26. Bruce R. McConkie, *A New Witness for the Articles of Faith* (Salt Lake City, UT: Deseret Book, 1985), 371.

27. Marvin J. Ashton, "There are Many Gifts," *Ensign,* Nov. 1987, 20.

Doctrine and Covenants Section 47

Keep a Regular History

Historical Context

IN A REVELATION GIVEN IN APRIL 1829, OLIVER COWDERY WAS CALLED TO "write for my servant Joseph" (Doctrine and Covenants 9:4). However, by the spring of 1831, Oliver was away leading the mission to the Lamanites, to which he had been called by revelation (see Doctrine and Covenants 28:8). In his absence, the need arose for a new scribe and historian to take Oliver's place. John Whitmer was already serving as Joseph's scribe in a number of capacities when the call came to him to fill the post of Church Historian. At first John was reluctant to serve in this calling. He later wrote, "I was appointed by the voice of the Elders to keep the Church record. Joseph Smith Jr. said unto me you must also keep the Church history. I would rather not do it but observed that the will of the Lord be done, and if he desires it, I desire that he would manifest it through Joseph the Seer. And thus came the word of the Lord."[1]

Although he accepted the calling reluctantly, John diligently worked to fulfill the Lord's command. A few months later, in June 1831, he began writing a history he titled "The Book of John Whitmer." His history records many important details about the early Saints and their struggles in Ohio and Missouri. However, it seems that John felt insecure about his work. In 1833 he wrote to Oliver Cowdery, saying, "I want you to remember me to Joseph in a special manner, and enquire of him respecting my clerkship[;] you very well know what I mean and also my great desire of doing all things according to the mind of the Lord."[2]

John was excommunicated from the Church in 1838 on a charge of "unchristian like conduct."[3] He left the Church along with several other members of the Whitmer family, including David Whitmer and their brother-in-law Oliver Cowdery. At the time John left, he refused to turn his history over to the Church. Joseph Smith and Sidney Rigdon wrote to John, saying, "We are still willing to honor you, if you can be made to know your own interest and give up your notes, so that they can be corrected, and made fit for the press." After John's refusal, in 1838 Joseph began working on a new history that contained much more detail about early events in the Church. In January 1844 John offered to sell his history to the Church. Willard Richards, who was then compiling the history of the Church, wrote back informing John that Church historians had "already compiled about 800 pages of church history . . . which covers all the ground you took notes, therefore anything which you wrote in the shape of church history would be of little or no consequence to the church at large."[4]

After Joseph Smith's death, John joined James Strang's movement and began writing in his history again. He later left Strang's group and crossed out the portions of his history that were about Strang. John never rejoined the Church, and after his passing in 1878 his history eventually came into the custody of the Community of Christ. The final document is ninety-six pages in length.

In recent years, John's reputation as a historian has been somewhat rehabilitated. Historians working to compile the Joseph Smith Papers have noted that the number of documents related to the history of the Church increased substantially after John was called as Church Historian. In addition, after he began his service, the minutes of Church conferences and other meetings generally contained more information. Most importantly, John did a superb job recording most of the early revelations given to Joseph Smith in Revelation Book 1. The rich documentary record of the early Church owes a great debt to this reluctant historian. In the last entry of his history, John wrote and then crossed out his own hopes for salvation, writing, "Therefore I close the history of the church of Latter Day Saints, Hoping that I may be forgiven of my faults, and my sins be blotted out and in the last day be saved in the kingdom of God notwithstanding my present situation, which I hope will soon be bettered and I find favor in the eyes of God and all men, his saints. Farewell."[5]

Verse-by-Verse Commentary

1 Behold, it is expedient in me that my servant John should write and keep a regular history, and assist you, my servant Joseph, in transcribing all things which shall be given you, until he is called to further duties.

2 Again, verily I say unto you that he can also lift up his voice in meetings, whenever it shall be expedient.

3 And again, I say unto you that it shall be appointed unto him to keep the church record and history continually; for Oliver Cowdery I have appointed to another office.

4 Wherefore, it shall be given him, inasmuch as he is faithful, by the Comforter, to write these things. Even so. Amen.

The commandment given here highlights the importance of keeping a history. Note that the two words the Lord uses to describe the history are "regular" and "continual" (verses 1, 3). Throughout his prophetic service, Joseph Smith made diligent attempts to keep a regular and continually written documentary record of the history of the Church. The Articles and Covenants of the Church of Christ contained a brief sketch of the rise and progress of the Church, totaling about sixteen verses in the current version of the revelation (see Doctrine and Covenants 20:1–16). Beginning with this revelation, John Whitmer began recording a history, "The Book of John Whitmer," which included copies of revelations, letters, and other materials important to the history of the Church. In the summer of 1832, the year after this revelation was given, Joseph Smith and Frederick G. Williams wrote a six-page account titled "A History of the Life of Joseph Smith" that contained the earliest account of the First Vision. Oliver Cowdery began another history in 1834 and continued it until 1836; it contains many journal entries and transcripts of newspaper articles.

Ironically, it was John Whitmer's departure in 1838 that fully prompted Joseph Smith to take the reins in compiling and writing the history of the Church. This was a collaborative effort involving the assistance of clerks such as James Mulholland, Willard Richards, Howard Coray, and Robert B. Thompson. By the time Joseph Smith was killed in 1844, the "manuscript history of the Church," as it came to be known, numbered 812 pages in two substantial volumes. The history directly overseen by Joseph Smith ran up to August 1838. After Joseph's death, Brigham Young directed other Church leaders, such as Willard Richards and Wilford Woodruff, to complete the work. They relied on accounts from diligent record keepers, such as Thomas Bullock, William Clayton, and Eliza R. Snow. By 1856 the work had been reviewed by the First Presidency and was published as "The History of Joseph Smith."[6]

The massive task of compiling Church history should not overshadow the importance of each individual member keeping his or her own history. Such personal works are critical in the composition of larger historical stories and are an invaluable resource to loved ones. Individual leaders such as Heber J. Grant and Spencer W. Kimball kept journals that provide important insights into their lives and times. Wilford Woodruff's journal was so important to the compilation of the history of the Church that one historian declared, "Wilford Woodruff largely made the glasses through which we see the [Latter-day Saint] past."[7]

Addressing some of the concerns around keeping a regular and continual history, President Kimball made this prophetic promise: "People often use the excuse that their lives are uneventful and nobody would be interested in what they have done. But I promise you that if you will keep your journals and records they will indeed be a source of great inspiration to your families, to your children, your grandchildren, and others, on through the generations."[8]

End Notes

1. John Whitmer, History, 1831–circa 1847, 24, josephsmithpapers.org.
2. Lyndon W. Cook, *The Revelations of the Prophet Joseph Smith: A Historical and Biographical Commentary of the Doctrine and Covenants* (Salt Lake City, UT: Deseret Book, 1985), 64–65.
3. Minute Book 2, 104–105, josephsmithpapers.org.
4. Journal, December 1842–June 1844; Book 3, 15 July 1843–29 February 1844, 274, footnote 543, josephsmithpapers.org.
5. John Whitmer, History, 1831–circa 1847, 85, josephsmithpapers.org. See also "Historical Introduction," Revelation, circa 8 March 1831–B [D&C 47], josephsmithpapers.org.
6. Introduction to History, 1838–1856 (Manuscript History of the Church), josephsmithpapers.org.
7. Steven C. Harper and Richard E. Turley Jr., *Preserving the History of the Latter-day Saints* (Salt Lake City, UT: Deseret Book, 2010), 117.
8. Spencer W. Kimball, "Hold Fast to the Iron Rod," *Ensign*, Nov. 1978, 4.

Doctrine and Covenants Section 48

Be Gathered with Your Families

Historical Context

IN THE SPRING OF 1831 THE SAINTS IN KIRTLAND FOUND THEMSELVES IN the midst of a refugee crisis. More than a hundred Church members from New York were making their way to Kirtland and the surrounding areas as part of the Lord's commandment to gather to Ohio (see Doctrine and Covenants 37). John Whitmer recorded in his history, "The time drew near for the brethren from the State of New York to arrive at Kirtland Ohio. And some had supposed that it was the place of gathering even the place of the New Jerusalem spoken of in the Book of Mormon, according to the visions and revelations received in the last days. There was no preparation made for the reception of the Saints from the East. The Bishop [Edward Partridge] being anxious to know something concerning the matter. Therefore, the Lord spake unto Joseph Smith Jr. as follows."[1]

According to John Whitmer's record, Church leaders faced two challenges. First, some members believed that the Kirtland area was the place for the New Jerusalem. In the revelation, the Lord addresses this misunderstanding by informing the Saints that He had not yet revealed the place for the city (see Doctrine and Covenants 48:5). Second, Bishop Partridge and others sought guidance on how to utilize the law of consecration, which had been revealed only one month earlier, to assist the Saints from the East who were gathering to Kirtland. In the revelation, the Lord emphasized the importance of flexibility in the implementation of the law, asking the bishop and other Church leaders to consider "every man according to his family, according to his circumstances" (Doctrine and Covenants 48:6).[2]

Verse-by-Verse Commentary

1 It is necessary that ye should remain for the present time in your places of abode, as it shall be suitable to your circumstances.

2 And inasmuch as ye have lands, ye shall impart to the eastern brethren;

3 And inasmuch as ye have not lands, let them buy for the present time in those regions round about, as seemeth them good, for it must needs be necessary that they have places to live for the present time.

In this revelation we see an early practical implementation of the law of consecration. With the Saints from the Eastern states expected to begin arriving in Kirtland, the Lord asked the Saints there to share their property to help those in need. One of the basic principles of consecration is that the resources of a group of people can make more of a difference than those of a single individual or family. While individual acts of charity are commendable, organized consecration among the Saints can help far more people.

Elder Christofferson taught that one of the major reasons "the Savior works through a church, His Church, . . . is to achieve needful things that cannot be accomplished by individuals or smaller groups. One clear example is dealing with poverty. It is true that as individuals and families we look after the physical needs of others, 'imparting to one another both temporally and spiritually according to their needs and their wants' (Mosiah 18:29). But together in the Church, the ability to care for the poor and needy is multiplied to meet the broader need, and hoped-for self-reliance is made a reality for very many."[3]

4 It must needs be necessary that ye save all the money that ye can, and that ye obtain all that ye can in righteousness, that in time ye may be enabled to purchase land for an inheritance, even the city.

5 The place is not yet to be revealed; but after your brethren come from the east there are to be certain men appointed, and to them it shall be given to know the place, or to them it shall be revealed.

6 And they shall be appointed to purchase the lands, and to make a commencement to lay the foundation of the city; and then shall ye begin to be gathered with your families, every man according to his family, according to his circumstances, and as is appointed to him by the presidency and the bishop of the church, according to the laws and commandments which ye have received, and which ye shall hereafter receive. Even so. Amen.

At this point, the location of the city of Zion was unrevealed. The location was given a few months later in Doctrine and Covenants 57:1–2. Nevertheless, the Lord gave the Saints a commandment to begin laying up reserves in anticipation of the sacrifices necessary to build the city. The Saints at this time could not have known the trials they would experience as they worked to build Zion and were driven from place to place.

In a similar manner, prophets and apostles in our time have advised the Saints to be careful with their spending and to keep a reserve in anticipation of future needs. Elder Joseph B. Wirthlin counseled:

During times of prosperity, save up for a day of want. Too often, people assume that they probably never will be injured, get sick, lose their jobs, or see their investments evaporate. To make matters worse, often people make purchases today based upon optimistic predictions of what they hope will happen tomorrow. The wise understand the importance of saving today for a rainy day tomorrow. They have adequate insurance that will provide for them in case of illness or death. Where possible, they store a year's supply of food, water, and other basic necessities of life. They set aside money in savings and investment accounts. They work diligently to reduce the debt they owe to others and strive to become debt free.

Brothers and sisters, the preparations you make today may one day be to you as the stored food was to the Egyptians and to Joseph's father's family.[4]

End *Notes*

1. John Whitmer, History, 1831–circa 1847, 23, josephsmithpapers.org.
2. See "Historical Introduction," Revelation, 10 March 1831 [D&C 48], josephsmithpapers.org.
3. D. Todd Christofferson, "Why the Church," *Ensign* or *Liahona*, Nov. 2015, 110.
4. Joseph B. Wirthlin, "Earthly Debts, Heavenly Debts," *Ensign* or *Liahona*, May 2004, 42.

$\mathcal{D}$octrine and $\mathcal{C}$ovenants
Section 49
Unto the Shakers

$\mathcal{H}$istorical $\mathcal{C}$ontext

WHEN LEMAN COPLEY CHOSE TO BE BAPTIZED IN 1831, HE WAS A PROSPER-ous farmer living in Thompson, Ohio, a settlement just a few miles away from Kirtland, where the Saints were gathering. Leman had previously been a member of the United Society of Believers in Christ's Second Appearing when missionaries arrived in his area and began sharing a message about the Book of Mormon. Members of Leman's former religion were more commonly known by the nickname Shakers because their worship services included, at times, a kind of euphoric dancing.

Leman may have been attracted to the new Church because of its similarities to the doctrine of the Shakers. The Saints and the Shakers both believed that there had been a general apostasy of the Christian faith, that men and women had agency, that the Lord had called new prophets, and that believers should share resources to reduce poverty. However, there were also sharp differences between the Shakers' doctrine and Leman's new faith. For example, the Shakers rejected the need for baptism and any other ordinance of the gospel. Some Shakers practiced vegetarianism. Shakers, along with others in America (though perhaps not to the same extent), also believed that celibacy was a higher form of life. One Shaker leader taught that celibacy was "the key to sinless perfection and salvation." This doctrine led to a segregation of the sexes and influenced all other aspects of Shaker life.[1] Finally, the Shakers believed that Jesus Christ had already returned to earth in the form of Mother Ann Lee (1736–1784), an early leader who defined many of the Shakers' beliefs.[2]

Leman Copley lived about thirty-five miles away from the primary Shaker community in the area and appears to not have fully involved himself in the lifestyle of the Shakers. After he was baptized into the Church, he was chided by Ashbel Kitchell, the local leader of the Shakers, for giving up on their plan of celibacy and for having "taken up with Mormonism as the easier plan."[3] Troubled over leaving the Shakers, Leman approached Joseph Smith and asked for a revelation clarifying some of the doctrines he had questions about. Joseph Smith later recorded, "About this time came Leman Copley, one of the sect called Shaking Quakers, and embraced the fulness of the everlasting gospel, apparently honest hearted, but still retained ideas that the Shakers were right in some particulars of their faith; and, in order to have more perfect understanding on the subject, I inquired of the Lord and received the following revelation [Doctrine and Covenants 49]"[4]

In the revelation, the Lord called Sidney Rigdon and Parley P. Pratt to accompany Copley on a visit to the Shakers. The three men were directed to read the revelation to the Shakers and to attempt to correct the Shakers' incorrect beliefs. With the revelation in hand, Sidney, Parley, and Leman set out to travel to a nearby Shaker community located in North Union, Ohio.[5]

$\mathcal{V}$erse-by-$\mathcal{V}$erse $\mathcal{C}$ommentary

1 Hearken unto my word, my servants Sidney, and Parley, and Leman; for behold, verily I say unto you, that I give unto you a commandment that you shall go and preach my gospel which ye have received, even as ye have received it, unto the Shakers.

2 Behold, I say unto you, that they desire to know the truth in part, but not all, for they are not right before me and must needs repent.

3 Wherefore, I send you, my servants Sidney and Parley, to preach the gospel unto them.

4 And my servant Leman shall be ordained unto this work, that he may reason with them, not according to that which he has received of them, but according to that which shall be taught him by you my servants; and by so doing I will bless him, otherwise he shall not prosper.

Sidney Rigdon and Parley P. Pratt were probably the most qualified missionaries among the Saints to minister to the Shakers. Parley grew up in New Lebanon, New York, close to the largest and most important Shaker community, the Mount Lebanon Shaker Society. Records also show that Parley had several extended family members who were Shakers. Sidney had been a minister in the region for several years and was a strong proponent of communalism, making it likely that he traded and had economic connections with the Shaker communities in North Union, Ohio.[6]

The Shakers had been visited earlier by Oliver Cowdery and the missionaries sent to preach to the Lamanites (see Doctrine and Covenants 28:8). Several copies of the Book of Mormon had been circulated among the Shakers, but the Shakers appeared to show little interest. Ashbel Kitchell later wrote that the missionaries left him with a copy of the Book of Mormon before they departed: "They thought it prudent to wait on us a while for the leaven to work, so that thing moved on smoothly for sometime and we had time for reflection."[7]

According to Kitchell's account of the meeting, there may have been some hesitation on Sidney Rigdon's part to share the revelation. Initially Sidney arrived accompanied only by Leman Copley, and the two men did not share the revelation right away. Kitchell recorded, "They tarried all night, and in the course of the evening, the doctrines of the cross and the Mormon faith were both investigated. . . . Thus the matter stood when we retired to rest, not knowing that they had in possession what they called a revelation or message from Jesus Christ to us." The next day, which was the Sabbath, Parley P. Pratt arrived and announced that "they had come with the authority of the Lord Jesus Christ, and the people must hear it." Shortly after, Sidney Rigdon read the message to the Shakers.[8]

5 Thus saith the Lord; for I am God, and have sent mine Only Begotten Son into the world for the redemption of the world, and have decreed that he that receiveth him shall be saved, and he that receiveth him not shall be damned—

6 And they have done unto the Son of Man even as they listed; and he has taken his power on the right hand of his glory, and now reigneth in the heavens, and will reign till he descends on the earth to put all enemies under his feet, which time is nigh at hand—

7 I, the Lord God, have spoken it; but the hour and the day no man knoweth, neither the angels in heaven, nor shall they know until he comes.

The revelation shows no hesitation in addressing the most important teaching of the Church: the mission of Jesus Christ to redeem the world. This teaching may have been a sharp point of disagreement between the missionaries and the Shakers. According to some sources, early Shakers tended to reject the vicarious Atonement of Jesus Christ, instead seeing "the role of Christ as an example for Believers."[9] The Lord directly addresses this belief, unequivocally stating that He came to redeem the world and that acceptance of this mission is a matter of salvation or damnation.

Surprisingly, Latter-day Saints have been accused of similarly downplaying the importance of the atoning acts of Jesus Christ. A 1980 article in *Newsweek* magazine incorrectly reported that "unlike orthodox Christians, Mormons believe that men . . . earn their way to godhood by the proper exercise of free will, rather than through the grace of Jesus Christ. Thus, Jesus' suffering and death in the Mormon view were brotherly acts of compassion, but they do not atone for the sins of others."[10] In contrast to this claim, the First Presidency and the Quorum of the Twelve Apostles have unanimously testified that Jesus Christ "gave His life to atone for the sins of all mankind. His was a great vicarious gift in behalf of all who would ever live upon the earth."[11]

Latter-day Saints must be careful to follow this example when introducing our beliefs to people of other faiths. We must begin by explaining clearly and carefully that Jesus Christ is the center of our faith. We are blessed to have a unique and expansive theology that embraces all facets of a person's existence, but none of our beliefs hold meaning without a knowledge of the saving work of Christ. President Nelson taught, "If we as a people and as individuals are to have access to the power of the Atonement of Jesus Christ—to cleanse and heal us, to strengthen and magnify us, and ultimately to exalt us—we must clearly acknowledge Him as the source of that power."[12]

8 Wherefore, I will that all men shall repent, for all are under sin, except those which I have reserved unto myself, holy men that ye know not of.

9 Wherefore, I say unto you that I have sent unto you mine everlasting covenant, even that which was from the beginning.

10 And that which I have promised I have so fulfilled, and the nations of the earth shall bow to it; and, if not of themselves, they shall come down, for that which is now exalted of itself shall be laid low of power.

11 Wherefore, I give unto you a commandment that ye go among this people, and say unto them, like unto mine apostle of old, whose name was Peter:

12 Believe on the name of the Lord Jesus, who was on the earth, and is to come, the beginning and the end;

13 Repent and be baptized in the name of Jesus Christ, according to the holy commandment, for the remission of sins;

14 And whoso doeth this shall receive the gift of the Holy Ghost, by the laying on of the hands of the elders of the church.

Here the Lord addresses the second great concern between the Saints and their Shaker neighbors, specifically that the Shakers believed no ordinances were necessary for salvation. The Lord makes reference to the "everlasting covenant" made possible through the ordinances of the gospel of Jesus Christ. In a later revelation, the Lord taught Joseph Smith that "in the ordinances thereof, the power of godliness is manifest. And without the ordinances thereof, and the authority of the priesthood, the power of godliness is not manifest unto men in the flesh" (Doctrine and Covenants 84:20–21). Simply put, the gospel of Jesus Christ is redemptive. As the Savior states in this revelation, the starting point of the gospel is an acknowledgment that all have sinned and fallen short of the glory of God (see Romans 3:23–24; Alma 34:9–10). The ordinances of the gospel allow men and women to be cleansed of their sins by entering into a covenant relationship with Jesus Christ.

While some aspects of salvation, such as physical resurrection, come to all people without ordinances, the highest blessings of the gospel require ordinances. In an 1844 discourse, Joseph Smith declared, "The question is frequently asked, can we not be saved without going through with all these ordinances? I would answer no, not the fulness of salvation."[13] The Savior invited the Shakers to enter into the most basic ordinance of the gospel—baptism—followed by confirmation and the gift of the Holy Ghost.

In our time, some have downplayed the importance of ordinances, in part because the majority of the human race has not been given the opportunity to receive them. However, the importance of ordinances in the teachings of the Savior and His prophets is indisputable (see Matthew 28:9; Mark 16:16; John 3:5; Ether 4:18; Doctrine and Covenants 112:28–29). Later revelations and keys given to Joseph Smith opened the door for all people, both the living and the dead, to receive the ordinances of the gospel of Jesus Christ.

> 15 And again, verily I say unto you, that whoso forbiddeth to marry is not ordained of God, for marriage is ordained of God unto man.
>
> 16 Wherefore, it is lawful that he should have one wife, and they twain shall be one flesh, and all this that the earth might answer the end of its creation;
>
> 17 And that it might be filled with the measure of man, according to his creation before the world was made.

Addressing the Shaker belief that celibacy was a higher form of life, the Lord upholds the sanctity of marriage, even identifying it as one of the purposes of the creation of the earth. In the New Testament, one of the epistles written to Timothy highlights "forbidding to marry" as one of the signs of apostasy (see 1 Timothy 4:3). Subsequent revelations to Joseph Smith also emphasized the importance of marriage in the plan of salvation (see Doctrine and Covenants 2; 131–132). In 1995 the First Presidency and Quorum of the Twelve Apostles paraphrased this section of the revelation in proclaiming that "marriage between a man and a woman is ordained of God and that the family is central to the Creator's plan for the eternal destiny of His children."[14]

The Lord's statement that "it is lawful that he should have one wife" was consistent with the Church's teachings at the time this revelation was given. In the 1835 edition of the Doctrine and Covenants, an article was included that specified "that one man should have one wife; and one woman, but one husband."[15] The article was not presented as a revelation and was generally attributed to Oliver Cowdery. The article was removed from the Doctrine and Covenants when section 132, which was a revelation, was placed in the scriptural canon, supplanting it in importance. Doctrine and Covenants 132 further underlined the idea that marriage was sacred and established that marriages performed by the proper authority and sealed by the Holy Spirit of promise would endure in the next life (see Doctrine and Covenants 132:19).

> 18 And whoso forbiddeth to abstain from meats, that man should not eat the same, is not ordained of God;
>
> 19 For, behold, the beasts of the field and the fowls of the air, and that which cometh of the earth, is ordained for the use of man for food and for raiment, and that he might have in abundance.
>
> 20 But it is not given that one man should possess that which is above another, wherefore the world lieth in sin.
>
> 21 And wo be unto man that sheddeth blood or that wasteth flesh and hath no need.

The revelation next addresses vegetarianism among the Shakers. It should be noted that the Lord does not disapprove of vegetarianism itself, only the act of forbidding others to eat meat. He specifies that the use of animals for food and clothing is appropriate as long as men and women act as wise stewards to their environment (see Genesis 1:26; Doctrine and Covenants 59:15–21). The Lord condemns the unnecessary shedding of blood or wasting of flesh. This is consistent with earlier scripture. The Lord instructed anciently that "surely, blood shall not be shed, only for meat, to save your lives; and the blood of every beast will I require at your hands" (Joseph Smith Translation, Genesis 9:11 [in Genesis 9:4, footnote a]).

Several years after this revelation was given, Joseph Smith reported an incident that illustrated this teaching. While Joseph was traveling with Zion's Camp, the men on the expedition encountered three rattlesnakes and were about to kill them when Joseph intervened. "I said let them alone, don't hurt them, how will the serpent ever lose its venom, while the servants of God possess the same disposition, and continue to make war upon them," Joseph later wrote in his history. He taught the brethren that "men must become harmless before the brute creation, and when men lose their vicious dispositions and cease to destroy the animal race, the lion and the lamb can dwell together, and the sucking child play with the serpent with safety."[16]

Following the Prophet's counsel, the men carefully lifted the snakes with sticks and carried them to a safe location. Joseph added, "I exhorted the brethren not to kill a serpent, bird, or any animal of any kind, during our journey unless it were necessary to preserve ourselves from hunger." Illustrating that he was not against the use of animals for food, Joseph also spoke of another occasion when he saw a group of men observing a squirrel in a tree: "To prove them and know if they would heed my counsel, I took one of their guns, shot the squirrel and passed on, leaving the Squirrel on the ground." Elder Orson Hyde, who was present, "came up, picked up the squirrel, and said, 'We will cook this, that nothing may be lost.'"[17]

> 22 And again, verily I say unto you, that the Son of Man cometh not in the form of a woman, neither of a man traveling on the earth.
>
> 23 Wherefore, be not deceived, but continue in steadfastness, looking forth for the heavens to be shaken, and the earth to tremble and to reel to and fro as a drunken man, and for the valleys to be exalted, and for the mountains to be made low, and for the rough places to become smooth—and all this when the angel shall sound his trumpet.

The revelation to the Shakers establishes two things about the Second Coming: first, that "no man . . . neither the angels in heaven" knows the time of the Savior's coming (see Doctrine and Covenants 49:7), and second, that the Savior would not return to earth in the same manner as His first coming. The Christmas story, with a helpless baby in a manger, would not be repeated (see Doctrine and Covenants 29:11; 34:7; 45:16; 65:5). This time, the Savior would return to earth in a glorified, resurrected body. The most accurate model for the Savior's return is found in the early chapters of 3 Nephi, where natural and societal upheavals led to disarray among the Nephites and Lamanites until the Savior arrived in glory.

In contrast, the Shakers believed that Jesus had already returned to the earth, being born again in the form of Ann Lee, the most important leader among the Shakers. The words of the Lord to the Shakers establishes that a mortal person claiming to be the reincarnated or returned Jesus Christ is in error or is deliberately trying to deceive. The return of the Savior might occur in an unexpected way, but it will be unmistakable when it occurs. Ancient and modern scripture agree that the Savior's return to earth will be a grand event seen by all the world (see Matthew 24:30; Revelation 1:7; Doctrine and Covenants 64:23).

Another error on the part of the Shakers is that they claimed the Savior's gender was changed when He returned. The Shakers believed that God had a dual nature that was both male and female. The Shakers' emphasis on the equality of men and women was admirable, but their understanding of the eternal nature of gender was flawed. In contrast, modern prophets and apostles have testified that "gender is an essential characteristic of individual premortal, mortal, and eternal identity and purpose."[18]

> 24 But before the great day of the Lord shall come, Jacob shall flourish in the wilderness, and the Lamanites shall blossom as the rose.
>
> 25 Zion shall flourish upon the hills and rejoice upon the mountains, and shall be assembled together unto the place which I have appointed.

At the time the Book of Mormon was published, there was a long-standing tradition of people of European ancestry claiming a link to the lost tribes of Israel. When the Book of Mormon was published, it challenged its readers to consider the possibility that throughout history, God has sent inspired teachers to people in different locations around the world. The title page of the Book of Mormon directly proclaims that "Jesus is the Christ, the Eternal God, manifesting himself unto all nations." The Lord has directed the Saints to extend the blessings of the gospel to many groups, including the Lamanites, who were initially understood to be the American Indians.

While early Church members applied these promises directly to the American Indians, the common conception of Lamanite identity has broadened over time to include Pacific Islanders and other people of native ancestry. The term *Lamanite* is used fluidly in the Book of Mormon, sometimes speaking of ancestry (see Mosiah 10:11–17) and sometimes speaking of an ideological alignment (see 4 Nephi 1:36–38). In the latter days, some Latter-day Saints have used the term *Lamanite* in a derogatory way, but for the most part it has been used as a term to extend and apply the scriptural blessings promised to the house of Israel. An official Church essay concerning Lamanite identity proclaims that "Saints who have identified as Lamanites have made substantial contributions to the Church and to their communities as they have aimed to realize the Lord's promises to His covenant people."[19]

Larry Echohawk, a Church leader of American Indian ancestry, spoke about his experience with the Book of Mormon, saying, "As I read the Book of Mormon, it seemed to me that it was about my American Indian ancestors." He further added, "I especially ask the remnant of the house of Israel, the descendants of the people of the Book of Mormon, wherever you may be, to read and reread the Book of Mormon. Learn of the promises contained in the Book of Mormon. Follow the teachings and example of Jesus Christ. Make and keep covenants with the Lord. Seek for and follow the guidance of the Holy Spirit."[20]

The Lord's promise that "Jacob shall flourish in the wilderness, and the Lamanites shall blossom as the rose" (verse 24) undoubtedly will be fulfilled in multiple ways. One of the most positive ways to apply the prophecy given by the Lord in this revelation is to see all people as potential heirs to the promises made to Israel, regardless of their background.

> 26 Behold, I say unto you, go forth as I have commanded you; repent of all your sins; ask and ye shall receive; knock and it shall be opened unto you.
>
> 27 Behold, I will go before you and be your rearward; and I will be in your midst, and you shall not be confounded.
>
> 28 Behold, I am Jesus Christ, and I come quickly. Even so. Amen.

The Shakers rejected the revelation given to them. After Sidney Rigdon finished reading the revelation, Ashbel Kitchell announced that "I would release them and their Christ from any further burden about us, and take all the responsibility on myself." Rigdon then asked to hear from the congregation who, according to Kitchell, declared "that they were fully satisfied with what they had." Kitchell further recorded that "upon hearing this Rigdon professed to be satisfied and put his paper by; but Parley P. Pratt arose and commenced shaking his coattail; he said he shook the dust from his garments as a testimony against us, that we had rejected the word of the Lord Jesus." Kitchell rebuked Parley and then accused Leman Copley of hypocrisy, reducing Copley to tears.[21]

The experience left Leman Copley shaken, and he began to vacillate between his commitment to the Church and to the Shakers. When he returned home, he refused to honor a prior agreement he had made to permit Church members migrating from Colesville, New York, to live on his farm (see Doctrine and Covenants 54). Over the next few years, Copley went back and forth between the Saints and the Shakers, eventually settling with neither. He joined several different Christian churches and remained near his home in Thompson, Ohio, until his death in 1862.[22]

As for the Shakers, they continued to grow throughout the nineteenth century, but in the twentieth century, their movement entered a sharp decline. At the movement's peak, there were 2,000–4,000 Shakers living in eighteen different communities. However, the Shaker belief in celibacy, combined with stricter laws making it illegal for religious groups to adopt children, meant that the Shaker population decreased swiftly. By the twenty-first century, there was only one remaining Shaker community, at Sabbathday Lake in Maine. Only a handful of Shakers remain today.[23]

End Notes

1. See Clarke Garrett, *From the old world to the new world: Origins of the Shakers* (Baltimore, MD: Johns Hopkins University Press, 1998), 152–153, 223, 233–234.

2. See Matthew McBride, "Leman Copley and the Shakers," in *Revelations in Context* (2016).

3. McBride, "Leman Copley and the Shakers."

4. Joseph Smith, in History, 1838–1856, volume A-1 [23 December 1805–30 August 1834], 112, josephsmithpapers.org.

5. See McBride, "Leman Copley and the Shakers." See also "Historical Introduction," Revelation, 7 May 1831 [D&C 49], josephsmithpapers.org.

6. See Mario S. De Pillis, *The Development of Mormon Communitarianism, 1826–1846* (Ann Arbor, MI: University Microfilms, 1960), 56–62, 65–66.

7. Lawrence R. Flake, "A Shaker View of a Mormon Mission," *BYU Studies* 20, no. 1 (1979): 2.

8. See Flake, "A Shaker View of a Mormon Mission," 2–3.

9. Stephen J. Stein, *The Shaker Experience in America: A History of the United Society of Believers* (New Haven, CT: Yale University Press, 1992), 75.

10. *Newsweek*, Sept. 1, 1980, 68.

11. "The Living Christ: The Testimony of the Apostles," Gospel Library.

12. Russell M. Nelson, "The Correct Name of the Church," *Ensign* or *Liahona*, Nov. 2018, 88.

13. Discourse, 21 January 1844, as Reported by Wilford Woodruff, 183, josephsmithpapers.org.

14. "The Family: A Proclamation to the World," Gospel Library.

15. Doctrine and Covenants, 1835, 251, josephsmithpapers.org.

16. Joseph Smith, in History, 1838–1856, volume A-1 [23 December 1805–30 August 1834], 8 [addenda], josephsmithpapers.org.

17. History, 1838–1856, volume A-1 [23 December 1805–30 August 1834], 8 [addenda], josephsmithpapers.org.

18. "The Family: A Proclamation to the World," Gospel Library.

19. Church History Topics, "Lamanite Identity," Gospel Library.

20. Larry Echohawk, "Come unto Me, O Ye House of Israel," *Ensign* or *Liahona*, Nov. 2012, 33.

21. See Flake, "A Shaker View of a Mormon Mission," 3.

22. See "Biography: Copley, Leman," Joseph Smith Papers, accessed Feb. 13, 2023, https://www.josephsmithpapers.org/person/leman-copley.

23. See Katherine Lucky, "The Last Shakers?," *Commonweal*, Nov. 28, 2019, https://www.commonwealmagazine.org/last-shakers.

Doctrine and Covenants
Section 50
Both Are Edified and Rejoice Together

Historical Context

FROM THE TIME JOSEPH SMITH ARRIVED IN OHIO, A MAJOR CAUSE FOR CONcern among the converts in Kirtland was their overabundance of religious enthusiasm. John Whitmer, the first Church leader from the East to arrive in Ohio, noted with some distress that "the enemy of all righteous had got hold of some of those who professed to be his followers, because they had not sufficient knowledge to detect him in all his devices." Describing the unusual manifestations among the converts in more detail, Whitmer recorded the following:

> Some had visions and could not tell what they saw, some would fancy to themselves that they had the sword of Laban, and would wield it as expert as a light dragoon, some would act like an Indian in the act of scalping, some would slide or scoot [on] the floor, with the rapidity of a serpent, which the[y] termed sailing in the boat to the Lamanites, preaching the

gospel. And many other vain and foolish maneuvers that are unseeming, and unprofitable to mention. Thus the devil blinded the eyes of some good and honest disciples.[1]

Parley P. Pratt, returning from his mission to the Lamanites, also noted disturbing manifestations among the individuals whom he had helped convert just a few months earlier. "As I went forth among the different branches, some very strange spiritual operations were manifested, which were disgusting, rather than edifying," he later wrote. "Some persons would seem to swoon away, and make unseemly gestures, and be drawn or disfigured in their countenances. Others would fall into ecstasies, and be drawn into contortions, cramp, fits, etc. Others would seem to have visions and revelations, which were not edifying, and which were not congenial to the doctrine and spirit of the gospel. In short, a false and lying spirit seemed to be creeping into the Church."[2]

Even people not affiliated with the Church began to notice these unsettling displays among the converts. A reporter from the nearby newspaper, the *Painesville Telegraph*, wrote, "A scene of the wildest enthusiasm was exhibited, chiefly, however, among the young people; they would fall, as without strength, roll upon the floor, and, so mad were they that even the females were seen in a cold winter day, lying under the bare canopy of heaven, with no couch or pillow but the fleecy snow." The *Telegraph* article also noted, "At other times they are taken with a fit of jabbering that which they neither understand themselves nor any body else, and this they call speaking foreign languages by divine inspiration. Again, the young men are seen running over the hills in pursuit, they say, of balls of fire which they see flying through the air."[3]

Some of these manifestations became physically dangerous. An early African American convert to the Church, known only in the record as "Black Pete," was almost seriously injured during one such incident. According to Elder George A. Smith (who was later the Church Historian), "Black Pete got sight of one of those revelations carried by a black angel. . . . He started after it, and ran off a steep wash bank twenty-five feet high, passed through a tree top into the Chagrin river beneath. He came out with a few scratches, and his ardor somewhat cooled."[4] A newspaper from the time also noted the incident, though it mixed up some of the details: "The Mormonites have among them an African (or, as [abolitionist William Lloyd] Garrison would say, an Africo American,) who fancies he can fly. . . . He accordingly chose the elevated bank of Lake Erie as a starting place, and, spreading his pinions, he lit on a tree-top, some fifty [feet] below, sustaining no other damage than the demolition of his faith in wings without feathers."[5]

Concerned over these manifestations, Church leaders asked Joseph Smith for a revelation to clarify the matter. John Whitmer later recorded, "These things grieved the servants of the Lord, and some conversed together on this subject, and others came in and we were at Joseph Smith Jr. the seers, and made it a matter of consultation, for many would not turn from their folly, unless God would give a revelation, therefore the Lord spake to Joseph."[6]

This revelation, now known as Doctrine and Covenants 50, was received in the presence of several people. Parley P. Pratt noted the way the revelation came to Joseph Smith: "Feeling our weakness and inexperience, and lest we should err in judgment concerning these spiritual phenomena, myself, John Murdock, and several other Elders, went to Joseph Smith and asked him to inquire of the Lord concerning these spirits or manifestations. After we had joined in prayer in his translating room, he dictated in our presence the following revelation [section 50]." Parley also recorded the manner in which Joseph dictated the revelation:

> Each sentence was uttered slowly and very distinctly, and with a pause between each, sufficiently long for it to be recorded, by an ordinary writer, in long hand. This was the manner in which all his written revelations were dictated and written. There was never any hesitation, reviewing, or reading back, in order to keep the run of the subject; neither did any of these communications undergo revisions, interlinings, or corrections. As he dictated them so they stood, so far as I have witnessed; and I was present to witness the dictation of several communications of several pages each.[7]

Verse-by-Verse Commentary

1 Hearken, O ye elders of my church, and give ear to the voice of the living God; and attend to the words of wisdom which shall be given unto you, according as ye have asked and are agreed as touching the church, and the spirits which have gone abroad in the earth.

2 Behold, verily I say unto you, that there are many spirits which are false spirits, which have gone forth in the earth, deceiving the world.

3 And also Satan hath sought to deceive you, that he might overthrow you.

4 Behold, I, the Lord, have looked upon you, and have seen abominations in the church that profess my name.

5 But blessed are they who are faithful and endure, whether in life or in death, for they shall inherit eternal life.

The events in Kirtland in the spring of 1831 show that during times of great spiritual progress, the adversary often takes advantage of the overzealous and leads them into wayward paths. While Satan uses different tactics during different times, his will to deceive remains constant.

More than a decade after Doctrine and Covenants 50 was received, an editorial entitled "Try the Spirits" was published in the *Times and Seasons* newspaper. The editorial was written under Joseph Smith's direction and was later published in Joseph Smith's official history. It reads in part, "Recent occurrences that have transpired amongst us render it an imperative duty devolving upon me to say something in relation to the spirits by which men are actuated. It is evident from the apostle's writings that many false spirits existed in their day, and had 'gone forth into the world,' and that it needed intelligence which God alone could impart to detect false spirits, and to prove what spirits were of God."

The editorial cites several scriptural examples in which evil spirits deceived men and women:

The Egyptians were not able to discover the difference between the miracles of Moses and those of the magicians until they came to be tested together; and if Moses had not appeared in their midst they would unquestionably have thought that the miracles of the magicians were performed through the mighty power of God; for they were great miracles that were performed by them: a supernatural agency was developed; and great power manifested.

"Try the spirits," says John, but who is to do it? The learned, the eloquent, the philosopher, the sage, the divine, all are ignorant . . . but no one can try his own, and what is the reason? because they have not a key to unlock, no rule wherewith to measure, and no criterion whereby they can test it; could anyone tell the length, breadth, or height of a building without a rule? test the quality of metals without a criterion, or point out the movements of the planetary system without a knowledge of astronomy? certainly not: and if such ignorance as this is manifested about a spirit of this kind who can describe an angel of light, if Satan should appear as one in glory? . . . We answer that no man can do this without the Priesthood, and having a knowledge of the laws by which spirits are governed; for as, 'no man knows the things of God but by the spirit of God,' so no man knows the spirit of the devil and his power and influence but by possessing intelligence which is more than human, and having unfolded through the medium of the Priesthood the mysterious operations of his devices.[8]

Satan and his servants are well practiced in carrying out deception. However, the Prophet teaches that through the priesthood, the influence of the Holy Ghost, and a knowledge of the laws of God, we can identify and counter the deceptions of the adversary. The editorial adds, "It requires the spirit of God, to know the things of God, and the spirit of the devil can only be unmasked through that medium."[9]

> 6 But wo unto them that are deceivers and hypocrites, for, thus saith the Lord, I will bring them to judgment.
>
> 7 Behold, verily I say unto you, there are hypocrites among you, who have deceived some, which has given the adversary power; but behold such shall be reclaimed;
>
> 8 But the hypocrites shall be detected and shall be cut off, either in life or in death, even as I will; and wo unto them who are cut off from my church, for the same are overcome of the world.
>
> 9 Wherefore, let every man beware lest he do that which is not in truth and righteousness before me.

During His ministry on earth, the Savior frequently condemned the sin of hypocrisy. He called out the scribes and Pharisees in His time for their hypocrisy (see Matthew 23:23; Luke 11:44). On one occasion, the Savior said, "Now do ye Pharisees make clean the outside of the cup and the platter; but your inward part is full of ravening and wickedness" (Luke 11:39). Similarly, the Savior is quick to condemn hypocrisy in the latter days. When the Savior spoke to Joseph Smith during the First Vision, He remarked that the religious leaders of the time "draw near to me with their lips while their hearts are far from me."[10]

Undoubtedly, there are still hypocrites within the Church today, just as there were in Kirtland. Each of us should take a hard look at our own hypocrisies and shortcomings and see how to best overcome them. In an 1843 discourse, Joseph Smith taught, "I do not think there have been many good men on the Earth since the days of Adam, but there was one good man, and his name was Jesus. Many persons think a Prophet must be a great deal better than anybody else. Suppose I would condescend, yes I will call it condescend, to be a great deal better than any of you. I would be raised up to the highest heaven, and who should I have to accompany me?" He added, "I love that man better who swears a stream as long as my arm, yet deals justice to his neighbors and mercifully deals his substance to the poor, than the long smooth faced hypocrite. I don't want you to think I am very righteous, for I am not. God judges men according to the use they make of the light which he gives them."[11]

> 10 And now come, saith the Lord, by the Spirit, unto the elders of his church, and let us reason together, that ye may understand;
>
> 11 Let us reason even as a man reasoneth one with another face to face.
>
> 12 Now, when a man reasoneth he is understood of man, because he reasoneth as a man; even so will I, the Lord, reason with you that you may understand.
>
> 13 Wherefore, I the Lord ask you this question—unto what were ye ordained?
>
> 14 To preach my gospel by the Spirit, even the Comforter which was sent forth to teach the truth.

Though the Savior is an omniscient being and could simply offer corrections by decree, He often employs the technique of reasoning. Gently but firmly, He leads His disciples to correct conclusions by asking questions that allow them to use their own intellect and knowledge. There is wisdom in asking inspired questions to a seeker of truth rather than just providing the answer. As the most inspired of teachers, the Savior models good teaching by asking the disciples to consider what they were ordained to in the first place and what it means to preach the gospel by the power of the Holy Ghost.

While the manifestations among the Saints in Kirtland appear strange to us today, there is still a tendency among members of the Church to look outward to less nourishing sources in our gospel learning. At times, we eschew the simple truths of the gospel in favor of flashier material that is less nourishing. President Holland warned, "When crises come in our lives—and they will—the philosophies of men interlaced with a few scriptures and poems just won't do. Are we really nurturing our youth and our new members in a way that will sustain them when the stresses of life appear? Or are we giving them a kind of theological Twinkie—spiritually empty calories? President John Taylor once called such teaching 'fried froth,' the kind of thing you could eat all day and yet finish feeling totally unsatisfied."[12]

It is worthwhile for all of us to ask from time to time, Unto what was I ordained? What is the Lord asking me to do, and am I doing it in the right way?

> 15 And then received ye spirits which ye could not understand, and received them to be of God; and in this are ye justified?
>
> 16 Behold ye shall answer this question yourselves; nevertheless, I will be merciful unto you; he that is weak among you hereafter shall be made strong.
>
> 17 Verily I say unto you, he that is ordained of me and sent forth to preach the word of truth by the Comforter, in the Spirit of truth, doth he preach it by the Spirit of truth or some other way?
>
> 18 And if it be by some other way it is not of God.
>
> 19 And again, he that receiveth the word of truth, doth he receive it by the Spirit of truth or some other way?
>
> 20 If it be some other way it is not of God.
>
> 21 Therefore, why is it that ye cannot understand and know, that he that receiveth the word by the Spirit of truth receiveth it as it is preached by the Spirit of truth?
>
> 22 Wherefore, he that preacheth and he that receiveth, understand one another, and both are edified and rejoice together.

The powers of persuasion, rhetoric, and learning can all play an important role in preaching the gospel. Any person asked to share the message of Jesus Christ should strive to be intellectually prepared and to use all of his or her gifts to be a persuasive teacher. As important as these tools are, the Savior gives a firm reminder that they pale in comparison to the importance of the Spirit in our teaching. The Spirit, brought into our teaching through righteous living and sincere testimony, is how people are converted to the gospel of Jesus Christ. In this way, the weak things of the world, assisted by a member of the Godhead, can open doors and soften hearts.

Around the time section 50 was received, Brigham Young began to have his first encounters with missionaries from the Church. In an 1852 discourse, he recounted how important the influence of the Spirit was in helping him gain his testimony:

> If all the talent, tact, wisdom, and refinement of the world had been sent to me with the Book of Mormon, and had declared, in the most exalted of earthly eloquence, the truth of it, undertaking to prove it by learning and worldly wisdom, they would have been to me like the smoke which arises only to vanish away. But when I saw a man without eloquence, or talents for public speaking, who could only say, "I know, by the power of the Holy Ghost, that the Book of Mormon is true, that Joseph Smith is a Prophet of the Lord," the Holy Ghost proceeding from that individual illuminated my understanding, and light, glory, and immortality were before me. I was encircled by them, filled with them, and I knew for myself that the testimony of the man was true.[13]

Brigham paused in the middle of the discourse to recognize the missionary who taught him by the Spirit: "My own judgment, natural endowments, and education bowed to this simple, but mighty testimony. There sits the man who baptized me, (brother Eleazer Miller.) It filled my system with light, and my soul with joy. The world, with all its wisdom and power, and with all the glory and gilded show of its kings or potentates, sinks into perfect insignificance, compared with the simple, unadorned testimony of the servant of God." He then added, "Sermonizing, dividing, and subdividing subjects, building up a fine superstructure, a fanciful and aerial building, calculated to fascinate the mind, coupled with the choicest eloquence in the world, will do no good to them. The sentiments of my mind, and the manner of my life, are to obtain knowledge by the power of the Holy Ghost."[14]

> 23 And that which doth not edify is not of God, and is darkness.
>
> 24 That which is of God is light; and he that receiveth light, and continueth in God, receiveth more light; and that light groweth brighter and brighter until the perfect day.
>
> 25 And again, verily I say unto you, and I say it that you may know the truth, that you may chase darkness from among you;

The Savior provides the simplest test to determine whether a communication comes from God: simply ask, Was it edifying? The word *edify* is defined by an 1828 dictionary as "to build, in a literal sense" or "to instruct and improve the mind in knowledge generally, and particularly in moral and religious knowledge, in faith and holiness."[15] *Edify* is also the root word in *edifice*, as in a sacred structure, such as a temple. True communications from God are edifying; they will communicate light and build a person up.

Joseph Smith commented on this aspect of true spiritual communication with God. Referring to the dramatic spiritual displays found in some Christian denominations of his time, Joseph said, "Others frequently possess a spirit that will cause them to lay down, and during its operation, animation is frequently entirely suspended; they consider it to be the power of God, and a glorious manifestation from God—a manifestation of what?—*Is there any intelligence communicated?* are the curtains of heaven withdrawn, or the purposes of God developed? have they seen and conversed with an angel; or have the glories of futurity burst upon their view?"[16]

The dual tests of edification and intelligence do not mean that a spiritual communication must be entirely understood. Speaking in an unknown tongue, for instance, is still one of the gifts of the Spirit. In September 1832 Brigham Young traveled with his friend Heber C. Kimball to meet the Prophet. According to Brigham's account, "We visited many friends on the way, and some branches of the Church. We exhorted them and prayed with them, and I spoke in tongues. Some pronounced it genuine and from the Lord, and others pronounced it of the devil." When Brigham and Heber arrived in Kirtland, they found Joseph Smith chopping and hauling wood. Brigham later commented, "Here my joy was full at the privilege of shaking the hand of the Prophet of God, and received the sure testimony, by the spirit of prophecy, that he was all that any man could."[17]

That evening, Brigham attended a meeting with several Church members from the area. He was asked to pray, and during the prayer he spoke in tongues. As soon as the prayer ended, those present at the meeting looked to Joseph Smith to see his reaction. Brigham later recalled, "He told them it was the pure Adamic language. Some said to him they expected he would condemn the gift Brother Brigham had, but he said, 'No, it is of God, and the time will come when Brother Brigham Young will preside over this Church.' The latter part of this conversation was in my absence."[18]

In this instance, Brigham spoke in an unknown tongue, but the experience was edifying and intelligence was communicated. Though Brigham did not understand the words he uttered, the meaning was given to the presiding officer at the meeting, Joseph Smith. Though it was years later when Brigham became aware of meaning of his utterance, the episode was a meaningful communication from God through the power of the Holy Ghost.

> 26 He that is ordained of God and sent forth, the same is appointed to be the greatest, notwithstanding he is the least and the servant of all.
>
> 27 Wherefore, he is possessor of all things; for all things are subject unto him, both in heaven and on the earth, the life and the light, the Spirit and the power, sent forth by the will of the Father through Jesus Christ, his Son.
>
> 28 But no man is possessor of all things except he be purified and cleansed from all sin.

Here the Savior accounts for another important factor in spiritual communication: personal purity. Of course, God can speak to all of His children regardless of their spiritual condition. Some of His children in the deepest throes of sin have received strong and compelling communications from God. Among these individuals are Laman and Lemuel, Alma the Younger, King Lamoni, and Saul (who became the apostle Paul). At the same time, these individuals received their messages through direct and forceful means, being rebuked by an angel or, in Paul's case, by the Lord Himself. This forceful communication was necessary because those deeply involved in sin have difficulty feeling the gentle promptings of the Holy Ghost. For instance, Nephi once chastised his brothers for not receiving the full power of the message an angel gave to them because they were "past feeling" (1 Nephi 17:45).

Communication through the Spirit of God is constant, but we need to be in tune to receive it. While serving as a mission president in Australia, Elder Bruce R. McConkie illustrated this principle in an object lesson to two of his sons. The family had toured a television broadcast facility on a mountain above a nearby city. That night, when the family returned to the valley below, Elder McConkie and his sons tuned their television set to the frequency being broadcast from the mountain. He explained the following to his sons:

The same thing applies in radio. If we had a radio here today and tuned it to the proper wave band, we would hear the symphonies that are being broadcast into this building. Or if we looked on television we would see in effect the visions that are coming forth in a similar way. Now in the same sense, if at any time we manage to tune our souls to the eternal wave band upon which the Holy Ghost is broadcasting, since he is a Revelator, we could receive the revelations of the Spirit. If we could attune our souls to the band on which he is sending forth the visions of eternity, we could see what the Prophet saw in Section 76, or anything else that it was expedient for us to see.[19]

29 And if ye are purified and cleansed from all sin, ye shall ask whatsoever you will in the name of Jesus and it shall be done.

30 But know this, it shall be given you what you shall ask; and as ye are appointed to the head, the spirits shall be subject unto you.

31 Wherefore, it shall come to pass, that if you behold a spirit manifested that you cannot understand, and you receive not that spirit, ye shall ask of the Father in the name of Jesus; and if he give not unto you that spirit, then you may know that it is not of God.

32 And it shall be given unto you, power over that spirit; and you shall proclaim against that spirit with a loud voice that it is not of God—

33 Not with railing accusation, that ye be not overcome, neither with boasting nor rejoicing, lest you be seized therewith.

34 He that receiveth of God, let him account it of God; and let him rejoice that he is accounted of God worthy to receive.

35 And by giving heed and doing these things which ye have received, and which ye shall hereafter receive—and the kingdom is given you of the Father, and power to overcome all things which are not ordained of him—

36 And behold, verily I say unto you, blessed are you who are now hearing these words of mine from the mouth of my servant, for your sins are forgiven you.

The Lord warns his servants against resorting to the methods of the adversary in seeking to overcome evil influences. Specifically, he speaks against "railing accusation" and "boasting or rejoicing" in a way that impedes the influence of the Spirit. While these methods can be tempting to use in our teaching, the Savior counsels that "he that hath the spirit of contention is not of me, but is of the devil, who is the father of contention, and he stirreth up the hearts of men to contend with anger, one with another" (3 Nephi 11:29).

Elder Parley P. Pratt wrote about those deceived by wicked spirits through unusual manifestations. He counseled, "We must, however, pity rather than ridicule or despise the subjects or advocates of these deceptions. Many of them are honest, but they have no Apostles nor other officers nor gifts to detect evil, or to keep them from being led to every delusive spirit."[20]

> 37 Let my servant Joseph Wakefield, in whom I am well pleased, and my servant Parley P. Pratt go forth among the churches and strengthen them by the word of exhortation;
>
> 38 And also my servant John Corrill, or as many of my servants as are ordained unto this office, and let them labor in the vineyard; and let no man hinder them doing that which I have appointed unto them—
>
> 39 Wherefore, in this thing my servant Edward Partridge is not justified; nevertheless let him repent and he shall be forgiven.
>
> 40 Behold, ye are little children and ye cannot bear all things now; ye must grow in grace and in the knowledge of the truth.
>
> 41 Fear not, little children, for you are mine, and I have overcome the world, and you are of them that my Father hath given me;
>
> 42 And none of them that my Father hath given me shall be lost.
>
> 43 And the Father and I are one. I am in the Father and the Father in me; and inasmuch as ye have received me, ye are in me and I in you.
>
> 44 Wherefore, I am in your midst, and I am the good shepherd, and the stone of Israel. He that buildeth upon this rock shall never fall.

45 And the day cometh that you shall hear my voice and see me, and know that I am.

46 Watch, therefore, that ye may be ready. Even so. Amen.

At the end of the revelation, the Lord provides direction and counsel to several of the people who were present when the revelation was given. Rather than giving strict guidelines to determine the difference between authentic and counterfeit communications of the Spirit, the Lord provided His servants with general principles to assist them in carrying out their duties. When a spiritual experience comes, particularly a dramatic spiritual experience, we must ask, Was it edifying? Was there intelligence communicated? Did it follow the patterns of operation set forth in the scriptures?

Parley P. Pratt took to the words he heard in the revelation. After the revelation was received, he followed the counsel given and traveled in the company of Joseph Wakefield, visiting several branches of the Church and "rebuking the wrong spirits which had crept in among them, setting in order things that were wanting; ordaining elders and officers; baptizing such as believed and repented of their sins; and administering the gift of the Holy Ghost by the laying on of hands."[21]

Unusual and dramatic spiritual experiences can come from God and are still experienced in the Church today. In section 50, the Lord does not discount supernatural events; He only asks that we look carefully and "test the spirits" to know which of them come from God. Only a few weeks after the revelation was given, Parley P. Pratt and Joseph Smith visited a young woman named Chloe Smith who "seemed at the point of death." When Joseph and Parley arrived to visit her, she was "lying very low with a lingering fever." According to Parley, "We kneeled down and prayed vocally all around, each in turn; after which President Smith went to the bedside, took her by the hand, and said unto her with a low voice, 'in the name of Jesus Christ arise and walk!' She immediately arose and was dressed by a woman in attendance, when she walked to a chair before the fire, and was seated and joined in singing a hymn. . . . From that minute she was perfectly restored to health."[22]

End Notes

1. John Whitmer, History, 1831–circa 1847, 10, 26–27, josephsmithpapers.org.
2. Parley P. Pratt, *Autobiography of Parley P. Pratt (Revised and Enhanced)* (Salt Lake City, UT: Deseret Book, 2000), 65.
3. "Mormonism," *Painesville Telegraph* (15 Feb. 1831): 1–2.
4. George A. Smith, in *Journal of Discourses,* 11:4.
5. "Mormonites," *The Philadelphia Sun*, Aug. 18, 1831.
6. John Whitmer, History, 1831–circa 1847, 26–27, josephsmithpapers.org.
7. Parley P. Pratt, *Autobiography of Parley P. Pratt,* 65–66. See also "Historical Introduction," Revelation, 9 May 1831 [D&C 50], josephsmithpapers.org.
8. "'Try the Spirits' Joseph Smith, Times and Seasons (April 1, 1842)," Joseph Smith Foundation, accessed Feb. 13, 2024, https://josephsmithfoundation.org/docs/try-the-spirits-joseph-smith-times-and-seasons-1-april-1842/.
9. "'Try the Spirits' Joseph Smith, Times and Seasons (April 1, 1842)."
10. History, circa Summer 1832, 3, josephsmithpapers.org.
11. Joseph Smith, in History, 1838–1856, volume D-1 [1 August 1842–1 July 1843], 1555, josephsmithpapers.org.
12. Jeffrey R. Holland, "A Teacher Come From God," *Ensign*, May 1998, 26–27.
13. Brigham Young, in *Journal of Discourses*, 1:16.
14. Brigham Young, in *Journal of Discourses*, 1:16.
15. *An American Dictionary of the English Language*, s.v. "edify," accessed February 13, 2024, https://webstersdictionary1828.com/Dictionary/edify.
16. Joseph Smith, in History, 1838–1856, volume C-1 [2 November 1838–31 July 1842], 1304–5, josephsmithpapers.org; emphasis added.
17. *Manuscript History of Brigham Young, 1801–1844,* comp. Elden Jay Watson (1968), 11.
18. *Manuscript History of Brigham Young, 1801–1844,* comp. Elden Jay Watson (1968), 4–5.
19. Joseph Fielding McConkie, *The Bruce R. McConkie Story: Reflections of a Son* (Salt Lake City, UT: Deseret Book, 2003), 225–226.
20. Parley P. Pratt, *Key to the Science of Theology* (1943), 117–118.
21. Parley P. Pratt, *Autobiography of Parley P. Pratt,* 65.
22. Parley P. Pratt, *Autobiography of Parley P. Pratt,* 79–80.

Doctrine and Covenants Section 51

A Faithful, a Just, and a Wise Steward

Historical Context

OBEDIENT TO THE LORD'S COMMANDMENT TO "ASSEMBLE TOGETHER AT the Ohio" (Doctrine and Covenants 37:3), the Knight family and other members of the Colesville Branch departed from their homes in mid-April 1831 to gather with the Saints in Kirtland. Led by Newel Knight, the members of the Colesville Branch were delayed for two weeks in Buffalo, New York, because the harbor was frozen over. After the ice thawed, they weathered the stormy journey over Lake Erie on their way to Kirtland. "Our voyage on [the] lake [was] very disagreeable, nearly all the company being seasick," Newel Knight later wrote. "However, we arrived in safety at our place of destination."[1]

The arrival of the Colesville Saints and the other Church members from New York proved to be the first test of leadership for Bishop Edward Partridge, who had been called only a few months earlier to look after the temporal needs of the Saints and to implement the law of consecration (see Doctrine and Covenants 41:9; 42:31–32). At Bishop Partridge's request, Joseph Smith sought instruction from the Lord and received a revelation providing guidance on how to help the refugees who were arriving from New York.

Orson Pratt was present when this revelation was received. In 1874 he recounted the experience in a discourse given in Brigham City, Utah. An account of Orson's discourse reads:

> Joseph was as calm as the morning sun. But he noticed a change in his countenance that he had never noticed before, when a revelation was given to him. Joseph's face was exceedingly white, and seemed to shine. The speaker [Orson] had been present many times when he was translating the New Testament, and wondered why he did not use the Urim and Thummim, as in translating the Book of Mormon. While this thought passed through the speaker's mind, Joseph, as if he read his thoughts, looked up and explained that the Lord gave him the Urim and Thummim when he was inexperienced with the Spirit of inspiration. But now he had advanced so far that he understood the operations of that Spirit, and did not need the assistance of that instrument.[2]

$\mathcal{V}$erse-by-$\mathcal{V}$erse $\mathcal{C}$ommentary

1 Hearken unto me, saith the Lord your God, and I will speak unto my servant Edward Partridge, and give unto him directions; for it must needs be that he receive directions how to organize this people.

2 For it must needs be that they be organized according to my laws; if otherwise, they will be cut off.

3 Wherefore, let my servant Edward Partridge, and those whom he has chosen, in whom I am well pleased, appoint unto this people their portions, every man equal according to his family, according to his circumstances and his wants and needs.

4 And let my servant Edward Partridge, when he shall appoint a man his portion, give unto him a writing that shall secure unto him his portion, that he shall hold it, even this right and this in-

heritance in the church, until he transgresses and is not accounted worthy by the voice of the church, according to the laws and
covenants of the church, to belong to the church.

5 And if he shall transgress and is not accounted worthy to belong to the church, he shall not have power to claim that portion which he has consecrated unto the bishop for the poor and
needy of my church; therefore, he shall not retain the gift, but
shall only have claim on that portion that is deeded unto him.

6 And thus all things shall be made sure, according to the laws
of the land.

7 And let that which belongs to this people be appointed unto
this people.

8 And the money which is left unto this people—let there be an
agent appointed unto this people, to take the money to provide
food and raiment, according to the wants of this people.

The Lord specifies that as the Church members from New York begin to
arrive in the Kirtland area, they must be organized according to His laws,
a likely reference to the law of consecration and other laws revealed a few
months earlier (see Doctrine and Covenants 42). Throughout the history
of the Church, the law of consecration has been a dynamic set of principles designed to be adjusted to fit the current needs of Church members.
Consecration was not going to be a one-size-fits-all affair. While it is true
that the Lord counseled Bishop Partridge to divide resources on an equal
basis, He also directed him to make determinations based on a family's circumstances, wants, and needs (see verse 3).

Rather than an arbitrary function, consecration was set up to be a ne-
gotiation in good faith between the bishop and the family in need of assistance. Two years later, as Bishop Partridge was laboring to set up the law of
consecration in Missouri, Joseph Smith wrote a letter to explain the roles of
the bishop and the Church member in determining stewardships. He wrote:

I will tell you that every man must be his own judge how much he should
receive, and how much he should suffer to remain in the hands of the
Bishop. . . . The matter of consecration must be done by the mutual consent of both parties—For, to give the Bishop power to say how much every
man shall have and he be obliged to comply with the Bishops judgment,
is giving to the Bishop more power than a King has and upon the other

hand, to let every man say how much he needs and the Bishop obliged to comply with his judgment, is to throw Zion into confusion and make a Slave of the Bishop. The fact is, there must be a balance or equilibrium of power between the bishop and the people, and thus harmony and good will may be preserved among you.[3]

> 9 And let every man deal honestly, and be alike among this people, and receive alike, that ye may be one, even as I have commanded you.
>
> 10 And let that which belongeth to this people not be taken and given unto that of another church.
>
> 11 Wherefore, if another church would receive money of this church, let them pay unto this church again according as they shall agree;
>
> 12 And this shall be done through the bishop or the agent, which shall be appointed by the voice of the church.

Fundamental to the successful implementation of consecration was honesty on the part of everyone involved. The bishop had to be honest about the available resources. He was also expected to be above reproach in his personal conduct and to model integrity for the people he served. When Edward Partridge was chosen to serve as bishop, the Lord had declared that his calling was "because his heart is pure before me, for he is like Nathanael of old, in whom there is no guile" (Doctrine and Covenants 41:11).

For consecration to work, honesty was required of Church members as well. Members needed to be clear and honest about their wants and needs. We do not know the particulars about the system of consecration used in the time of Christ, but the book of Acts sternly notes the punishment by death of Ananias and Sapphira when they tried to defraud the leaders of the Church (see Acts 5:1–11). Nothing so dramatic happened in the time of the Restoration, but without honesty, jealousy and contention could grow among Church members, and this would be fatal to consecration.

The other churches referred to in these verses (see verses 10–12) are other branches of the Church. Consecration asks Church members to maintain a wider perspective and seek after not only the welfare of their own family or their own Church unit but the kingdom of God as a whole. Members in more developed congregations and countries sacrifice to assist those in less developed areas. While individual acts of charity are important, the great work is overseen by leaders who see the big picture and can direct the resources of the Church in the most efficient way possible.

> 13 And again, let the bishop appoint a storehouse unto this church; and let all things both in money and in meat, which are more than is needful for the wants of this people, be kept in the hands of the bishop.
>
> 14 And let him also reserve unto himself for his own wants, and for the wants of his family, as he shall be employed in doing this business.
>
> 15 And thus I grant unto this people a privilege of organizing themselves according to my laws.

The establishment of a storehouse operated and administered by the bishop is mentioned in the original instructions given with the law of consecration (see Doctrine and Covenants 42:34). The frequent use in these verses of the term *wants* as opposed to *needs* emphasizes that consecration was meant to provide the means not only for surviving but also for flourishing. Church members who have consecrated themselves to the Lord enjoy access to the fellowship, talents, and resources of a community. The Lord speaks of organizing according to His laws as "a privilege" (Doctrine and Covenants 42:34).

We sometimes speak of consecration from this time as a failed experiment. It is true that the Colesville Saints in particular suffered because of those who refused to live the law of consecration, but many Saints who gathered to Kirtland prospered under the law. Emily M. Coburn Austin was among the members of the extended Knight family who joined the Church in Colesville and then gathered to Kirtland. Though Emily eventually left the Church, she looked back on the system of consecration in Kirtland with fond memories. "The church had become numerous within a year or two after we arrived, and we were in a new country," she recalled of her first impression upon her arrival. She continued:

> Probably it is indispensably requisite to say that all the money belong[ed] to the wealthy members of the church treasury; and one man had the entire charge of financial affairs. Had it not been thus, there would have been great suffering among the poor and aged, who were in this way both fed and clothed. Probably this is the true origin of the report that they had all things in common; and this is true. The poor were provided for, as well

as those who had put their money in the treasury. They were all satisfied and happy to all appearance, and all seemed to enjoy themselves.[4]

> 16 And I consecrate unto them this land for a little season, until I, the Lord, shall provide for them otherwise, and command them to go hence;
>
> 17 And the hour and the day is not given unto them, wherefore let them act upon this land as for years, and this shall turn unto them for their good.
>
> 18 Behold, this shall be an example unto my servant Edward Partridge, in other places, in all churches.
>
> 19 And whoso is found a faithful, a just, and a wise steward shall enter into the joy of his Lord, and shall inherit eternal life.
>
> 20 Verily, I say unto you, I am Jesus Christ, who cometh quickly, in an hour you think not. Even so. Amen.

The settlement of the Colesville Saints was planned to be "an example . . . in other places, in all churches" (Doctrine and Covenants 51:18). The faithful Saints of this branch were intended to set up a covenant community to be replicated in other locations. President Lorenzo Snow, using the terminology common in his time to describe the law of consecration, taught that consecration "was not confined to any particular locality, but in that revelation [Doctrine and Covenants 51] it was told to the Bishop that this should be an example unto him in organizing in all Churches. So that wherever Edward Partridge should find a Church, he would have the privilege of organizing them according to the United Order, the Celestial Law, or the Order of Enoch."[5]

Unfortunately, the members of the Colesville Branch stayed in Ohio only a short time. Because of transgression, their covenant community was abandoned in its infancy (see commentary for Doctrine and Covenants 54). Instead, the Colesville Branch was commanded to move on to Missouri, and these Saints were among the first members of the Church to live the law of consecration in the land of Zion (see Doctrine and Covenants 54:8). Joined by Bishop Partridge, the Prophet Joseph Smith, and a small band of missionaries, they would be present when the Lord identified the precise location for the New Jerusalem to "be built up upon this land" (Ether 13:6).

End Notes

1. William G. Hartley and Michael Hubbard MacKay, *The Rise of the Latter-day Saints: The Journals and Histories of Newell K. Knight* (Salt Lake City, UT: Deseret Book, 2019), 33.
2. *Millennial Star,* Aug. 11, 1874, 498–499. See also "Historical Introduction," Revelation, 20 May 1831 [D&C 51], josephsmithpapers.org.
3. Letter to Church Leaders in Jackson County, Missouri, 25 June 1833, 2, josephsmithpapers.org.
4. Janiece Johnson and Jennifer Reeder, *The Witness of Women: Firsthand Experiences and Testimonies from the Restoration* (Salt Lake City, UT: Deseret Book, 2016), 82.
5. Lorenzo Snow, in *Journal of Discourses*, 19:344.

Doctrine and Covenants
Section 52
Journey to the Land of Missouri

Historical Context

IN A REVELATION GIVEN IN FEBRUARY 1831, JOSEPH SMITH WAS COMMAND-ed "that the elders of my church should be called together, from the east and from the west, and from the north and from the south" (Doctrine and Covenants 44:1–2). In obedience to this commandment, a conference was held in early June 1831 in Kirtland, Ohio, with all the elders of the Church who could attend. The conference lasted several days, from around June 3–6 (sources are unclear on the precise dates). The conference minutes identify sixty-two participants, including forty-three elders, nine priests, and ten teachers. They assembled in a schoolhouse near the home of Isaac Morley.[1]

The Lord promised to "pour out my Spirit upon them in the day that they assemble themselves together" (Doctrine and Covenants 44:2). In fulfillment of this promise, several unusual spiritual experiences took place at the conference. John Whitmer recorded, "The Spirit of the Lord fell upon

Joseph in an unusual manner. And prophesied that John the Revelator was then among the ten tribes of Israel who had been led away . . . to prepare them for their return, from their long dispersion, to again possess the land of their fathers. He prophesied many more things." The Spirit fell upon Lyman Wight as well, and he prophesied "concerning the coming of Christ. . . . He will appear in his brightness, and consume all before him." He also foretold that "some of my brethren shall suffer martyrdom, for the sake of the religion of Jesus Christ, and seal the testimony of Jesus with their blood. . . . He said that God would work a work in these Last days that tongue cannot express, and the mind is not capable to conceive."[2] John Whitmer also wrote that Joseph prophesied "that the man of sin should be revealed" (2 Thessalonians 2:3).

The outpouring of the Spirit was also accompanied by opposition from the adversary. Whitmer's history recorded, "While the Lord poured out his spirit, upon his servants, the Devil took occasion, to make known his power, he bound Harvey Whitlock and John Murdock so that he could not speak, and others were affected, but the Lord showed to Joseph the Seer, the design of this thing, he commanded the devil in the name of Christ and he departed to our Joy and comfort."[3] In an 1839 history John Corrill remembered, "Some curious things took place. The same visionary and marvelous spirits, spoken of before, got hold of some of the elders; it threw one from his seat to the floor; it bound another, so that for some time he could not use his limbs nor speak; and some other curious effects were experienced, but, by a mighty exertion, in the name of the Lord, it was exposed and shown to be from an evil source."[4]

In his own history Joseph Smith wrote about the conference, saying, "I conferred, the high priesthood for the first time, upon several of the elders. It was clearly evident that the Lord gave us power in proportion to the work to be done and strength according to the race set before us; and grace and help as our needs required."[5] What this ordination refers to is not exactly clear. Later in the Church, the term *high priesthood* became synonymous with *Melchizedek Priesthood*, but it seems unlikely that the June 1831 conference was the first time the Melchizedek Priesthood was given to officers of the Church. The Book of Mormon uses the phrase *high priesthood* in several places and ties it to Melchizedek Priesthood but does not connect the two names directly (see Alma 13:1–19).

The ordinations at the conference appear to have bestowed a higher authority on those already ordained to the office of elder; these were the first distinctive ordinations to the office of high priest. This may have been a partial fulfillment of the Lord's promise that Church members would be "endowed with power from on high" after they gathered to Ohio (see Doctrine and Covenants 37:32). Parley P. Pratt, who was present at the meeting, explained, "Several were then selected by revelation, through President Smith, and ordained to the High Priesthood after the order of the Son of God; which is after the order of Melchizedek. This was the first occasion in which this priesthood had been revealed and conferred upon the Elders in this dispensation, although the office of an Elder is the same in a certain degree, but not in the fulness. On this occasion I was ordained to this holy ordinance and calling by President Smith."[6] John Corrill likewise recorded, "The Melchizedek Priesthood was then for the first time introduced and conferred on several of the elders. In this chiefly consisted the endowment—it being a new order—and bestowed authority."[7]

At a conference held a few months later in October 1831, the minutes recorded the "names of those ordained to the High priesthood" separately from the elders, teachers, and deacons, implying that the high priesthood was recognized as a distinct office in the Church. Other sources seem to indicate this as well. Jared Carter, for instance, believed that those ordained to the high priesthood gained the ability to perform miraculous healings.[8] Joseph Smith taught in October 1831 that "the order of the High priesthood is that they have power given to them to seal up the Saints unto eternal life."[9]

Doctrine and Covenants 52 was received on the last day of the conference. Joseph Smith said that the revelation was given "by an heavenly vision."[10] The revelation commanded fourteen pairs of elders, including Joseph Smith and Sidney Rigdon, to travel to Independence, Missouri. The elders were commanded to preach the gospel along their journey and to hold a conference upon their arrival in Missouri. The Lord promised that, upon their arrival, "it shall also, inasmuch as they are faithful, be made known unto them the land of your inheritance" (Doctrine and Covenants 52:5).[11]

Verse-by-Verse Commentary

1 Behold, thus saith the Lord unto the elders whom he hath called and chosen in these last days, by the voice of his Spirit—

2 Saying: I, the Lord, will make known unto you what I will that ye shall do from this time until the next conference, which shall be held in Missouri, upon the land which I will consecrate unto my people, which are a remnant of Jacob, and those who are heirs according to the covenant.

This is the first reference to the state of Missouri in the revelations of Joseph Smith. The Lord revealed the location for the city of Zion line upon line, and this revelation demonstrates that the time was near for the Church to know at last where the city would be built. A revelation given in September 1830 had indicated that the city would be built "on the borders by the Lamanites" (Doctrine and Covenants 28:9). In the months following, Oliver Cowdery had led a mission to the boundaries of the United States and, while in the area, had brought most of the new converts in Kirtland into the Church. Because of Oliver's efforts, the geographic center of the Church shifted westward to Kirtland, but Ohio was not the location of Zion. The Lord now commanded Joseph to travel to the frontier himself to know the final location of the city.

The Lord promises to consecrate the land there to the "remnant of Jacob" (verse 2), a term that typically refers to the twelve tribes of Israel. The descendants of Lehi were "among the ancestors of the American Indians" (introduction to the Book of Mormon) and therefore heirs to the covenants made to Abraham. The promises made to Abraham, Isaac, and Jacob in the Holy Bible were familiar to Joseph Smith and his contemporaries. A few years after this revelation, Joseph translated the book of Abraham, which reiterated the blessings of the covenant. The Lord told Abraham, "I give unto thee a promise that this right shall continue in thee, and in thy seed after thee (that is to say, the literal seed, or the seed of the body) shall all the families of the earth be blessed, even with the blessings of the Gospel, which are the blessings of salvation, even of life eternal" (Abraham 2:11).

3 Wherefore, verily I say unto you, let my servants Joseph Smith, Jun., and Sidney Rigdon take their journey as soon as preparations can be made to leave their homes, and journey to the land of Missouri.

4 And inasmuch as they are faithful unto me, it shall be made known unto them what they shall do;

5 And it shall also, inasmuch as they are faithful, be made known unto them the land of your inheritance.

6 And inasmuch as they are not faithful, they shall be cut off, even as I will, as seemeth me good.

The Lord assigned fourteen companionships to travel to Missouri for the next conference. The journey was challenging, and as the Lord indicates, it brought blessings to the faithful and also resulted in several of the missionaries leaving the Church (see verses 5–6). Ezra Booth was commanded to travel along with Isaac Morley (see Doctrine and Covenants 52:23). Ezra had been a Methodist minister and had converted after he witnessed Joseph Smith heal Elsa Johnson's arm (see commentary for Doctrine and Covenants 42:19–20). During the journey to Missouri, he became disillusioned with Joseph, and he disparaged the land the Lord chose, seeing it as dreary and underdeveloped.[12]

When Ezra returned from Missouri, he apostatized from the Church and wrote a series of nine letters in the *Ohio Star,* a local newspaper. He said, "A journey of one thousand miles to the west, has taught me far more abundantly, than I should have probably learned from any other source. It has taught me . . . the imbecility of human nature, and especially my own weakness. . . . But thanks be to God! The spell is dissipated."[13] Elder George A. Smith later commented on the reason for Booth's apostasy, saying, "He had formerly been a Methodist minister, commenced preaching the Gospel without purse or scrip, and he did so until he found, (using a common expression,) it did not pay."[14]

7 And again, verily I say unto you, let my servant Lyman Wight and my servant John Corrill take their journey speedily;

8 And also my servant John Murdock, and my servant Hyrum Smith, take their journey unto the same place by the way of Detroit.

9 And let them journey from thence preaching the word by the way, saying none other things than that which the prophets and apostles have written, and that which is taught them by the Comforter through the prayer of faith.

10 Let them go two by two, and thus let them preach by the way in every congregation, baptizing by water, and the laying on of the hands by the water's side.

11 For thus saith the Lord, I will cut my work short in righteousness, for the days come that I will send forth judgment unto victory.

Others who left on the journey to Missouri experienced miracles and saw their faith strengthened. John Murdock, assigned as a companion to Hyrum Smith (see verses 8–9), left Kirtland under extremely trying circumstances. Only a month before he was called on his mission, his wife, Julia, died just six hours after giving birth to twins. Overcome with grief, John asked Joseph and Emma Smith if they would raise the twins for him. He then left Kirtland with the rest of the elders bound for Missouri, placing the rest of his five children in the care of other families in the area.

John struggled with his health during the journey. He later recorded, "I was so weak I fell from the horse and lay till the brethren came and picked me up." When he arrived in Jackson County, he was still ill and was taken to the home of a local member. "I lay sick two or three months, so much so that 2 or 3 days was lost time to me. Although I was so very sick that I could not pray vocally, yet my belief was so firm that it could not be moved. I believe[d] that I could not die because my work was not yet done." During another bout of sickness he wrote:

> I lay and thought on our mission and our calling of God. We had but very little money and while sick we were continually on expense. I saw we could not stand it, so I determined in the name of the Lord Jesus Christ to arise and pursue my journey. I called Bro. P. [Brother Pratt] to the bed and told him my determination, and requested him to lay hands on me in the name of the Lord. I arose from my bed, we took dinner and gave the widow a Book of Mormon for her kindness and started on our journey.[15]

Strengthened by continual blessings from Parley P. Pratt, John was able to make his way home to Kirtland and reunite with his children. Unfortunately, upon his return he found that one of the twins born before his departure, Joseph, had died in part because of a mob attack made on Joseph Smith at the John Johnson home. He noted the baby's death, and he also wrote, "But my daughter was still doing well with Bro. Joseph, the Prophet."[16] During the winter of 1832–33 he saw a vision of the Savior. John later served several missions for the Church, including the first to Australia. He maintained his faith in the gospel and later wrote, "I would that I could thunder it loud enough to be heard through the world . . . that the mountains might tremble, and the inhabitants thereof with those on the valleys and everywhere else, give heed, and in truth and righteousness, and a candid upright step, act accordingly."[17] John Murdock died in 1871, firm in the faith.[18]

> 12 And let my servant Lyman Wight beware, for Satan desireth to sift him as chaff.
>
> 13 And behold, he that is faithful shall be made ruler over many things.
>
> 14 And again, I will give unto you a pattern in all things, that ye may not be deceived; for Satan is abroad in the land, and he goeth forth deceiving the nations—
>
> 15 Wherefore he that prayeth, whose spirit is contrite, the same is accepted of me if he obey mine ordinances.
>
> 16 He that speaketh, whose spirit is contrite, whose language is meek and edifieth, the same is of God if he obey mine ordinances.
>
> 17 And again, he that trembleth under my power shall be made strong, and shall bring forth fruits of praise and wisdom, according to the revelations and truths which I have given you.
>
> 18 And again, he that is overcome and bringeth not forth fruits, even according to this pattern, is not of me.
>
> 19 Wherefore, by this pattern ye shall know the spirits in all cases under the whole heavens.
>
> 20 And the days have come; according to men's faith it shall be done unto them.
>
> 21 Behold, this commandment is given unto all the elders whom I have chosen.

The instructions given to the missionaries in these verses constitute an early missionary guide. Echoing the early commandments given in Doctrine and Covenants 46 and 50, the Lord warns the elders of opposition from the adversary during their mission and gives them a formula for avoiding deception. The Lord asks the missionaries to pray contritely and obey the commandments. Those who represent the Lord must sincerely commit to a course of obedience. *Ordinances* as used here refers to all of the Lord's commandments. Earlier the Lord gave a strong warning about the avoidance of hypocrisy (see Doctrine and Covenants 50:7–8), and this warning was reemphasized for this select group who had been asked to seek out and identify the land of Zion.

The Lord provided these instructions to assist the missionaries in knowing the honest and sincere in heart during their journey to Missouri. He also intended for them to know the honest and sincere among their own number by the actions and dedication they showed to the teachings of the gospel along the way.

22 And again, verily I say unto you, let my servant Thomas B. Marsh and my servant Ezra Thayre take their journey also, preaching the word by the way unto this same land.

23 And again, let my servant Isaac Morley and my servant Ezra Booth take their journey, also preaching the word by the way unto this same land.

24 And again, let my servants Edward Partridge and Martin Harris take their journey with my servants Sidney Rigdon and Joseph Smith, Jun.

25 Let my servants David Whitmer and Harvey Whitlock also take their journey, and preach by the way unto this same land.

26 And let my servants Parley P. Pratt and Orson Pratt take their journey, and preach by the way, even unto this same land.

27 And let my servants Solomon Hancock and Simeon Carter also take their journey unto this same land, and preach by the way.

28 Let my servants Edson Fuller and Jacob Scott also take their journey.

29 Let my servants Levi W. Hancock and Zebedee Coltrin also take their journey.

30 Let my servants Reynolds Cahoon and Samuel H. Smith also take their journey.

31 Let my servants Wheeler Baldwin and William Carter also take their journey.

32 And let my servants Newel Knight and Selah J. Griffin both be ordained, and also take their journey.

33 Yea, verily I say, let all these take their journey unto one place, in their several courses, and one man shall not build upon another's foundation, neither journey in another's track.

34 He that is faithful, the same shall be kept and blessed with much fruit.

35 And again, I say unto you, let my servants Joseph Wakefield and Solomon Humphrey take their journey into the eastern lands;

36 Let them labor with their families, declaring none other things than the prophets and apostles, that which they have seen and heard and most assuredly believe, that the prophecies may be fulfilled.

37 In consequence of transgression, let that which was bestowed upon Heman Basset be taken from him, and placed upon the head of Simonds Ryder.

38 And again, verily I say unto you, let Jared Carter be ordained a priest, and also George James be ordained a priest.

39 Let the residue of the elders watch over the churches, and declare the word in the regions round about them; and let them labor with their own hands that there be no idolatry nor wickedness practiced.

40 And remember in all things the poor and the needy, the sick and the afflicted, for he that doeth not these things, the same is not my disciple.

41 And again, let my servants Joseph Smith, Jun., and Sidney Rigdon and Edward Partridge take with them a recommend from the church. And let there be one obtained for my servant Oliver Cowdery also.

42 And thus, even as I have said, if ye are faithful ye shall assemble yourselves together to rejoice upon the land of Missouri, which is the land of your inheritance, which is now the land of your enemies.

43 But, behold, I, the Lord, will hasten the city in its time, and will crown the faithful with joy and with rejoicing.

44 Behold, I am Jesus Christ, the Son of God, and I will lift them up at the last day. Even so. Amen.

Following the Lord's instructions, the missionaries took different paths on their way to Missouri in order to preach to as many people as possible. According to John Corrill, who was one of the elders called on the journey, the missionaries were commanded "two by two; no two were to travel in the track of the others, and they were to preach the gospel by the way."[19] Their destination lay more than eight hundred miles away and would require them to travel great distances by wagon, stage coach, and steamboat. After arriving in St. Louis, Missouri, Joseph and a few other men crossed the state on foot, traversing a distance of 240 miles, and arrived in Independence on July 14, 1831.[20] It was the first of four journeys Joseph Smith made to Missouri over the next six years.[21]

In the revelation, the Lord provides an ominous warning, calling Missouri the "land of your inheritance, which is now the land of your enemies" (verse 42). The journey was perhaps the most consequential that Joseph Smith undertook in his life. Throughout the remainder of Joseph Smith's life, his fate was tied to the state of Missouri. The sacred land promised to the Saints as the place where a city of peace would be built would become the site of more strife, sorrow, and blood spilt among the Saints than any other place in the history of the Church. At the same time, the Prophet's journey to Missouri in the summer of 1831 was key to unlocking the role of the land of Missouri in the last days and the promise it held for the Saints to one day become "a land of peace, a city of refuge, a place of safety for the saints of the Most High God" (Doctrine and Covenants 45:66).

End Notes

1. See Minutes, circa 3–4 June 1831, 3–4, josephsmithpapers.org.

2. John Whitmer, History, 1831–circa 1847, 28–29, josephsmithpapers.org.

3. John Whitmer, History, 1831–circa 1847, 29, josephsmithpapers.org.

4. John Corrill, *A Brief History of the Church of Christ of Latter Day Saints*, 1839, 18, josephsmithpapers.org.

5. Joseph Smith, in History, 1838–1856, volume A-1 [23 December 1805–30 August 1834], 118, josephsmithpapers.org.

6. Parley P. Pratt, *Autobiography of Parley P. Pratt (Revised and Enhanced)* (Salt Lake City, UT: Deseret Book, 2000), 82.

7. John Corrill, *A Brief History of the Church of Christ of Latter Day Saints*, 1839, 18, josephsmithpapers.org.

8. See "John S. Carter journal, 1831 December-1833 September," Church History Catalog, accessed Feb. 13, 2024, https://catalog.churchofjesuschrist.org/record/20b260ae-89ea-4268-be5d-906fc303eedd/0.

9. Minutes, 25–26 October 1831, 11, josephsmithpapers.org.

10. Letter to the Elders of the Church, 2 October 1835, 179, josephsmithpapers.org.

11. See "Historical Introduction," Revelation, 6 June 1831 [D&C 52], josephsmithpapers.org. See also, "Historical Introduction," Minutes, circa 3–4 June 1831, josephsmithpapers.org.

12. See *Saints: The Story of the Church of Jesus Christ in the Latter Days*, vol. 1, *The Standard of Truth, 1815–1846* (2018), 129.

13. Eber Howe, *Mormonism Unvailed* (1834), letter I.

14. George A. Smith, in *Journal of Discourses*, 11:5.

15. "John Murdock, 1792–1871," Book of Abraham Project, accessed Feb. 13, 2024, http://boap.org/LDS/Early-Saints/JMurdock.html.

16. "John Murdock, 1792–1871."

17. "John Murdock, 1792–1871."

18. See Susan Easton Black, *Who's Who in the Doctrine & Covenants* (Salt Lake City, UT: Bookcraft, 1997), 201–204.

19. John Corrill, *A Brief History of the Church of Christ of Latter Day Saints*, 1839, 18, josephsmithpapers.org.

20. See Casey Paul Griffiths, Susan Easton Black, and Mary Jane Woodger, *What You Don't Know About the 100 Most Important Events in Church History* (Salt Lake City, UT: Deseret Book, 2017), 46.

21. See Karl R. Anderson, *Joseph Smith's Kirtland: Eyewitness Accounts* (Salt Lake City, UT: Deseret Book, 1996), 63–64.

Doctrine and Covenants Section 53

Be an Agent unto This Church

Historical Context

ALGERNON SIDNEY GILBERT WAS THE BUSINESS PARTNER OF NEWEL K. Whitney. The two men had opened a small store in Kirtland under the name of N. K. Whitney and Company. Their store became a hub for Church activity after Joseph Smith arrived in Kirtland. Along with his business partner, Sidney Gilbert was baptized in 1830 when Oliver Cowdery and the first missionaries arrived in Kirtland.[1] He may have been present at the conference of elders held in Kirtland in early June, but he was not among those who were called to travel to Missouri in the revelation given at that time (see Doctrine and Covenants 52). Two days later, at the request of Sidney Gilbert, Joseph received this revelation on his behalf.[2]

*V*erse-by-*V*erse *C*ommentary

1 Behold, I say unto you, my servant Sidney Gilbert, that I have heard your prayers; and you have called upon me that it should be made known unto you, of the Lord your God, concerning your calling and election in the church, which I, the Lord, have raised up in these last days.

2 Behold, I, the Lord, who was crucified for the sins of the world, give unto you a commandment that you shall forsake the world.

3 Take upon you mine ordination, even that of an elder, to preach faith and repentance and remission of sins, according to my word, and the reception of the Holy Spirit by the laying on of hands;

4 And also to be an agent unto this church in the place which shall be appointed by the bishop, according to commandments which shall be given hereafter.

5 And again, verily I say unto you, you shall take your journey with my servants Joseph Smith, Jun., and Sidney Rigdon.

6 Behold, these are the first ordinances which you shall receive; and the residue shall be made known in a time to come, according to your labor in my vineyard.

7 And again, I would that ye should learn that he only is saved who endureth unto the end. Even so. Amen.

Section 53 is the only place in the Doctrine and Covenants where the phrase "calling and election" appears (see verse 1). However, in this case, the calling in question refers only to Sidney Gilbert's *church* calling at the time, or his appointed role among the Saints. Sidney is the first person asked in the revelations to serve as an agent for the Church. He was commanded to travel along with Joseph Smith and Sidney Rigdon to Missouri. Once he arrived there, he was commanded by the Lord to "establish a store, that he may sell goods without fraud . . . and thus provide for my saints" (Doctrine and Covenants 57:8, 10). Sidney did establish a store in Missouri and served among the Saints in Zion. In 1833 his store was ransacked during the persecutions against Church members in Jackson County, and Sidney was taken to jail. The only possessions he took with him when he was arrested were a

Bible and several revelations of Joseph Smith that he had personally copied. Sidney later died during a cholera outbreak among the volunteers in Zion's Camp, a relief mission sent to the Saints in Missouri.[3]

Sidney lived for only four years after joining the Church, but his influence lived on through the family members he helped bring into the gospel. After his sister's husband died in a shipwreck on Lake Ontario, Sidney had taken his sister and her children into his home. When the missionaries arrived in Kirtland a few years later with the Book of Mormon, Sidney helped introduce the book to his sister and her family, which included his niece, Mary Elizabeth Rollins. When Mary first heard of the Book of Mormon, she went to the home of Isaac Morley, who had a copy of the book. When he saw Mary's interest in it, Morley agreed to loan her the book. Mary ran home, proclaiming to Sidney, "Oh Uncle I have the Golden Bible." She stayed up late that night, studying the book with her family.

Mary woke up early the next day to study the book. She later remembered, "I learned the first paragraph by heart." When she brought the book back to Brother Morley, he told her, "You are early, I guess you did not read much of it." Mary showed him how far she had read and repeated an "outline of the history of Nephi." In response, Morley looked at her in surprise, telling her, "Child, you take this back and finish it, I can wait." A few days later, Joseph Smith visited Sidney Gilbert's home, saw the copy of the Book of Mormon, and remarked, "I sent that book to Brother Morley." Sidney explained how Mary had obtained it, and Joseph sent for her. She later remembered, "He came and put his hands on my head and gave me a great blessing, the first I ever received, and made me a present of the book, and said he would give Brother Morley another." Mary later moved with her uncle to Missouri and was instrumental in saving the early manuscripts of Joseph Smith's revelations from a mob.[4]

End Notes

1. See Lyndon W. Cook, *The Revelations of the Prophet Joseph Smith: A Historical and Biographical Commentary of the Doctrine and Covenants* (Salt Lake City, UT: Deseret Book, 1985), 84.

2. See History, 1838–1856, volume A-1 [23 December 1805–30 August 1834], 121, josephsmithpapers.org. See also "Historical Introduction," Revelation, 8 June 1831 [D&C 53], josephsmithpapers.org.

3. See Susan Easton Black, *Who's Who in the Doctrine & Covenants* (Salt Lake City, UT: Bookcraft, 1997), 102–103.

4. See "Mary Elizabeth Rollins Lightner," *Utah Genealogical and Historical Magazine* 17 (July 1826): 193–205, 250.

$\mathcal{D}$octrine and $\mathcal{C}$ovenants
Section 54
Be Patient in Tribulation

$\mathcal{H}$istorical $\mathcal{C}$ontext

WHEN JOSEPH SMITH HAD FIRST ARRIVED IN KIRTLAND IN FEBRUARY 1831, one of the most welcoming of the new converts had been Leman Copley. Copley had offered for Joseph and Sidney Rigdon to live with him in Thompson, Ohio, and had even offered them housing and provisions. Joseph and Sidney found other living arrangements, but, encouraged by Copley's generosity, Joseph made plans for the emigrating members of the Colesville Branch to settle on Copley's property.

While the Colesville Saints were traveling to Kirtland, Leman Copley was called to accompany Sidney Rigdon and Parley P. Pratt on a mission to members of his former faith, the Shakers. Unfortunately, the mission to the Shakers failed to convert anyone, and Copley's faith was shaken. He soon returned to the Shaker community and reconciled with them. Afterward, he returned to his home with Shaker leader Ashbel Kitchell, apparently with the intent to evict any Church members on his property. When Kitchell arrived on Copley's farm, members of the Colesville Branch were already there. Kitchell became involved in a discussion with Newel Knight, the leader of the Colesville Branch, that elevated into a shouting match with Joseph Knight Sr.[1]

Following the altercation, the members of the Colesville Branch were forced to leave Copley's land. Joseph Knight Jr. later recalled bitterly, "We had to leave his [Copley's] farm and pay sixty dollars damage . . . for fitting up his houses and planting his ground."[2] With no place to go, the evicted Saints approached Joseph Smith for direction and guidance. Newel K. Whitney later recalled, "We commenced work in all good faith, thinking to obtain a living by the sweat of the brow. We had not lingered long before the above-named Copley broke the engagement which he made with us. At this time, I went to Kirtland to see Brother Joseph."[3]

Verse-by-Verse Commentary

1 Behold, thus saith the Lord, even Alpha and Omega, the beginning and the end, even he who was crucified for the sins of the world—

2 Behold, verily, verily, I say unto you, my servant Newel Knight, you shall stand fast in the office whereunto I have appointed you.

3 And if your brethren desire to escape their enemies, let them repent of all their sins, and become truly humble before me and contrite.

4 And as the covenant which they made unto me has been broken, even so it has become void and of none effect.

5 And wo to him by whom this offense cometh, for it had been better for him that he had been drowned in the depth of the sea.

6 But blessed are they who have kept the covenant and observed the commandment, for they shall obtain mercy.

Leman Copley's actions did not destroy the work of consecration in Kirtland but did demonstrate one of its vulnerabilities. Consecration depended on the voluntary contribution of resources from those who participated.

The Lord had urged the Saints to enter into "a covenant and a deed which cannot be broken" (Doctrine and Covenants 42:30), but at the same time Church leaders respected the principle of agency. The Lord laments the selfish and incorrect decision made by Copley in withdrawing the assistance he had offered to the Church members arriving in the area. However, Church leaders continued to work with him and bring him to repentance. Fellowship with Copley was withdrawn in the summer of 1831 but was extended again to him by October 1832. He continued to be involved in the Church until the Saints left the Kirtland area entirely and he refused to follow.[4]

In the same revelation, Newel Knight is told to "stand fast" in his office (see verse 2). As the leader of the Colesville Branch, Newel may have felt that their misfortune occurred because of his actions. It can be difficult, but those called to lead in the Church must also accept the agency of the people they serve. It can be gut-wrenching to see some make the wrong decision, but it is worse when, as in the case of Leman Copley, a poor decision affects many other people in a negative way. Nevertheless, the agency of an individual and their power to make both good and bad choices must always be respected.

7 Wherefore, go to now and flee the land, lest your enemies come upon you; and take your journey, and appoint whom you will to be your leader, and to pay moneys for you.

8 And thus you shall take your journey into the regions westward, unto the land of Missouri, unto the borders of the Lamanites.

9 And after you have done journeying, behold, I say unto you, seek ye a living like unto men, until I prepare a place for you.

10 And again, be patient in tribulation until I come; and, behold, I come quickly, and my reward is with me, and they who have sought me early shall find rest to their souls. Even so. Amen.

Because of Leman Copley's refusal to help, the members of the Colesville Branch were commanded to continue on their journey to the land of Missouri. They had already traveled more than 350 miles to arrive in Kirtland, and now a journey of 800 more miles lay before them. Newel Knight worried over the health of his mother, Polly, wondering if she could even survive such a journey. "My mother's health was very poor and had been for a considerable length of time," he later wrote. "Yet she would not consent to stop traveling. Her only, or her greatest desire, was to set her feet upon the land of Zion, and to have her body interred in that land." Newel went so far as to purchase lumber before their departure, in case his mother died along the way and he needed to make a coffin for her.[5]

Nevertheless, the Knight family and the rest of the Colesville Branch began preparations to start the next portion of their journey. "We now understood that [Ohio] was not the land of our inheritance—the land of promise," Newel Knight recorded. "For it was made known in a revelation that Missouri was the place chosen for the gathering of the church, and several were called to lead the way to that state."[6] The Colesville Saints chose to have Newel continue to preside over them. He was released from his previous calling as a missionary (see Doctrine and Covenants 52:32) and given leave to look after his family during their journey (see Doctrine and Covenants 56:6–7). Newel later reflected, "This was the first branch of the Church which had emigrated to the land of Zion. I had found it required all of the wisdom I had to lead this company through so long a journey in the midst of enemies; yet so great were the mercies and blessings of God to us that not one of us were harmed, and we made our journey in safety."[7]

End Notes

1. See Lawrence R. Flake, "A Shaker View of a Mormon Mission," *BYU Studies* 20, no. 1 (1979): 4.

2. See "Historical Introduction," Revelation, 10 June 1831 [D&C 54], footnote 10, josephsmithpapers.org.

3. William G. Hartley and Michael Hubbard MacKay, *The Rise of the Latter-day Saints: The Journals and Histories of Newell K. Knight* (Salt Lake City, UT: Deseret Book, 2019), 33–34. See also "Historical Introduction," Revelation, 10 June 1831 [D&C 54], josephsmithpapers.org.

4. See Susan Easton Black, *Who's Who in the Doctrine & Covenants* (Salt Lake City, UT: Bookcraft, 1997), 68–69.

5. See Hartley and MacKay, *The Rise of the Latter-day Saints*, 36.

6. Joseph F. Darowski, "Journey of the Colesville Branch," in *Revelations in Context* (2016), 42–43.

7. Hartley and MacKay, *The Rise of the Latter-day Saints*, 36.

Doctrine and Covenants Section 55

That Little Children Also May Receive Instruction

Historical Context

WILLIAM WINES PHELPS WAS THE EDITOR OF A NEWSPAPER, THE *ONTARIO Phoenix*, when he began to hear tales of a new book of scripture brought forth by a prophet in the nearby community of Palmyra. Phelps was acquainted with several early members of the Church, including Martin Harris and Thomas B. Marsh. Many other early converts lived near Phelps's home in Canandaigua, New York, including Brigham Young and Ezra Thayer. In April 1830 Phelps purchased several copies of the Book of Mormon. He stayed up the entire night comparing the new book with the Bible. Soon he and his wife, Sally, became convinced that the Book of Mormon was the word of God. Though he hesitated to join the new church, he later wrote, "My heart was there from the time I became acquainted with the Book of Mormon, and my hope, steadfast like an anchor, and my faith increased like the grass after a refreshing shower."[1]

Phelps held off on joining the Church but was still subject to persecution because of his promotion of the Book of Mormon. In the spring of 1831 Phelps was in Palmyra researching the beginnings of the new movement when two men from his hometown of Canandaigua brought charges against him, arresting him for indebtedness. Newspapermen like Phelps often operated on credit, but apparently it wasn't the debt that caused the arrest. When Phelps arrived at the jail, he was informed that the action was taken to "keep him from joining the Mormons." Jailed for thirty days, Phelps wrote a letter of outrage to the local newspapers. "Is this religion?" he demanded. "Is it liberty to jail someone who is investigating to find the truth? Is this humanity?" While he languished in jail, Phelps resigned his editorship of the *Ontario Phoenix* and began preparations to leave with his family to join the gathering Church in Kirtland, Ohio.

In his final message to his readers, he wrote, "We live in an eventful day. According to the Psalmist, truth springs out of the earth, and righteousness looks down from heaven, and as twin-angels they will sweep through the world like a mighty torrent, till mankind, untrammeled by secret bondage, sings as the sons of glory, 'we are one—peace on earth—virtue endures forever!'" William and Sally left Canandaigua on June 9, traveling to Kirtland via the Erie Canal and over Lake Erie to Kirtland. The Phelps family arrived in Kirtland on June 14, 1831, and immediately went to see Joseph Smith, who was then residing northeast of Kirtland on the Morley farm. When William arrived, he told Joseph Smith he was willing "to do the will of the Lord" and asked Joseph to seek a revelation on his behalf. Joseph agreed, receiving the following revelation.[2]

Verse-by-Verse Commentary

1 Behold, thus saith the Lord unto you, my servant William, yea, even the Lord of the whole earth, thou art called and chosen; and after thou hast been baptized by water, which if you do with an eye single to my glory, you shall have a remission of your sins and a reception of the Holy Spirit by the laying on of hands;

2 And then thou shalt be ordained by the hand of my servant Joseph Smith, Jun., to be an elder unto this church, to preach

repentance and remission of sins by way of baptism in the name of Jesus Christ, the Son of the living God.

3 And on whomsoever you shall lay your hands, if they are contrite before me, you shall have power to give the Holy Spirit.

William W. Phelps was baptized shortly after this revelation was given. In an 1835 letter, Phelps gives the date of his baptism as June 10, 1831. However, several different sources give the date of this revelation as June 14, 1831, and at the time the revelation was given, Phelps was not baptized.[3]

In the revelation, the Lord directs that William be immediately ordained an elder, a step that was rare in the early Church. The Lord may have recognized the earlier struggles William had experienced and knew his talents as a leader and writer. William was among the most influential of the early converts to the Church, and the works produced by his pen continue to resound in the Church today. William wrote the words of a number of beloved Latter-day Saint hymns, including "Now Let Us Rejoice," "Redeemer of Israel," "Praise to the Man," "If You Could Hie to Kolob," and "The Spirit of God."

Phelps also possessed a strong testimony of the Book of Mormon, refined by his trials before he joined the Church. He later wrote of the importance of the Book of Mormon in helping him join the Church: "Whenever I have meditated upon the Book of Mormon, and looked ahead at the glory which will be brought to pass by that, and the servants of God, I have been filled with hope; filled with light; filled with joy; and filled with satisfaction. What a wonderful volume! What a glorious treasure! By that book I learned the right way to God; by that book I received the fulness of the everlasting gospel; by that book I found the new covenant."[4]

4 And again, you shall be ordained to assist my servant Oliver Cowdery to do the work of printing, and of selecting and writing books for schools in this church, that little children also may receive instruction before me as is pleasing unto me.

5 And again, verily I say unto you, for this cause you shall take your journey with my servants Joseph Smith, Jun., and Sidney Rigdon, that you may be planted in the land of your inheritance to do this work.

6 And again, let my servant Joseph Coe also take his journey with them. The residue shall be made known hereafter, even as I will. Amen.

William was commanded to accompany Joseph Smith and Sidney Rigdon on their journey to Missouri. He departed along with them on June 19, 1831, just three days after his baptism. He was also selected for a special work: alongside Oliver Cowdery, he was to write books for the schools of the Church "that little children also may receive instruction" (verse 4). This is the earliest revelation relating to the educational initiatives of the Church. Later Parley P. Pratt and others were told that "there should be a school in Zion" (Doctrine and Covenants 97:3).

In later revelations, the Lord directed not only the creation of schools for children but also the building of educational programs for adults (see Doctrine and Covenants 88:78–80). The revelatory command for William W. Phelps to serve as an educator in Zion serves as a precursor to the Church's emphasis on education. Throughout its history the Church has engaged in a myriad of educational programs. President Uchtdorf succinctly summarized the Church's approach to education when he said, "For members of the Church, education is not merely a good idea—it's a commandment."[5]

End Notes

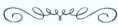

1. Bruce Van Orden, *We'll Sing and We'll Shout: The Life and Times of W. W. Phelps* (Salt Lake City, UT: Deseret Book, 2018), 32.

2. See Van Orden, *We'll Sing and We'll Shout*, 34–36. See also "Historical Introduction," Revelation, 14 June 1831 [D&C 55], josephsmithpapers.org.

3. See "Letter No. 6," *Latter-day Saints' Messenger and Advocate* 1 (Apr. 1835): 97.

4. "Letter No. 10," *Latter-day Saints' Messenger and Advocate* 12 (Sept. 1835): 177–78.

5. Dieter F. Uchtdorf, "Two Principles for Any Economy," *Ensign* or *Liahona*, Nov. 2009, 58.

Doctrine and Covenants Section 56

These Words Shall Not Pass Away

Historical Context

THOMAS B. MARSH AND EZRA THAYER WERE BOTH CALLED BY REVELATION to travel to Missouri (see Doctrine and Covenants 52:22). This revelation was received just days before the elders called in the revelation had planned to depart from Kirtland to begin their journey. Complications arose when Thayer said that he would have to delay his departure for the mission. We do not know the precise reason why Thayer had to delay, but it is likely that the situation was linked to his investment in a piece of real estate. Doctrine and Covenants 56 refers to a "former commandment" given to Thayer "concerning the place upon which he lives" (Doctrine and Covenants 56:8). This revelation was not placed in the Doctrine and Covenants but is found in Revelation Book 1.[1] Ezra appears to have been concerned over his duties on the Frederick G. Williams farm where Joseph Smith's family was staying at the time. The property was being shared by at least three different parties, and Thayer apparently wanted his payment on his portion of the land secured before he left on his mission (see Doctrine and Covenants 56:9).

Thomas B. Marsh recorded his perspective on the controversy, writing, "In June 1831 I received an appointment to go to Missouri with Ezra Thayer and preach by the way. In consequence of Ezra Thayer delaying for so long, I went to Joseph who received the word of the Lord appointing Selah J. Griffin with whom I journeyed to Missouri preaching by the way."[2] John Whitmer simply recorded, "Thomas [B.] Marsh was desirous to know what he should do as the Lord had commanded him & Ezra Thayer to take their journey to the land of Missouri, but Thayer could not get ready as soon as Thomas wanted that he should."[3]

Verse-by-Verse Commentary

1 Hearken, O ye people who profess my name, saith the Lord your God; for behold, mine anger is kindled against the rebellious, and they shall know mine arm and mine indignation, in the day of visitation and of wrath upon the nations.

2 And he that will not take up his cross and follow me, and keep my commandments, the same shall not be saved.

3 Behold, I, the Lord, command; and he that will not obey shall be cut off in mine own due time, after I have commanded and the commandment is broken.

4 Wherefore I, the Lord, command and revoke, as it seemeth me good; and all this to be answered upon the heads of the rebellious, saith the Lord.

While we do not know the exact details surrounding the actions of Ezra Thayer, it is clear from the revelation that the Lord was concerned over more than just a financial transaction gone wrong. The actions taken by Ezra Thayer, combined with the complications arising from Leman Copley's actions (see Doctrine and Covenants 54), threatened the call of several of the missionaries to Missouri. In response to these events, the Lord adjusted the earlier commandments given to the elders, revoking a portion of them.

In a revelation given shortly after, the Lord explained, "I command and men obey not; I revoke and they receive not the blessing" (Doctrine and Covenants 58:32). The Lord respects our agency and adjusts His expectations and blessings based on the good and bad decisions we make. An example of such a situation can be found in the Bible. Anciently, the children of Israel received a command to possess the land of Canaan. When returning spies gave a negative report of the walled cites of the inhabitants of Canaan, the children of Israel began to murmur against Moses and Aaron and make plans to return to Egypt (see Numbers 14:2–4). In consequence of this behavior, the Lord commanded instead that the people wander in the wilderness until the rebellious generation had passed away. He then reinstituted the commandment for their righteous posterity to occupy Canaan. Likewise, the rebellious actions of a small number of the Saints in Kirtland caused the Lord to adjust His earlier commands.

> 5 Wherefore, I revoke the commandment which was given unto my servants Thomas B. Marsh and Ezra Thayre, and give a new commandment unto my servant Thomas, that he shall take up his journey speedily to the land of Missouri, and my servant Selah J. Griffin shall also go with him.

> 6 For behold, I revoke the commandment which was given unto my servants Selah J. Griffin and Newel Knight, in consequence of the stiffneckedness of my people which are in Thompson, and their rebellions.

> 7 Wherefore, let my servant Newel Knight remain with them; and as many as will go may go, that are contrite before me, and be led by him to the land which I have appointed.

> 8 And again, verily I say unto you, that my servant Ezra Thayre must repent of his pride, and of his selfishness, and obey the former commandment which I have given him concerning the place upon which he lives.

> 9 And if he will do this, as there shall be no divisions made upon the land, he shall be appointed still to go to the land of Missouri;

> 10 Otherwise he shall receive the money which he has paid, and shall leave the place, and shall be cut off out of my church, saith the Lord God of hosts;

> 11 And though the heaven and the earth pass away, these words shall not pass away, but shall be fulfilled.

12 And if my servant Joseph Smith, Jun., must needs pay the money, behold, I, the Lord, will pay it unto him again in the land of Missouri, that those of whom he shall receive may be rewarded again according to that which they do;

13 For according to that which they do they shall receive, even in lands for their inheritance.

In consequence of Ezra Thayer's negative actions, the Lord adjusted His commandments to the other missionaries departing for Missouri. Selah J. Griffin was appointed instead to travel with Thomas B. Marsh, and Newel Knight was given charge to assist his family and the other members of the Colesville Branch in their journey to Missouri. The troubles with Ezra Thayer freed up Newel Knight to care for his family, which was a source of relief to them and the rest of the Colesville Saints.

The former commandment given to Ezra Thayer that is mentioned in the revelation (see verse 8) warned him directly against pride. While the revelation was not selected for publication in the Doctrine and Covenants, it foreshadowed the difficulties caused by Ezra in this instance. It reads in part, "Let my servant Ezra humble himself and at the conference meeting he shall be ordained unto power from on high and he shall go from thence, if he be obedient unto my commandments." In a revelation given the same day, but not directed specifically to Ezra Thayer, the Lord gave this general counsel concerning financial matters: "What shall the Brethren do with their money[?] Ye shall go forth and seek diligently among the Brethren and obtain lands and save the money that it may be consecrated to purchase lands in the west for an everlasting inheritance."[4]

14 Behold, thus saith the Lord unto my people—you have many things to do and to repent of; for behold, your sins have come up unto me, and are not pardoned, because you seek to counsel in your own ways.

15 And your hearts are not satisfied. And ye obey not the truth, but have pleasure in unrighteousness.

16 Wo unto you rich men, that will not give your substance to the poor, for your riches will canker your souls; and this shall be your lamentation in the day of visitation, and of judgment, and of indignation: The harvest is past, the summer is ended, and my soul is not saved!

17 Wo unto you poor men, whose hearts are not broken, whose spirits are not contrite, and whose bellies are not satisfied, and whose hands are not stayed from laying hold upon other men's goods, whose eyes are full of greediness, and who will not labor with your own hands!

18 But blessed are the poor who are pure in heart, whose hearts are broken, and whose spirits are contrite, for they shall see the kingdom of God coming in power and great glory unto their deliverance; for the fatness of the earth shall be theirs.

19 For behold, the Lord shall come, and his recompense shall be with him, and he shall reward every man, and the poor shall rejoice;

20 And their generations shall inherit the earth from generation to generation, forever and ever. And now I make an end of speaking unto you. Even so. Amen.

Money is neither good nor evil. It can keep a person from entering the kingdom of God or be a means of building the kingdom of God. The New Testament recounts the story of a rich young man who approached the Savior and affirmed that he kept all the commandments of God. In response to this, Christ told him:

> Yet lackest thou one thing: sell all that thou hast, and distribute unto the poor, and thou shalt have treasure in heaven: and come, follow me.
> And when he heard this, he was very sorrowful: for he was very rich.
> And when Jesus saw that he was very sorrowful, he said, How hardly shall they that have riches enter into the kingdom of God!
> For it is easier for a camel to go through a needle's eye, than for a rich man to enter into the kingdom of God.
> And they that heard it said, Who then can be saved?
> And he said, The things which are impossible with men are possible with God. (Luke 18:22–27)

When Joseph Smith translated the last verse of this passage, it was re-written to read, "And he said unto them, It is impossible for them who trust in riches, to enter into the kingdom of God; but he who forsaketh the things which are of this world, it is possible with God, that he should enter in" (Joseph Smith Translation, Luke 18:27 [in Luke 18:27, footnote a]). The context of these warnings, given so close to the implementation of the law of consecration, demonstrates the way the Lord tried to show that the weakness of both the rich and the poor could be offset by sacrifice and unselfish service in the kingdom of God.

End Notes

1. See Revelation, 15 May 1831, josephsmithpapers.org.
2. Lyndon W. Cook, *The Revelations of the Prophet Joseph Smith: A Historical and Biographical Commentary of the Doctrine and Covenants* (Salt Lake City, UT: Deseret Book, 1985), 88.
3. Revelation Book 1, 91, josephsmithpapers.org. See also "Historical Introduction," Revelation, 15 June 1831 [D&C 56]; "Historical Introduction," Revelation, 15 May 1831., josephsmithpapers.org.
4. Revelation, 15 May 1831, 85, josephsmithpapers.org.

$\mathcal{D}$octrine and $\mathcal{C}$ovenants Section 57

The Place for the City of Zion

$\mathcal{H}$istorical $\mathcal{C}$ontext

FULFILLING THE LORD'S COMMANDMENT (SEE DOCTRINE AND COVENANTS 52:2), Joseph Smith and the other elders who had been called in the revelation left Kirtland on June 19, 1831. They arrived in Independence, Jackson County, Missouri, on July 14. Upon their arrival, Joseph was greeted by Oliver Cowdery, other members of the Lamanite mission, and a small handful of converts from the area. Joseph Smith later wrote, "The meeting of our brethren, who had long waited our arrival, was a glorious one and moistened with many tears. It seemed good and pleasant for brethren to meet together in unity." Joseph's thoughts weren't only with the members in his presence, however. While "standing now upon the confines, or western limits of the united States, and looking into the vast wilderness," he reflected on the plight of the American Indians.[1]

Joseph wrote that "after viewing the country, seeking diligently at the hand of God, he manifested himself unto me, and designated to me and others, the very spot upon which he designed to commence the work of the gathering, and the upbuilding of an holy city, which should be called Zion:—Zion because it is to be a place of righteousness, and all who build thereon, are to worship the true and living God—and all believe in one doctrine even the doctrine of our Lord and Savior Jesus Christ."[2] The revelation, received a few days after Joseph arrived in Missouri, was based on the following questions: "When will the wilderness blossom as the rose; when will Zion be built up in her glory, and where will thy Temple stand unto which all nations shall come in the last days?"[3]

*V*erse-by-*V*erse *C*ommentary

1 Hearken, O ye elders of my church, saith the Lord your God, who have assembled yourselves together, according to my commandments, in this land, which is the land of Missouri, which is the land which I have appointed and consecrated for the gathering of the saints.

2 Wherefore, this is the land of promise, and the place for the city of Zion.

3 And thus saith the Lord your God, if you will receive wisdom here is wisdom. Behold, the place which is now called Independence is the center place; and a spot for the temple is lying westward, upon a lot which is not far from the courthouse.

The journey of Joseph Smith and his companions to the land of Missouri was the culmination of many hopes and promises for the early members of the Church. The first mention of this city was given to Joseph as he translated the words of Jesus Christ to the Nephites. The Savior prophesied that "the remnant of Jacob, and also as many of the house of Israel as shall come . . . may build a city, which shall be called the New Jerusalem. And then shall they assist my people that they may be gathered in, who are scattered upon all the face of the land, in unto the New Jerusalem" (3 Nephi 21:23–34).

Later, as Joseph began his translation of the Old Testament, he learned of the city of Enoch named Zion that was built anciently. The Lord told

Enoch, "Truth will I cause to sweep the earth as with a flood, to gather out mine elect from the four quarters of the earth, unto a place which I shall prepare, an Holy City, that my people may gird up their loins, and be looking forth for the time of my coming; for there shall be my tabernacle, and it shall be called Zion, a New Jerusalem" (Moses 7:62–64).

At the heart of the city of Zion will be a temple, and the city of Zion, along with a rebuilt and restored Jerusalem, is to be the center of the millennial kingdom of Jesus Christ (see Ether 13:10–11). From there the borders of Zion will spread to encompass the entire earth—Jackson County was just the starting place. Brigham Young recalled an instance when a woman asked if Jackson County was large enough to hold all who would gather to Zion. In response, he said, "Zion will extend, eventually, all over this earth. There will be no nook or corner upon the earth but what will be in Zion. It will all be Zion. . . . We are going to gather as many as we can, bless them, give them their endowments, etc., preach to them the truth, lay the principles of eternal life before them."[4]

> 4 Wherefore, it is wisdom that the land should be purchased by the saints, and also every tract lying westward, even unto the line running directly between Jew and Gentile;
>
> 5 And also every tract bordering by the prairies, inasmuch as my disciples are enabled to buy lands. Behold, this is wisdom, that they may obtain it for an everlasting inheritance.
>
> 6 And let my servant Sidney Gilbert stand in the office to which I have appointed him, to receive moneys, to be an agent unto the church, to buy land in all the regions round about, inasmuch as can be done in righteousness, and as wisdom shall direct.
>
> 7 And let my servant Edward Partridge stand in the office to which I have appointed him, and divide unto the saints their inheritance, even as I have commanded; and also those whom he has appointed to assist him.

Once the location of the city was identified, the revelation directed the Saints toward the practical aspects of obtaining the land to build the city. The "line running directly between Jew and Gentile" (verse 4) is a reference to the boundary between the American Indians and the European settlers in Jackson County. With the Nephites and the Lamanites among the ancestors of the American Indians, they were designated as part of the house of Israel, referred to here simply as relatives to the Jewish people. Independence was located only twelve miles down the Missouri River from the state line that also served as the border to Indian Territory, which had been established by the United States Congress in the Indian Removal Act of 1830. Oliver Cowdery and the members of the Lamanite mission, who had arrived in the region months earlier, had made attempts to cross into Indian Territory, but they were rebuffed by federal Indian agents for not holding licenses to teach among the native people.

The European settlers already in Missouri were also a cause of concern to the Saints who were gathering there. When Newel Knight and the members of the Colesville Branch arrived in the area, he was taken aback by the roughness of the local settlers. He later acknowledged, "We could not but feel deeply the contrast as we now stood upon the western limits of the USA and were obliged to mingle and associate with those who had known nothing but a frontier life, until they were but a little above the native in the point of education and refinement." Newel felt that the settlers were "full of bigotry, superstition, and prejudice, the natural result of ignorance."[5] Despite the roughness of the land and the people, the Saints were commanded to enter the scene as peacemakers. A later commandment given to Joseph Smith instructed the Saints to "carefully gather together, as much in one region as can be, consistently with the feelings of the people" (Doctrine and Covenants 105:24).

8 And again, verily I say unto you, let my servant Sidney Gilbert plant himself in this place, and establish a store, that he may sell goods without fraud, that he may obtain money to buy lands for the good of the saints, and that he may obtain whatsoever things the disciples may need to plant them in their inheritance.

9 And also let my servant Sidney Gilbert obtain a license—behold here is wisdom, and whoso readeth let him understand—that he may send goods also unto the people, even by whom he will as clerks employed in his service;

10 And thus provide for my saints, that my gospel may be preached unto those who sit in darkness and in the region and shadow of death.

11 And again, verily I say unto you, let my servant William W. Phelps be planted in this place, and be established as a printer unto the church.

12 And lo, if the world receive his writings—behold here is wisdom—let him obtain whatsoever he can obtain in righteousness, for the good of the saints.

13 And let my servant Oliver Cowdery assist him, even as I have commanded, in whatsoever place I shall appoint unto him, to copy, and to correct, and select, that all things may be right before me, as it shall be proved by the Spirit through him.

14 And thus let those of whom I have spoken be planted in the land of Zion, as speedily as can be, with their families, to do those things even as I have spoken.

15 And now concerning the gathering—Let the bishop and the agent make preparations for those families which have been commanded to come to this land, as soon as possible, and plant them in their inheritance.

16 And unto the residue of both elders and members further directions shall be given hereafter. Even so. Amen.

Consistent throughout the revelation is the commandment for the missionaries to "plant" themselves in the new land. The Colesville Branch, after a journey of over 1,100 miles, had at last found a home. Edward Partridge, the bishop of the Church, and Sidney Gilbert, the agent of the Church, were directed to begin preparations for the new home of the Colesville Branch, who settled near the Big Blue River near Independence. The first Sunday after their arrival, the elders held a worship service. Historian B. H. Roberts later reflected that "such a congregation was present as was only possible in an American frontier district." The group included American Indians, enslaved African Americans, "and all classes and conditions of people from the surrounding counties—Universalists, Atheists, Deists, Presbyterians, Methodists, Baptists, both priests and people—a motley crowd truly!" After the service, two people who had already been meeting with the missionaries came forth and were baptized.[6]

This moment captured all of the promise and peril in building the city of Zion. A diverse group of people met together, listening to the hopes of a shining new city of God to be built in their midst. At the same time,

DOCTRINE AND COVENANTS COMMENTARY

ominous signs emerged on the horizon. B. H. Roberts noted that, other than a small handful of converts, "the Church was made up wholly of Northern people, and therefore constituted a different class of settlers from the old inhabitants of Independence, who came chiefly from the south."[7] The millennial hopes of the Saints would soon collide with the culture of the frontier. But for now, Joseph and the other members of the Church rejoiced that at last the location of the New Jerusalem was known.

End Notes

1. Joseph Smith, in History, 1838–1856, volume A-1 [23 December 1805–30 August 1834], 127, josephsmithpapers.org.
2. Letter to the Elders of the Church, 2 October 1835, 179, josephsmithpapers.org.
3. History, 1838–1856, volume A-1 [23 December 1805–30 August 1834], 127, josephsmithpapers.org). See also "Historical Introduction," Revelation, 20 July 1831 [D&C 57], josephsmithpapers.org.
4. Brigham Young, in *Journal of Discourses, 9:138.*
5. William G. Hartley and Michael Hubbard MacKay, *The Rise of the Latter-day Saints: The Journals and Histories of Newell K. Knight* (Salt Lake City, UT: Deseret Book, 2019), 37.
6. See B. H. Roberts, *The Missouri Persecutions* (Salt Lake City, UT: Bookcraft, 1965), 43.
7. Roberts, *The Missouri Persecutions,* 43.

$\mathcal{D}$octrine and $\mathcal{C}$ovenants
Section 58
After Much Tribulation Come the Blessings

$\mathcal{H}$istorical $\mathcal{C}$ontext

JOSEPH SMITH RECEIVED THIS REVELATION A FEW DAYS AFTER THE LORD revealed that Jackson County, Missouri, would be the place for the city of Zion (see Doctrine and Covenants 57). The elders who had traveled from Kirtland had mixed reactions upon learning of the city's location. The missionaries led by Oliver Cowdery worked among the local settlers for several months, but they had managed to convert only a handful of people, fewer than ten, to the teachings of the gospel. According to one source, Edward Partridge and Joseph Smith argued over the quality of the land, creating contention between the two.[1] Sidney Rigdon accused Bishop Partridge of "having insulted the Lord's prophet in particular and assumed authority over him in open violation of the laws of God."[2] It took several months for Joseph and Edward to reconcile. In a Church conference held later, Bishop

Partridge demonstrated his contrition by announcing that "if Br. Joseph has not forgiven him he hopes he will, as he is and has always been sorry."[3]

The argument between Joseph and Edward was a small moment in what was a hopeful day for the missionaries. In his personal history written years after the disputes, Joseph recalled the promise of the moment and the diversity of the population living in the frontier settlement. He wrote, "The first Sabbath after our arrival in Jackson county, brother W[illiam] W. Phelps preached to a western audience, over the boundary of the United States, wherein were present specimens of 'all the families of the earth' for there were several of the Indians; quite a respectable number of Negroes; and the balance was made up of citizens of the surrounding country, and fully represented themselves as pioneers of the west."[4]

The same week this revelation was received, Joseph and the other missionaries noted the arrival of the Colesville Branch, the first Latter-day Saint emigrants to arrive in Missouri. The last part of the revelation provides instruction to these newly arrived settlers.[5]

$\mathcal{V}$erse-by-$\mathcal{V}$erse $\mathcal{C}$ommentary

1 Hearken, O ye elders of my church, and give ear to my word, and learn of me what I will concerning you, and also concerning this land unto which I have sent you.

2 For verily I say unto you, blessed is he that keepeth my commandments, whether in life or in death; and he that is faithful in tribulation, the reward of the same is greater in the kingdom of heaven.

3 Ye cannot behold with your natural eyes, for the present time, the design of your God concerning those things which shall come hereafter, and the glory which shall follow after much tribulation.

4 For after much tribulation come the blessings. Wherefore the day cometh that ye shall be crowned with much glory; the hour is not yet, but is nigh at hand.

5 Remember this, which I tell you before, that you may lay it to heart, and receive that which is to follow.

When Joseph Smith and the other missionaries arrived in Missouri, the first questions they asked of the Lord were "When will the wilderness blossom as the rose? And when will Zion be built up in her glory?"[6] To the elders who had just arrived in Jackson County, the stretch of land before them was a poor prospect for the divine city of God prophesied of in the scriptures. The Lord asked them to look with an eye of faith and see the possibilities. Later in the revelation, the Lord warned them that it would be "many years" before the city could be fully established. But the grand vision for the city was then only beginning to unfold.

The Lord also provided the first indications that before the city would be built, the Saints would suffer tribulation (see verses 4–5). At this time the Church was less than two years old, and nearly all the missionaries in Missouri were converts of less than one year. The Lord was trying to prepare the Saints for the challenges to come. Most of them could not imagine the opposition they would eventually face in attempting to build Zion in its chosen location. Ugly scenes of persecution awaited the Saints in Missouri, but so did the return of the city of Enoch. The road to Zion lay filled with challenges and promise.

6 Behold, verily I say unto you, for this cause I have sent you— that you might be obedient, and that your hearts might be prepared to bear testimony of the things which are to come;

7 And also that you might be honored in laying the foundation, and in bearing record of the land upon which the Zion of God shall stand;

8 And also that a feast of fat things might be prepared for the poor; yea, a feast of fat things, of wine on the lees well refined, that the earth may know that the mouths of the prophets shall not fail;

9 Yea, a supper of the house of the Lord, well prepared, unto which all nations shall be invited.

10 First, the rich and the learned, the wise and the noble;

11 And after that cometh the day of my power; then shall the poor, the lame, and the blind, and the deaf, come in unto the marriage of the Lamb, and partake of the supper of the Lord, prepared for the great day to come.

12 Behold, I, the Lord, have spoken it.

This preliminary group of missionaries had been sent to Missouri in part to prepare a group of witnesses who could share their testimony of the city's purpose and the place where the city was to be built. Sidney Rigdon was specifically appointed to write a description of Jackson County to encourage Church members to emigrate and help to build Zion (see Doctrine and Covenants 58:50–51). The Lord quoted Isaiah in describing a "feast of fat things" for all who choose to attend (see Isaiah 25:6). The "wine on the lees well refined" is a phrase used in the King James Version of the Bible. The *lees* are also known as the dregs, or the most concentrated portion of the wine. The lees contained the strongest and sweetest part of the wine and were similar to a jelly or a preserve; they were considered a great delicacy.

While those with advantages of wealth and education might be the first to receive the gospel, the Lord promises that His power will lift up "the poor, the lame, and the blind, and the deaf" (verse 11) until all can come into the marriage of the Lamb. An integral part of the Church's work in the latter days is to spread education and help people become self-reliant. To fulfill these aims, the Lord commanded the creation of a school in Zion (see Doctrine and Covenants 55:4; 97:3–5). The Lord also later commanded that those who wished to settle in Zion first enter into the law of consecration (see Doctrine and Covenants 72:15–17). The feast of fat things described by the Lord was both temporal and intellectual. The Lord intended to eradicate the twin plagues of ignorance and poverty within the city of Zion.

13 And that the testimony might go forth from Zion, yea, from the mouth of the city of the heritage of God—

14 Yea, for this cause I have sent you hither, and have selected my servant Edward Partridge, and have appointed unto him his mission in this land.

15 But if he repent not of his sins, which are unbelief and blindness of heart, let him take heed lest he fall.

16 Behold his mission is given unto him, and it shall not be given again.

17 And whoso standeth in this mission is appointed to be a judge in Israel, like as it was in ancient days, to divide the lands of the heritage of God unto his children;

18 And to judge his people by the testimony of the just, and by the assistance of his counselors, according to the laws of the kingdom which are given by the prophets of God.

Edward Partridge was reproved in the revelation for his doubts about Zion's location, and to his everlasting credit, he repented and worked to build Zion. Edward received other rebukes in the revelations (see Doctrine and Covenants 64:17), and each time he bore his chastisement with humility and worked to fulfill the Lord's commands. It is important to remember that Edward and his family had already made considerable sacrifices for the gospel. They took in and supported many of the penniless Saints emigrating from New York and Pennsylvania. While assisting these families, members of the Partridge family came down with the measles, which were transmitted from some of the refugees. It was during this trying time that Edward left to travel to Missouri, perhaps heightening his anxiety and leading to the conflict with Joseph over the land.

Lydia Partridge, Edward's wife, later remembered, "My eldest daughter was taken down with lung fever, and while she was at the worst, my husband was called by revelation to go with a number of others to Missouri to locate a place for the gathering of the Saints, the unbelievers thought he must be crazy, or he would not go. And I thought myself that I had reason to think my trials had commenced, and so [they] had, but this trial like all others was followed with blessings for our daughter recovered."[7]

A few days after this revelation was given, Edward wrote in a letter to Lydia, "You know I stand in an important station, and as I am occasionally chastened I sometimes fear my station is above what I can perform to the acceptance of my Heavenly Father. I hope you and I may conduct ourselves as at last to land our souls in the heaven of eternal rest. Pray that I may not fall."[8] Other members of the missionary expedition to Missouri, most notably Ezra Booth, were disappointed in the land's appearance and the local settlers' demeanor. But in contrast to Booth, who left the Church and became a bitter enemy of the Saints, Edward Partridge stood fast in his place, fulfilled his duties, and received his just reward (see Doctrine and Covenants 124:19, 21).

19 For verily I say unto you, my law shall be kept on this land.

20 Let no man think he is ruler; but let God rule him that judgeth, according to the counsel of his own will, or, in other words, him that counseleth or sitteth upon the judgment seat.

21 Let no man break the laws of the land, for he that keepeth the laws of God hath no need to break the laws of the land.

22 Wherefore, be subject to the powers that be, until he reigns whose right it is to reign, and subdues all enemies under his feet.

23 Behold, the laws which ye have received from my hand are the laws of the church, and in this light ye shall hold them forth. Behold, here is wisdom.

While Latter-day Saints see themselves as citizens of the kingdom of God, they also hold a responsibility to serve as upright citizens of the countries they reside in. The Lord directed the Saints in Jackson County to keep the laws of the Church and the laws of the land and to "be subject to the powers that be" (verse 21). In a similar vein, Joseph Smith declared as one of the articles of faith that Church members "believe in being subject to kings, presidents, rulers, and magistrates, in obeying, honoring, and sustaining the law" (Articles of Faith 1:12).

Church members are asked not only to honor and obey the law but also to be full participants in the governance of the societies they live in. Elder Ronald A. Rasband counseled, "The opportunity to be involved in the political process is a privilege given to every citizen. Our laws and legislation play an important teaching role in shaping our social and moral culture. We need every individual in society to take an active role in engaging in civic dialogue that helps frame laws and legislation that are fair for everyone."[9]

24 And now, as I spake concerning my servant Edward Partridge, this land is the land of his residence, and those whom he has appointed for his counselors; and also the land of the residence of him whom I have appointed to keep my storehouse;

25 Wherefore, let them bring their families to this land, as they shall counsel between themselves and me.

Prior to his conversion to the Church, Edward Partridge was a successful hatter in Painesville, Ohio. Relocating himself and his family to Missouri was a great sacrifice. Shortly after this commandment was given, he wrote to his wife, Lydia, informing her that he needed to stay in Missouri "for the present, contrary to [his] expectations" and that he wanted her to stay in Painesville until the spring so she would be more comfortable there. Then he wrote of his feelings about leaving his home of more than a decade: "When I left Painesville, I told people I was coming back and bade none a farewell but for a short time, consequently I feel a great desire to return once more and bid your connection and my friends and acquaintances an eternal farewell, unless they should be willing to forsake all for the sake of Christ, and be gathered with the saints of the most high God."[10]

Several months later, Lydia Partridge undertook the journey to Missouri. Because Edward had been assigned to look after the needs of the Church in Missouri, Lydia had to manage the journey on her own. In addition to moving all of the family's clothing and possessions, she had to look after their five daughters, ranging in age from eleven years to seventeen months old. Emily Partridge later reflected on her parents' sacrifices, saying, "It seemed, to him, a very great undertaking for mother to break up her home and prepare for such a journey, with a family of little children, without her husband to advise and make arrangements for her. She was then quite young, and inexperienced in such things. But if my father could have looked forward into the future and beheld what his family would have to go through I think he would have felt still more anxious."[11]

During their journey to Missouri, Lydia and her daughters were assisted by Church members such as Isaac Morley and his family, who were also traveling to the new Zion. Emily later reflected, "Whatever suffering and privation my mother had to endure she never murmured or complained, but rejoiced that she was counted worthy to endure tribulation for the Gospel's sake. She felt that she had enlisted in a good cause and she looked forward to the happy time that had been promised to the saints. Her religion compensated her for all the hardships she had to endure."[12]

> 26 For behold, it is not meet that I should command in all things; for he that is compelled in all things, the same is a slothful and not a wise servant; wherefore he receiveth no reward.
>
> 27 Verily I say, men should be anxiously engaged in a good cause, and do many things of their own free will, and bring to pass much righteousness;
>
> 28 For the power is in them, wherein they are agents unto themselves. And inasmuch as men do good they shall in nowise lose their reward.

29 But he that doeth not anything until he is commanded, and receiveth a commandment with doubtful heart, and keepeth it with slothfulness, the same is damned.

The doctrine of agency is further explored in this revelation, adding to the doctrine that had been revealed to Joseph Smith during his translation of the book of Genesis (see Moses 4:1–4) and in a revelation received almost a year earlier (see Doctrine and Covenants 29). The Lord had revealed to the Prophet that Lucifer's objective in premortality was to "destroy the agency of man, which I, the Lord God, had given him" (Moses 4:3). Doctrine and Covenants 29 added that Satan and his followers turned away from God "because of their agency" (verse 36). The devil and his angels play a role in helping men and women learn the power of their agency. The Lord revealed that "it must needs be that the devil should tempt the children of men, or they could not be agents unto themselves; for if they never should have bitter they could not know the sweet" (Doctrine and Covenants 29:39). For people to exercise the power to choose, they must have a good choice and a bad choice.

Now, as the first missionaries stood in the land of Zion, the Lord again wanted to emphasize their power to do good. While the Lord provides commandments and counsel, His ultimate aim is to empower men and women to see the ways they can bring about God's purposes and then move proactively to do good. The Lord gives direction, but He wants us to eventually learn to see what needs to be accomplished and do good works of our own free will. Learning to use our personal agency to bless and help those around us is the Lord's ultimate aim of giving us agency.

30 Who am I that made man, saith the Lord, that will hold him guiltless that obeys not my commandments?

31 Who am I, saith the Lord, that have promised and have not fulfilled?

32 I command and men obey not; I revoke and they receive not the blessing.

33 Then they say in their hearts: This is not the work of the Lord, for his promises are not fulfilled. But wo unto such, for their reward lurketh beneath, and not from above.

Along with agency must come accountability. The Lord gives commandments to men and women and therefore must hold them accountable. In recent years Church leaders have discouraged the use of the term *free agency* because it suggests that a person's freedom to choose comes without consequences for their actions. The term *free agency* does not appear in the scriptures. The Lord instead uses the term *moral agency* (see Doctrine and Covenants 101:78). In the time this revelation was received, an *agent* was defined as one "entrusted with the business of another."[13] The connotation is similar to saying that someone can act as an attorney or representative of someone or something else. To say a person had *moral agency* was to say that a person was entrusted to act on behalf of morality.

Today when we speak of someone as a *free agent*, we mean that the person is committed to no group or organization to act on his or her behalf. However, understanding our premortal existence, we also understand that we committed to live the plan when we came to earth. Therefore, we are not *free agents* during our life here on earth but *moral agents* committed to live the laws of God. The Lord gives us opportunities to recommit to the cause through baptism and other covenants. But just as a player signed to a sports team is not allowed to act as an agent for another team, we are committed to use our power to act to forward the purposes of God, working as moral agents.

34 And now I give unto you further directions concerning this land.

35 It is wisdom in me that my servant Martin Harris should be an example unto the church, in laying his moneys before the bishop of the church.

36 And also, this is a law unto every man that cometh unto this land to receive an inheritance; and he shall do with his moneys according as the law directs.

37 And it is wisdom also that there should be lands purchased in Independence, for the place of the storehouse, and also for the house of the printing.

38 And other directions concerning my servant Martin Harris shall be given him of the Spirit, that he may receive his inheritance as seemeth him good;

39 And let him repent of his sins, for he seeketh the praise of the world.

Martin Harris, one of the Three Witnesses, was among those the Lord commanded to travel as missionaries to identify the location of Zion (see Doctrine and Covenants 52:24). Though he is remembered primarily for his role in the coming forth of the Book of Mormon, Martin also deserves to be remembered for the sacrifices he made to build the city of Zion. In a sermon given just a few days after Martin Harris's death, Elder Orson Pratt noted:

> Martin Harris was the first man that the Lord called by name to consecrate his money and lay the same at the feet of the Bishop in Jackson County, Mo., according to the order of consecration. He willingly did it; he knew the work to be true; he knew that the word of the Lord through the Prophet Joseph was just as sacred as any word that ever came from the mouth of any Prophet from the foundation of the world. He consecrated his money and his substance, according to the word of the Lord. What for? As the revelation states, as an example to the rest of the Church (see Doctrine and Covenants 58:35).[14]

40 And also let my servant William W. Phelps stand in the office to which I have appointed him, and receive his inheritance in the land;

41 And also he hath need to repent, for I, the Lord, am not well pleased with him, for he seeketh to excel, and he is not sufficiently meek before me.

42 Behold, he who has repented of his sins, the same is forgiven, and I, the Lord, remember them no more.

43 By this ye may know if a man repenteth of his sins—behold, he will confess them and forsake them.

William W. Phelps was among the men set apart to serve as agents for the Church in Missouri. The Lord reproves him in these verses for the sin of "seeking to excel" (verse 41). While seeking excellence is not a sin, it is implied here that William was seeking to be placed on a higher plane than his fellow servants called to the work in Missouri, with the Lord pointing out that he was not "sufficiently meek" (verse 41).

For sins like the one William was struggling with, or any other kind of spiritual malady, the remedy is repentance. The Lord calls on William to repent and points out two of the most important actions accompanying repentance: to confess and to forsake the sin. Sincere confession to oneself, to God, and, if necessary, to priesthood leaders is a sign of contrition that demonstrates the beginning of a change within a person's heart. Forsaking the sin is more than just refraining from committing it again. The word *forsake* indicates a mighty change of heart, of losing the disposition to commit the sin. The people of King Benjamin spoke of a "mighty change in us, or in our hearts, that we have no more disposition to do evil, but to do good continually" (Mosiah 5:2). One of the most simple ways to measure repentance is just to ask, "Am I the sort of person who would commit that sin again?" An honest answer to that question determines if a real change of heart has taken place.

> 44 And now, verily, I say concerning the residue of the elders of my church, the time has not yet come, for many years, for them to receive their inheritance in this land, except they desire it through the prayer of faith, only as it shall be appointed unto them of the Lord.
>
> 45 For, behold, they shall push the people together from the ends of the earth.
>
> 46 Wherefore, assemble yourselves together; and they who are not appointed to stay in this land, let them preach the gospel in the regions round about; and after that let them return to their homes.
>
> 47 Let them preach by the way, and bear testimony of the truth in all places, and call upon the rich, the high and the low, and the poor to repent.
>
> 48 And let them build up churches, inasmuch as the inhabitants of the earth will repent.
>
> 49 And let there be an agent appointed by the voice of the church, unto the church in Ohio, to receive moneys to purchase lands in Zion.
>
> 50 And I give unto my servant Sidney Rigdon a commandment, that he shall write a description of the land of Zion, and a statement of the will of God, as it shall be made known by the Spirit unto him;

51 And an epistle and subscription, to be presented unto all the churches to obtain moneys, to be put into the hands of the bishop, of himself or the agent, as seemeth him good or as he shall direct, to purchase lands for an inheritance for the children of God.

52 For, behold, verily I say unto you, the Lord willeth that the disciples and the children of men should open their hearts, even to purchase this whole region of country, as soon as time will permit.

Sidney Rigdon was commanded in this revelation to write a description of the land of Zion to help people understand conditions there. Sidney's description is found in part in Joseph Smith's official history, where Joseph Smith noted:

As we had received a commandment for Elder [Sidney] Rigdon to write a description of the land of Zion, we sought for all the information necessary to accomplish so desirable an object. Unlike the timbered states in the east, except upon the rivers and water courses, which were verdantly dotted with trees from one to three miles wide,—as far as the eye can glance the beautiful rolling prairies lay spread be around like a sea of meadows. . . . The soil is rich and fertile, from three to ten feet deep, and generally composed of a rich black mould, intermingled with clay and sand. It produces in abundance, wheat, corn, and many other common agricultural commodities, together with sweet potatoes and cotton.[15]

Describing the climate of Missouri, Sidney Rigdon wrote:

The season is mild and delightful nearly three quarters of the year, and as the land of Zion situated at about equal distances from the Atlantic and Pacific oceans. . . . The winters are milder than in the Atlantic states of the same parallel of latitude; and the weather is more agreeable, so that were the virtues of the inhabitants only equal to the blessings of the Lord which he permits to crown the industry and efforts of those inhabitants, there would be a measure of the good things of life, for the benefit of the saints, full, press down and running over, even an hundred fold.[16]

Sidney's description of Zion also sought to give those who wanted to emigrate to Missouri an honest assessment of the land's challenges: "The disadvantages here, like all new countries, are self-evident: lack of mills and schools, together with the natural privations and inconveniences, which the hand of industry, and the refinement of society with the polish of science, overcome. But all these impediments, banish when it is recollected what the prophets have said concerning Zion in the last days."[17]

> 53 Behold, here is wisdom. Let them do this lest they receive none inheritance, save it be by the shedding of blood.
>
> 54 And again, inasmuch as there is land obtained, let there be workmen sent forth of all kinds unto this land, to labor for the saints of God.
>
> 55 Let all these things be done in order; and let the privileges of the lands be made known from time to time, by the bishop or the agent of the church.
>
> 56 And let the work of the gathering be not in haste, nor by flight; but let it be done as it shall be counseled by the elders of the church at the conferences, according to the knowledge which they receive from time to time.
>
> 57 And let my servant Sidney Rigdon consecrate and dedicate this land, and the spot for the temple, unto the Lord.
>
> 58 And let a conference meeting be called; and after that let my servants Sidney Rigdon and Joseph Smith, Jun., return, and also Oliver Cowdery with them, to accomplish the residue of the work which I have appointed unto them in their own land, and the residue as shall be ruled by the conferences.

The day after this revelation was given, Joseph Smith and Sidney Rigdon led several ceremonies dedicating the land of Zion. Joseph Smith recorded:

> On the 2nd day of August, I assisted the Colesville branch of the church to lay the first log for a house as a foundation of Zion, in Kaw township, twelve miles west of Independence. The log was carried and placed by twelve men in honor of the twelve tribes of Israel. At the same time, through prayer, the land of Zion was consecrated and dedicated for the gathering of the Saints by Elder [Sidney] Rigdon; and it was a season of joy to those present, and afforded a glimpse of the future, which time will yet unfold to the satisfaction of the faithful.[18]

John Whitmer included more details about the dedication in his history, where he wrote:

Brother Sidney Rigdon stood up and asked saying:

"Do you receive this land for the land of your inheritance with thankful hearts from the Lord?"

Answer from all: "we do."

"Do you pledge yourselves to keep the laws of God on this land, which you have never have kept in your own land?"

"We do."

"Do you pledge yourselves to see that others of your brethren, who shall come hither do keep the laws of God?"

"We do."

After prayer he arose and said, "I now pronounce this land consecrated and dedicated to the Lord for a possession and inheritance for the Saints, (in the name of Jesus Christ having authority from him.) And for all the faithful Servants of the Lord to the remotest ages of time. Amen."[19]

John Whitmer also recorded that the following day, eight elders—"Joseph Smith Jr., Oliver Cowdery, Sidney Rigdon, Peter Whitmer Jr., Frederick G. Williams, Wm. W. Phelps, Martin Harris, and Joseph Coe"—met together at the future site of the temple in Zion. Sidney Rigdon offered a prayer dedicating "the ground where the city is to Stand: and Joseph Smith Jr. laid a stone at the North east corner of the contemplated Temple in the name of the Lord Jesus of Nazareth. After all present had rendered thanks to the great ruler of the universe. Sidney Rigdon pronounced this Spot of ground wholly dedicated unto the Lord forever: Amen."[20]

59 And let no man return from this land except he bear record by the way, of that which he knows and most assuredly believes.

60 Let that which has been bestowed upon Ziba Peterson be taken from him; and let him stand as a member in the church, and labor with his own hands, with the brethren, until he is sufficiently chastened for all his sins; for he confesseth them not, and he thinketh to hide them.

Ziba Peterson was among the original missionaries sent to Missouri to preach to the Lamanites under the leadership of Oliver Cowdery (see Doctrine and Covenants 32:3). While we do not know the exact nature of Peterson's transgression, Ezra Booth later wrote that Peterson was guilty of conduct "on a parallel" with a man who "enters into a matrimonial contract with a young lady, and obtains the consent of her parents; but as soon as his back is turned upon her, he violates his engagements, and prostitutes his honor by becoming the gallant of another, and resolves in his heart, and expresses resolutions to marry her." Peterson confessed his transgression at the conference held on August 4, and a week later he married Rebecca Hopper of Lafayette County, Missouri.[21]

> 61 Let the residue of the elders of this church, who are coming to this land, some of whom are exceedingly blessed even above measure, also hold a conference upon this land.
>
> 62 And let my servant Edward Partridge direct the conference which shall be held by them.
>
> 63 And let them also return, preaching the gospel by the way, bearing record of the things which are revealed unto them.
>
> 64 For, verily, the sound must go forth from this place into all the world, and unto the uttermost parts of the earth—the gospel must be preached unto every creature, with signs following them that believe.
>
> 65 And behold the Son of Man cometh. Amen.

Many of the missionaries sent to Missouri were still on their way when this revelation was received. Some, including Samuel Smith, Hyrum Smith, and David Whitmer, did not arrive until later in August (see Doctrine and Covenants 62), while others did not arrive until October or November of that year.[22] Edward Partridge was directed to hold a conference with these elders upon their arrival. There was no reproval for these elders because their arrival was delayed. In a later revelation, the Lord told several of the elders, "Ye are blessed, for the testimony which ye have borne" (Doctrine and Covenants 62:3).

Along the way to accomplish our given tasks, we must remember the Lord's overarching command to share the gospel, to assist in lifting others up, and to build God's kingdom through good works. Zion is often created by the good carried out along the way as we strive to reach the holy city.

End Notes

1. See Ezra Booth, "Mormonism—No. VII," *Ohio Star* (Ravenna), Nov. 24, 1831.
2. Minute Book 2, 23, josephsmithpapers.org.
3. Minute Book 2, 23, josephsmithpapers.org.
4. Joseph Smith, in History, 1838–1856, volume A-1 [23 December 1805–30 August 1834], 129, josephsmithpapers.org.
5. See History, 1838–1856, volume A-1 [23 December 1805–30 August 1834], 129, josephsmithpapers.org. See also "Historical Introduction," Revelation, 1 August 1831 [D&C 58], josephsmithpapers.org.
6. History, 1838–1856, volume A-1 [23 December 1805–30 August 1834], 127, josephsmithpapers.org.
7. Joseph Smith Papers, Documents, Vol. 1, 330, footnote 458, josephsmithpapers.org.
8. Scott H. Partridge, "Edward Partridge in Painesville, Ohio," *BYU Studies* 41, no. 1: 64.
9. Ronald A. Rasband, "Religious Freedom and Fairness for All" (Brigham Young University devotional, Sept. 15, 2015), 1–2, speeches.byu.edu.
10. Partridge, "Edward Partridge in Painesville, Ohio," 64.
11. Partridge, "Edward Partridge in Painesville, Ohio," 65.
12. "Emily Partridge Young, 1824-1899," Book of Abraham Project, accessed Feb. 13, 2024, http://boap.org/LDS/Early-Saints/EmPart.html.
13. *An American Dictionary of the English Language*, s.v. "agent," accessed February 13, 2024, https://webstersdictionary1828.com/Dictionary/agent.
14. Orson Pratt, in *Journal of Discourses,* 18:160–161.
15. Joseph Smith, in History, 1838–1856, volume A-1 [23 December 1805–30 August 1834], 137–139, josephsmithpapers.org.
16. History, 1838–1856, volume A-1 [23 December 1805–30 August 1834], 137–139, josephsmithpapers.org.
17. History, 1838–1856, volume A-1 [23 December 1805–30 August 1834], 137–139, josephsmithpapers.org.
18. Joseph Smith, in History, 1838–1856, volume A-1 [23 December 1805–30 August 1834], 137, josephsmithpapers.org.
19. John Whitmer, History, 1831–circa 1847, 30–31, josephsmithpapers.org.
20. John Whitmer, History, 1831–circa 1847, 30–31, josephsmithpapers.org.
21. See Revelation, 1 August 1831 [D&C 58], footnote 51, josephsmithpapers.org.
22. See Revelation, 1 August 1831 [D&C 58], footnote 52, josephsmithpapers.org.

Doctrine and Covenants Section 59

Blessed Are They Whose Feet Stand upon the Land of Zion

Historical Context

THE FIRST WEEK OF AUGUST 1831 THE MEMBERS OF THE COLESVILLE Branch began arriving in the Independence region. Polly Knight, the matriarch of the Knight family, was ill during the entire journey to Missouri. Her son Newel Knight was leading the Colesville Branch during their journey. As mentioned earlier, he was so concerned over his mother's health that he purchased lumber in case he needed to make a coffin for her during the journey. He noted, "But the Lord gave her the desire of her heart, for she lived to stand upon that land [Missouri]." Newel later wrote, "On the Sixth [of August] my mother died. She quietly fell asleep in death rejoicing in the new and everlasting covenant of the gospel, and praising God that she had lived to see the land of Zion, and that her body would rest in peace after suffering as she had done from the persecution of the wicked, and journeying to this place."[1]

We do not know if Joseph Smith was aware of Polly Knight's death when the revelation was received, but the first two verses appear to acknowledge her death, speaking of "those that shall die and rest from their labors" (Doctrine and Covenants 59:2).

Another concern addressed in the revelation is the local settlers' coarse manner of living. William W. Phelps later noted that most of the residents of Jackson County were "emigrants from Tennessee, Kentucky, Virginia, and the Carolinas . . . with customs, manner, modes of living and a climate entirely different from the northerners."[2] In a later history Joseph Smith noted that "we could not associate with our neighbors who were many of them of the basest of men and had fled from the face of civilized society, to the frontier country to escape the hand of justice, in their midnight revels, their sabbath breaking, horseracing, and gambling."[3]

It appears that Christian living, particularly Sabbath worship, was a low priority for the local settlers. In response to this lifestyle, the members of the Church who were settling in the region were commanded to live the commandments and to take special care to make the Sabbath day an important part of their lives. These basic instructions to the Church added to earlier commandments given in the Articles and Covenants (see Doctrine and Covenants 20) and the Laws of the Church of Christ (see Doctrine and Covenants 42).[4]

Verse-by-Verse Commentary

1 Behold, blessed, saith the Lord, are they who have come up unto this land with an eye single to my glory, according to my commandments.

2 For those that live shall inherit the earth, and those that die shall rest from all their labors, and their works shall follow them; and they shall receive a crown in the mansions of my Father, which I have prepared for them.

3 Yea, blessed are they whose feet stand upon the land of Zion, who have obeyed my gospel; for they shall receive for their re-

ward the good things of the earth, and it shall bring forth in its strength.

4 And they shall also be crowned with blessings from above, yea, and with commandments not a few, and with revelations in their time—they that are faithful and diligent before me.

The opening words of this revelation were given to comfort the Knight family on the loss of their matriarch, Polly, and to reassure all those who made sacrifices on the road to Zion. The Knight family arrived in Missouri under difficult conditions. Joseph Knight Jr. recalled that "we had no tents, and my father and I slept in a hen coop two weeks, until we got a shelter."[5]

Polly Knight passed away the same day this revelation was received. Joseph Knight Sr. later wrote in his history, "There was one Joshua Lewis that had Come into the Church the winter Before, he and his wife. And they ware faithful and good to us and took us in to their house, my wife Being sick as before stated. She Died the Seventh Day of August and Joseph and Sidney attended her funeral on the Eighth. She was buried in the woods a spot chosen out by ourselves." Further noting the difficult conditions, Father Knight added, "I was along by where she was buried a few Days after, and I found the hogs had begun to root where she was Buried. I being very unwell, but I took my axe the next Day and went and built a pen round it. It was the last [thing] I done for her."[6]

Joseph Smith preached Polly Knight's funeral sermon the next day, declaring, "I can say a worthy member sleeps in Jesus till the resurrection."[7]

5 Wherefore, I give unto them a commandment, saying thus: Thou shalt love the Lord thy God with all thy heart, with all thy might, mind, and strength; and in the name of Jesus Christ thou shalt serve him.

6 Thou shalt love thy neighbor as thyself. Thou shalt not steal; neither commit adultery, nor kill, nor do anything like unto it.

7 Thou shalt thank the Lord thy God in all things.

8 Thou shalt offer a sacrifice unto the Lord thy God in righteousness, even that of a broken heart and a contrite spirit.

While the Ten Commandments were originally given to Moses on Mount Sinai, they are also part of the higher law of Jesus Christ and not just a part of the "law of carnal commandments" given to the Israelites (see

Hebrews 7:16; Doctrine and Covenants 84:7). Given anew in this dispensation, these commandments remain hallmarks of Jehovah's followers in any age.

While several of the original commandments remain in these verses, the wording of some commandments was updated to reflect the conditions of our time. For instance, instead of "Thou shalt have no other gods before me" (Exodus 20:3), the commandment given here is "Thou shalt love the Lord thy God with all thy heart, with all thy might, mind, and strength" (verse 5). Instead of "Thou shalt not make unto thee any graven images" (Exodus 20:4), the Lord teaches us to serve "in the name of Jesus Christ" (verse 5). The Lord further commands us to "love thy neighbor as thyself" (verse 6). He builds on the command "Thou shalt not kill" (Exodus 20:13) by adding "nor do anything like unto it" (verse 6). He also commands his disciples to "thank the Lord thy God in all things" (verse 7) and expounds greatly on the meaning and purpose of the Sabbath day (see verses 9–12).

All of these commandments are encompassed in the Lord's command to "offer a sacrifice unto the Lord thy God in righteousness even that of a broken heart and contrite spirit" (verse 8). The concept of a "broken heart and a contrite spirit" is where the law of Moses and the law of Christ connect. Both laws require a sacrifice to point toward the great sacrifice of Jesus Christ. But while the old law included a complex system of physical sacrifice, the new law asks that we give our whole heart and mind to God. Elder Neal A. Maxwell explained, "The submission of one's will is really the only uniquely personal thing we have to place on God's altar. . . . When you and I finally submit ourselves, by letting our individual wills be swallowed up in God's will, then we are really giving something to Him! It is the only possession which is truly ours to give!"[8]

> 9 And that thou mayest more fully keep thyself unspotted from the world, thou shalt go to the house of prayer and offer up thy sacraments upon my holy day;
>
> 10 For verily this is a day appointed unto you to rest from your labors, and to pay thy devotions unto the Most High;
>
> 11 Nevertheless thy vows shall be offered up in righteousness on all days and at all times;

12 But remember that on this, the Lord's day, thou shalt offer thine oblations and thy sacraments unto the Most High, confessing thy sins unto thy brethren, and before the Lord.

13 And on this day thou shalt do none other thing, only let thy food be prepared with singleness of heart that thy fasting may be perfect, or, in other words, that thy joy may be full.

14 Verily, this is fasting and prayer, or in other words, rejoicing and prayer.

Latter-day Saints do not worship on Sunday, or on any other day, in imitation of ancient people. We hallow and worship on the Sabbath day because of the Lord's commandment in this dispensation to do so. The principle of the Sabbath is setting aside a day to rest from our ordinary labors and devote time to worshipping the Lord. An *oblation*, as defined in the time this revelation was given, is "anything offered or presented in worship or sacred service; an offering; a sacrifice."[9] Church members can present as their offering a testimony, a portion of their time devoted to Church service or study, or an act of kindness to others.

We must be careful not to become too legalistic about the Sabbath day. Some Church members become obsessed with rules about the Sabbath while overruling the general principles the Lord teaches about this day. President Nelson counseled:

> In my much younger years, I studied the work of others who had compiled lists of things to do and things *not* to do on the Sabbath. It wasn't until later that I learned from the scriptures that my conduct and my attitude on the Sabbath constituted a *sign* between me and my Heavenly Father. With that understanding, I no longer needed lists of dos and don'ts. When I had to make a decision whether or not an activity was appropriate for the Sabbath, I simply asked myself, "What *sign* do I want to give to God?" That question made my choices about the Sabbath day crystal clear.[10]

15 And inasmuch as ye do these things with thanksgiving, with cheerful hearts and countenances, not with much laughter, for this is sin, but with a glad heart and a cheerful countenance—

The Lord is not opposed to happiness, cheerfulness, or laughter, as evidenced by the last half of this verse. While humor can sometimes be inappropriate or even blasphemous, this verse does not constitute a ban on humor among the Saints. There are three places in the Doctrine and Covenants where the Lord gives commandments concerning laughter. He commands his disciples to avoid "much laughter" (Doctrine and Covenants 59:15), to cast away an "excess of laughter" (Doctrine and Covenants 88:69), and to cease from "all laughter" (Doctrine and Covenants 88:121).

In each of these cases, it is important to consider the context of these commandments. In Doctrine and Covenants 59, the setting the Lord speaks of is fasting, prayer, and Sabbath worship, a place where "much" laughter should be avoided. In Doctrine and Covenants 88, the Lord is speaking of His house, the temple, where the spirit of reverence must abide and where laughter may be inappropriate.

The Prophet Joseph Smith was well known for his propensity toward laughter and merriment. Benjamin F. Johnson, a close friend of Joseph Smith, recalled that he "took great delight in his society and friendship. When with us, there was no lack of amusement for with jokes, games, etc., he was always ready to provoke merriment, one phase of which was matching couplets in rhyme, by which we were at times in rivalry; and his fraternal feeling, in great degree did away with his disparity of age or greatness of his calling."[11]

16 Verily I say, that inasmuch as ye do this, the fulness of the earth is yours, the beasts of the field and the fowls of the air, and that which climbeth upon the trees and walketh upon the earth;

17 Yea, and the herb, and the good things which come of the earth, whether for food or for raiment, or for houses, or for barns, or for orchards, or for gardens, or for vineyards;

18 Yea, all things which come of the earth, in the season thereof, are made for the benefit and the use of man, both to please the eye and to gladden the heart;

19 Yea, for food and for raiment, for taste and for smell, to strengthen the body and to enliven the soul.

20 And it pleaseth God that he hath given all these things unto man; for unto this end were they made to be used, with judgment, not to excess, neither by extortion.

The earth and all of its resources exist for men and women to use, enjoy, and protect. Even the Word of Wisdom, given later, does not forbid the use of substances as much as it counsels against their misuse. There is an appropriate and functional purpose for everything in our environment. While these things are given for the "benefit and use of man" (verse 18), we have an obligation to be wise stewards of the resources at hand. An official Church statement counsels, "The earth and all things on it should be used responsibly to sustain the human family. However, all are stewards—not owners—over this earth and its bounty and will be accountable before God for what they do with His creations. . . . The state of the human soul and the environment are interconnected, with each affecting and influencing the other."[12]

> 21 And in nothing doth man offend God, or against none is his wrath kindled, save those who confess not his hand in all things, and obey not his commandments.
>
> 22 Behold, this is according to the law and the prophets; wherefore, trouble me no more concerning this matter.
>
> 23 But learn that he who doeth the works of righteousness shall receive his reward, even peace in this world, and eternal life in the world to come.
>
> 24 I, the Lord, have spoken it, and the Spirit beareth record. Amen.

The Savior sums up the counsel given "according to the law and the prophets" (verse 22) by declaring that the root of many of our sorrows is a lack of acknowledgment of the Lord's hand in our lives and a lack of appreciation for the blessings He has given to us. As the Saints in Missouri entered into their great experiment in consecration, the Lord reminded them that the central tenet of that law was that nothing is really consecrated to God because everything already belongs to Him. Rather, we make our blessings holy by recognizing the holy source of our blessings.

Like the Saints in Zion did, we live in a world filled with challenges and complexity. President Russell M. Nelson reminded the Saints that "there is no medication or operation that can fix the many spiritual woes and maladies that we face." Then he added, "There is, however, a remedy—one that may seem surprising—because it flies in the face of our natural intuitions. . . . Nevertheless, its effects have been validated by scientists as well as men and women of faith. I am referring to the healing power of *gratitude*. Counting our blessings is far better than recounting our problems."[13]

End Notes

1. William G. Hartley and Michael Hubbard MacKay, *The Rise of the Latter-day Saints: The Journals and Histories of Newell K. Knight* (Salt Lake City, UT: Deseret Book, 2019), 36–39.
2. "Historical Introduction," Revelation, 7 August 1831, josephsmithpapers.org.
3. "Church History," 1 March 1842, 708, josephsmithpapers.org.
4. See "Historical Introduction," Revelation, 7 August 1831 [D&C 59], josephsmithpapers.org.
5. Arnold K. Garr and Clark V. Johnson, ed., *Regional Studies in Latter-day Saint History: Missouri* (Provo, UT: Department of Church History and Doctrine, 1994), 292.
6. Dean Jessee, "Joseph Knight's Recollection of Early Mormon History," *BYU Studies* 17, no. 1 (1977): 13.
7. William G. Hartley, *Stand by My Servant Joseph: Story of the Joseph Knight Family and the Restoration* (Salt Lake City, UT: Joseph Fielding Smith Institute, 2003), 135.
8. Neal A. Maxwell, "Swallowed Up in the Will of the Father," *Ensign*, Nov. 1995, 24.
9. *An American Dictionary of the English Language*, s.v. "oblation," accessed February 13, 2024, https://webstersdictionary1828.com/Dictionary/oblation.
10. Russell M. Nelson, "The Sabbath Is a Delight," *Ensign* or *Liahona*, May 2015, 130.
11. Mark L. McConkie, *Remembering Joseph: Personal Recollections of Those Who Knew the Prophet Joseph Smith* (Salt Lake City, UT: Deseret Book, 2003), 86.
12. "Environmental Stewardship and Conversation," newsroom.ChurchofJesusChrist.org.
13. "The Prophet Releases a Message on the Healing Power of Gratitude," Nov. 20, 2020, newsroom.ChurchofJesusChrist.org.

Doctrine and Covenants Section 60

I Am Able to Make You Holy

Historical Context

WITH THE LAND OF ZION DEDICATED AND THE EMIGRANTS FROM THE Church building their homes, it was time for the majority of the elders in Missouri to return home. Some elders, including Edward Partridge, would stay behind to assist the Saints in gathering and building the city. The Lord commanded most of the elders to return to Ohio and provided instructions for how to carry out the journey. In his history Joseph Smith introduced the revelation by simply noting, "On the 8th, as there had been some inquiry among the elders, what they were to do, I received the following."[1]

$\mathcal{V}$erse-by-$\mathcal{V}$erse $\mathcal{C}$ommentary

1 Behold, thus saith the Lord unto the elders of his church, who are to return speedily to the land from whence they came: Behold, it pleaseth me, that you have come up hither;

2 But with some I am not well pleased, for they will not open their mouths, but they hide the talent which I have given unto them, because of the fear of man. Wo unto such, for mine anger is kindled against them.

3 And it shall come to pass, if they are not more faithful unto me, it shall be taken away, even that which they have.

4 For I, the Lord, rule in the heavens above, and among the armies of the earth; and in the day when I shall make up my jewels, all men shall know what it is that bespeaketh the power of God.

Here the Lord references the parable of the talents found in Matthew 25:14–30. In the parable, three servants are given talents, a large monetary measure that equaled about twenty years' wages for the average day laborer.[2] Two of the servants wisely utilized their talents, doubling their investment, while the third servant took his talent "and digged in the earth, and hid his lord's money" (Matthew 25:18). When the master of the parable held an accounting of the three servants, he commended the first two for their wise stewardship. He then chastised the servant who hoarded his talent, and the master took the talent back.

Likewise, the Savior chastened a number of the missionaries in Missouri who were withholding their gifts and refusing to share the gospel with others. As with all of His servants, the Lord wants us to use the gifts and knowledge we have been given to bless and help others.

5 But, verily, I will speak unto you concerning your journey unto the land from whence you came. Let there be a craft made, or bought, as seemeth you good, it mattereth not unto me, and take your journey speedily for the place which is called St. Louis.

6 And from thence let my servants, Sidney Rigdon, Joseph Smith, Jun., and Oliver Cowdery, take their journey for Cincinnati;

7 And in this place let them lift up their voice and declare my word with loud voices, without wrath or doubting, lifting up holy hands upon them. For I am able to make you holy, and your sins are forgiven you.

8 And let the residue take their journey from St. Louis, two by two, and preach the word, not in haste, among the congregations of the wicked, until they return to the churches from whence they came.

9 And all this for the good of the churches; for this intent have I sent them.

Part of the elders' petition to the Lord apparently included a question about how to travel home to Kirtland. Some of the missionaries proposed traveling by canoe or by some other method. The Lord told the missionaries that their method of travel did not matter to Him and that they could decide for themselves. While the Lord is deeply involved in the details of our lives, there are many times when He desires us to use our own wisdom and agency to make decisions. Seeking personal revelation or guidance from a priesthood leader in every decision is not necessary and may impede our personal growth. In these verses, the Lord gives counsel to the elders about preaching the gospel during their journey, but He leaves the method of travel open to their judgment.

President Oaks spoke of two lines of communication to God. The first is the personal line, which is "of paramount importance in personal decisions and in the governance of the family." The second is "the priesthood line, which operates principally to govern heavenly communications on Church matters." President Oaks counseled, "We must use both the personal line and the priesthood line in proper balance to achieve the growth that is the purpose of mortal life. If personal religious practice relies too much on the personal line, individualism erases the importance of divine authority. If personal religious practice relies too much on the priesthood line, individual growth suffers. The children of God need both lines to achieve their eternal destiny. The restored gospel teaches both, and the restored Church provides both."[3]

10 And let my servant Edward Partridge impart of the money which I have given him, a portion unto mine elders who are commanded to return;

11 And he that is able, let him return it by the way of the agent; and he that is not, of him it is not required.

12 And now I speak of the residue who are to come unto this land.

13 Behold, they have been sent to preach my gospel among the congregations of the wicked; wherefore, I give unto them a commandment, thus: Thou shalt not idle away thy time, neither shalt thou bury thy talent that it may not be known.

14 And after thou hast come up unto the land of Zion, and hast proclaimed my word, thou shalt speedily return, proclaiming my word among the congregations of the wicked, not in haste, neither in wrath nor with strife.

The Lord provided a warning against idleness and hiding away talents to those who were coming to Zion. Often the work of the Lord is hindered not only by those who are afraid to share their witness but also by those who refuse to actively engage in the work. The Lord's counsel continues the theme that the members of the Church must be "anxiously engaged" and use their own free will and judgment to move the work forward (see Doctrine and Covenants 58:26–27). While the way may not always be clear, it is imperative that members of the Church continue to move forward. Idleness was one of the sure ways to create contention and strife among the Saints. The Lord commanded in an earlier revelation, "Thou shalt not be idle; for he that is idle shall not eat the bread nor wear the garments of the laborer" (Doctrine and Covenants 42:42).

15 And shake off the dust of thy feet against those who receive thee not, not in their presence, lest thou provoke them, but in secret; and wash thy feet, as a testimony against them in the day of judgment.

16 Behold, this is sufficient for you, and the will of him who hath sent you.

17 And by the mouth of my servant Joseph Smith, Jun., it shall be made known concerning Sidney Rigdon and Oliver Cowdery. The residue hereafter. Even so. Amen.

For more information on the phrase "shake off the dust of thy feet" (verse 15), see commentary for Doctrine and Covenants 24:15–19.

End Notes

1. Joseph Smith, in History, 1838–1856, volume A-1 [23 December 1805–30 August 1834], 141, josephsmithpapers.org. See also "Historical Introduction," Revelation, 8 August 1831 [D&C 60], josephsmithpapers.org.
2. See *Lexham Bible Dictionary* (Bellingham, WA: Lexham Press, 2016), s.v. "talent."
3. Dallin H. Oaks, "Two Lines of Communication," *Ensign or Liahona,* Nov. 2010, 86.

Doctrine and Covenants Section 61

All Flesh Is in Mine Hand

Historical Context

ON AUGUST 9, 1831, JOSEPH SMITH AND A GROUP OF MISSIONARIES SET OUT for Kirtland, choosing to travel part of the way by canoe on the Missouri River. The travelers in the party included Oliver Cowdery and Peter Whitmer Jr., two of the original missionaries to the Lamanites. Joseph Smith later noted, "Nothing very important occurred till the third day, when many of the dangers, so common upon the western waters, manifested themselves."[1] Anxiety over the river's turbulence was compounded by contention among the group. Ezra Booth noted that "a spirit of animosity and discord" was manifested among the group and that "the conduct of the elders became very displeasing to Oliver Cowdery." Oliver prophesied that "as the Lord God liveth, if you do not behave better some accident will befall you."[2]

None of the elders had much experience traveling by canoe, and shortly after Oliver's warning, Joseph Smith and Sidney Rigdon's canoe became snagged on a "sawyer," meaning a tree submerged below the surface of the water. Terrified by this near catastrophe, Joseph instructed the group to get off the river. The men exited the river at a place Joseph Smith labeled "McIlwaine's Bend," which is near present-day Miami, Missouri. Some of the men accused Joseph of cowardice for leaving the river.

At the camp, the elders held a council. Some of the elders expressed anger over Oliver Cowdery's earlier rebuke, while others accused Joseph of being "quite dictatorial." The council continued into the night until everyone had reconciled.[3] Joseph later noted in his history, "The next morning, after prayer, I received the following."[4]

Verse-by-Verse Commentary

1 Behold, and hearken unto the voice of him who has all power, who is from everlasting to everlasting, even Alpha and Omega, the beginning and the end.

2 Behold, verily thus saith the Lord unto you, O ye elders of my church, who are assembled upon this spot, whose sins are now forgiven you, for I, the Lord, forgive sins, and am merciful unto those who confess their sins with humble hearts;

3 But verily I say unto you, that it is not needful for this whole company of mine elders to be moving swiftly upon the waters, whilst the inhabitants on either side are perishing in unbelief.

This revelation came after a night of discussion over the contention developing among the elders. The journeys to and from Missouri were a test for the elders, strengthening the faith of some and weakening the faith of others. The difficulty was less about the circumstances they traveled in and more about their response to the adversity they faced. The Lord allowed the elders to choose the manner in which they traveled home to Kirtland (see Doctrine and Covenants 60:5). But here He expressed concern that the elders focused on returning home in the quickest way possible rather than seeing their journey as an opportunity to preach the gospel. The Lord had commanded the elders to travel "not in haste" (Doctrine and Covenants 60:7–8), but once the journey commenced, they neglected His counsel. As a result, contention erupted among the elders when their journey was delayed, even when Joseph Smith instructed them to leave the river for their own safety.

However, after the elders spent an evening counseling together and confessing their wrongs, the Lord provided reassurance that their mistakes could be forgiven as long as they recognized and confessed their sins.

> 4 Nevertheless, I suffered it that ye might bear record; behold, there are many dangers upon the waters, and more especially hereafter;
>
> 5 For I, the Lord, have decreed in mine anger many destructions upon the waters; yea, and especially upon these waters.
>
> 6 Nevertheless, all flesh is in mine hand, and he that is faithful among you shall not perish by the waters.
>
> 7 Wherefore, it is expedient that my servant Sidney Gilbert and my servant William W. Phelps be in haste upon their errand and mission.
>
> 8 Nevertheless, I would not suffer that ye should part until you were chastened for all your sins, that you might be one, that you might not perish in wickedness;
>
> 9 But now, verily I say, it behooveth me that ye should part. Wherefore let my servants Sidney Gilbert and William W. Phelps take their former company, and let them take their journey in haste that they may fill their mission, and through faith they shall overcome;
>
> 10 And inasmuch as they are faithful they shall be preserved, and I, the Lord, will be with them.
>
> 11 And let the residue take that which is needful for clothing.
>
> 12 Let my servant Sidney Gilbert take that which is not needful with him, as you shall agree.

After the harrowing experience of the previous day, the Lord warned the elders about the dangers of traveling on the waters. He also promised to protect them as they traveled. While the Lord will explain in Doctrine and Covenants 61:13–18 what He decreed generally upon the waters in the latter days, here He speaks of "these waters," meaning the Missouri River.

At the time, the Missouri River was considered one of the most hazardous waterways in all of North America. It was thought to be navigable only three months out of the year and was referred to as "mad water" in an 1837 atlas published in Missouri. This atlas also noted "the ever-varying channel of the river." The river was so dangerous that pilot wages and insurance were higher for those traveling the Missouri. In the heading of the revelation, John Whitmer gave the Missouri the name "the River Destruction" because of the hazards the elders faced.[5]

> 13 And now, behold, for your good I gave unto you a commandment concerning these things; and I, the Lord, will reason with you as with men in days of old.
>
> 14 Behold, I, the Lord, in the beginning blessed the waters; but in the last days, by the mouth of my servant John, I cursed the waters.
>
> 15 Wherefore, the days will come that no flesh shall be safe upon the waters.
>
> 16 And it shall be said in days to come that none is able to go up to the land of Zion upon the waters, but he that is upright in heart.

Doctrine and Covenants 61:13–22 is among the most misunderstood and misquoted passages of scripture. A number of folklore traditions have grown up surrounding it, including beliefs like "Satan controls the waters" or that the cursing of the waters is why missionaries are prohibited from swimming. To connect any of these traditions back to this revelation is to twist or misunderstand the Lord's words to Joseph Smith.

According to scriptural accounts of the Creation, the Lord blessed the waters to bring forth life in abundance (see Moses 2:20). At some point, a servant of the Lord named John was directed to curse the waters. We do not know the context of this incident or even which John the Lord is speaking about. It is possible that this cursing is linked to the author of the book of Revelation who witnessed a vision that "a great mountain burning with fire was cast into the sea: and the third part of the sea became blood; and a third part of the creatures which were in the sea, and had life, died; and the third part of the ships were destroyed" (Revelation 8:8–9). The John of the book of Revelation also saw a vision in which a star called Wormwood fell from the heavens and poisoned a "third part of the waters" (Revelation 8:11).

While many interpretations of John's visions have been offered over the years, it is best to approach these passages with caution since we have not been given an interpretation of what the visions mean. The Prophet Joseph Smith counseled, "I make this broad declaration, that where God ever gives a vision of an image, or beast or figure of any kind he always holds himself responsible to give a revelation or interpretation of the meaning thereof, otherwise we are not responsible or accountable for our belief in it. Don't be afraid of being damned for not knowing the meaning of a vision or figure where God has not given a revelation or interpretation on the subject."[6]

There are a number of ways the revelation given to Joseph Smith may find fulfillment. In the nineteenth century, a large number of deaths could be traced to waterborne diseases such as cholera. In 1834, when Joseph Smith led a group called Zion's Camp to assist the Saints in Missouri, an outbreak of cholera led to fifteen deaths. Cholera outbreaks throughout the nineteenth century led to millions of deaths worldwide, and such outbreaks continue to be deadly in our time. Other dramatic examples such as tsunamis, hurricanes, and other destructive weather patterns have led to great loss of life and property. But to assign too specific an interpretation to this passage while the Lord has chosen not to do so may be unwise.

> 17 And, as I, the Lord, in the beginning cursed the land, even so in the last days have I blessed it, in its time, for the use of my saints, that they may partake the fatness thereof.
>
> 18 And now I give unto you a commandment that what I say unto one I say unto all, that you shall forewarn your brethren concerning these waters, that they come not in journeying upon them, lest their faith fail and they are caught in snares;

The Lord's cursing of the land is most likely a reference to the words pronounced to Adam and Eve when they were expelled from the Garden of Eden. The Lord told Adam that "cursed shall be the ground for thy sake; in sorrow shalt thou eat of it all the days of thy life. Thorns also, and thistles shall it bring forth to thee, and thou shalt eat the herb of the field. By the sweat of thy face shalt thou eat bread, until thou return unto the ground" (Moses 4:23–25).

Here the Lord tells the elders that He has blessed the land in the last days, echoing earlier prophecies of Isaiah that the "desert shall rejoice, and blossom as the rose" (Isaiah 35:1) and that "instead of the thorn shall come up the fir tree" (Isaiah 55:13). In a later revelation to Joseph Smith, the Lord promised to "make solitary places to bud and to blossom, and to bring forth in abundance" (Doctrine and Covenants 117:7). Both the waters and the land will find revitalization when "the earth will be renewed and receive its paradisiacal glory" (Articles of Faith 1:10).

> 19 I, the Lord, have decreed, and the destroyer rideth upon the face thereof, and I revoke not the decree.
>
> 20 I, the Lord, was angry with you yesterday, but today mine anger is turned away.
>
> 21 Wherefore, let those concerning whom I have spoken, that should take their journey in haste—again I say unto you, let them take their journey in haste.
>
> 22 And it mattereth not unto me, after a little, if it so be that they fill their mission, whether they go by water or by land; let this be as it is made known unto them according to their judgments hereafter.

In his official history Joseph Smith recorded that William W. Phelps "in an open vision, by daylight, saw the Destroyer, in his most horrible power, ride upon the face of the waters." He also noted that "others heard the noise, but saw not the vision."[7] We do not know the significance of the vision. Two other members of the group who wrote accounts of the journey, Ezra Booth and Reynolds Cahoon, make no mention of the vision in their description of the incident. The vision was likely included in Joseph Smith's history because Phelps assisted him in preparing it.[8]

It is unclear whether the "destroyer" as mentioned here is a servant of God or of Satan. Most of the other mentions of a destroyer in scripture are associated with the power of God and not the power of Satan. For instance, an 1834 revelation given to Joseph Smith reads, "Behold, the destroyer I have sent forth to destroy and lay waste mine enemies; and not many years hence they shall not be left to pollute mine heritage, and to blaspheme my name upon the lands which I have consecrated for the gathering together of my saints" (Doctrine and Covenants 105:15). However, in the Doctrine and Covenants there is one possible reference to Satan as the destroyer, specifically where the Lord tells a parable about the Saints in Zion. The Lord tells the Saints that if they had heeded His instructions, they might have "saved my vineyard from the hands of the destroyer" (Doctrine and Covenants 101:54).

Joseph Smith's history does not provide enough context for us to make a final determination on who the destroyer is in this context. However, given the circumstances, it is likely that the destroyer is a reference to death. In the book of Exodus, the Lord promised the Israelites that if they followed the instructions that He gave through Moses, He would "not suffer the destroyer to come in unto your houses to smite you" (Exodus 12:23). The Lord associating the waters with death appears to be consistent with the way the term "destroyer" was used in Protestant America in the 1830s.[9]

> 23 And now, concerning my servants, Sidney Rigdon, Joseph Smith, Jun., and Oliver Cowdery, let them come not again upon the waters, save it be upon the canal, while journeying unto their homes; or in other words they shall not come upon the waters to journey, save upon the canal.
>
> 24 Behold, I, the Lord, have appointed a way for the journeying of my saints; and behold, this is the way—that after they leave the canal they shall journey by land, inasmuch as they are commanded to journey and go up unto the land of Zion;
>
> 25 And they shall do like unto the children of Israel, pitching their tents by the way.
>
> 26 And, behold, this commandment you shall give unto all your brethren.
>
> 27 Nevertheless, unto whom is given power to command the waters, unto him it is given by the Spirit to know all his ways;
>
> 28 Wherefore, let him do as the Spirit of the living God commandeth him, whether upon the land or upon the waters, as it remaineth with me to do hereafter.
>
> 29 And unto you is given the course for the saints, or the way for the saints of the camp of the Lord, to journey.

Joseph Smith, Sidney Rigdon, and Oliver Cowdery—the presiding elders of the group—were commanded to travel by land rather than by water, with the exception of man-made waterways such as canals. The presiding elders were also given assurance that the Lord can give His servants power to command the waters and that He can protect His servants from possible harm. The Savior Himself exercised this power over the waters in the New Testament (see Matthew 8:23–27; Mark 4:35–41; Luke 8:22–25). The same power has been wielded by holders of the priesthood in the latter days.

Mary Ann Weston Maughan, who crossed the Atlantic in 1841, recalled one raging storm that was lulled by the Lord's power. She later wrote:

> When near the banks of Newfoundland we had a dreadful storm. Our main mast broke off deck and the jib boom also broke, and as it came around on deck struck a sailor on his head nearly killing him. . . . Soon after our mast [broke], a young man in our company took off his shoes and went on deck going to the fore part of the ship. He raised his right hand to heaven and in the name of Jesus Christ rebuked the wind and the waves and prophesied that the storm should abate and the good ship *Harmony* would carry her load of Saints in safety to their destination and this came true, for all landed safe in [Quebec].[10]

On another occasion, in 1851, the ship *Olympus* was struck by a severe Atlantic storm. The captain, Horace A. Wilson, sent his second mate to speak with the leader of a company of Latter-day Saint emigrants, telling them "that if the God of the Mormons can do anything to save this ship and the people, they had better be calling on him to do so, for we are now sinking at the rate of a foot an hour; and if the storm continues we shall all be at the bottom of the ocean before daylight." William Howell, the leader of the Saints on the voyage, sent back word that "our God will protect us." He then invited twelve men to join him in prayer. The pitching and rolling of the ship ceased, and the storm abated. Both the captain of the ship and the Saints attributed their salvation to God's intervention. Fifty people were baptized during the remainder of the voyage.[11]

> 30 And again, verily I say unto you, my servants, Sidney Rigdon, Joseph Smith, Jun., and Oliver Cowdery, shall not open their mouths in the congregations of the wicked until they arrive at Cincinnati;
>
> 31 And in that place they shall lift up their voices unto God against that people, yea, unto him whose anger is kindled against their wickedness, a people who are well-nigh ripened for destruction.
>
> 32 And from thence let them journey for the congregations of their brethren, for their labors even now are wanted more abun-

dantly among them than among the congregations of the wicked.

33 And now, concerning the residue, let them journey and declare the word among the congregations of the wicked, inasmuch as it is given;

34 And inasmuch as they do this they shall rid their garments, and they shall be spotless before me.

35 And let them journey together, or two by two, as seemeth them good, only let my servant Reynolds Cahoon, and my servant Samuel H. Smith, with whom I am well pleased, be not separated until they return to their homes, and this for a wise purpose in me.

While Sidney, Joseph, and Oliver were commanded to travel quickly to Cincinnati and preach there, the rest of the elders were commanded to continue their journey and to preach along the way. Sharing the gospel would help the elders to "rid their garments, and they shall be spotless" (verse 34). Those with a responsibility to share the gospel also bear a burden for those whom they could have warned (see Ezekiel 3:18). The Nephite prophet Jacob spoke in a similar manner of "taking upon us the responsibility, answering the sins of the people upon our own heads if we did not teach them the word of God with all diligence," adding that "by laboring with our might their blood might not come upon our garments" (Jacob 1:19).

36 And now, verily I say unto you, and what I say unto one I say unto all, be of good cheer, little children; for I am in your midst, and I have not forsaken you;

37 And inasmuch as you have humbled yourselves before me, the blessings of the kingdom are yours.

38 Gird up your loins and be watchful and be sober, looking forth for the coming of the Son of Man, for he cometh in an hour you think not.

39 Pray always that you enter not into temptation, that you may abide the day of his coming, whether in life or in death. Even so. Amen.

After the harrowing experiences of the day before, it must have come as a comfort for the elders to hear that the Savior had not forsaken them (see verse 36). They did, however, receive counsel to gird up their loins, be watchful, and be sober. The use of the word *sober* makes no reference to the Word of Wisdom, which was not yet revealed. Common use of the word at the time suggests being "habitually temperate."[12] The Lord uses the word *sober* to emphasize the nearness of His coming and the need for the elders to stay focused on the work of salvation.

In a letter written to Moses Nickerson, a Canadian member of the Church, Joseph Smith spoke of this virtue:

> When I contemplate the rapidity with which the great and glorious day of the coming of the Son of Man advances, when he shall come to receive his saints unto himself where they shall dwell in his presence and be crowned with glory & immortality; when I consider that soon the heavens are to be shaken, and the earth tremble and reel to and fro; and that the heavens are to be unfolded as a scroll when it is rolled up, that every mountain and island are to flee away I cry out in my heart, What manner of person ought I to be in all holy conversation and godliness![13]

End Notes

1. Joseph Smith, in History, 1838–1856, volume A-1 [23 December 1805–30 August 1834], 142, josephsmithpapers.org.

2. Ezra Booth to Edward Partridge, "Mormonism—No. VII," *Ohio Star* (Ravenna), Nov. 24, 1831.

3. See Ezra Booth to Edward Partridge, "Mormonism—No. VII."

4. Joseph Smith, in History, 1838–1856, volume A-1 [23 December 1805–30 August 1834], 142, josephsmithpapers.org. See also "Historical Introduction," Revelation, 12 August 1831 [D&C 61], josephsmithpapers.org.

5. See "Historical Introduction," Revelation, 12 August 1831, josephsmithpapers.org.

6. Discourse, 8 April 1843, as Reported by William Clayton–B, 3–4, josephsmithpapers.org.

7. Joseph Smith, in History, 1838–1856, volume A-1 [23 December 1805–30 August 1834], 142., josephsmithpapers.org.

8. See "Historical Introduction," Revelation, 12 August 1831 [D&C 61], footnote 4, josephsmithpapers.org.

9. See Revelation, 12 August 1831 [D&C 61], footnote 18, josephsmithpapers.org.

10. Fred E. Woods, "Seagoing Saints," *Ensign,* Sept. 2001, 57–58.

11. See Fred E. Woods, "Seagoing Saints," 59.

12. *An American Dictionary of the English Language*, s.v. "sober," accessed February 13, 2024, https://webstersdictionary1828.com/Dictionary/sober.

13. Letter to Moses Nickerson, 19 November 1833, 64, josephsmithpapers.org.

Doctrine and Covenants
Section 62
Ye Are Blessed for the Testimony Which Ye Have Borne

Historical Context

AFTER THEIR EXPERIENCE ON THE MISSOURI RIVER, JOSEPH SMITH AND his traveling companions crossed the river at Chariton, Missouri. They were delighted to find Hyrum Smith, John Murdock, David Whitmer, and Harvey Whitlock in the small settlement. John had become ill in the early part of August, delaying Hyrum on his journey to Missouri. Hyrum waited in Chariton while John recovered, and shortly after, the two were joined by David and Harvey. Joseph later wrote in his history, "On the 13th I met several of the Elders on their way to the land of Zion, and after the joyful salutations with which brethren meet each other who are actually 'contending for the faith once delivered to the saints,' I received the following."[1]

*V*erse-by-*V*erse *C*ommentary

1 Behold, and hearken, O ye elders of my church, saith the Lord your God, even Jesus Christ, your advocate, who knoweth the weakness of man and how to succor them who are tempted.

2 And verily mine eyes are upon those who have not as yet gone up unto the land of Zion; wherefore your mission is not yet full.

3 Nevertheless, ye are blessed, for the testimony which ye have borne is recorded in heaven for the angels to look upon; and they rejoice over you, and your sins are forgiven you.

This revelation presents an interesting contrast with the revelation received only the day before (see Doctrine and Covenants 61). While the elders in Doctrine and Covenants 61 were exhorted to "rid their garments" to become spotless (see Doctrine and Covenants 61:34), the elders at Chariton were blessed and promised forgiveness of their sins because of the testimonies they had shared. Missionary work is an act of salvation for both the testifier and the hearer. As James taught, "He which converteth the sinner from the error of his way shall save a soul from death, and shall hide a multitude of sins" (James 5:20).

President Joseph F. Smith taught that "a testimony of truth is more than a mere assent of the mind. It is a conviction of the heart, a knowledge that fills the whole soul of its recipient."[2] For a testimony to be powerful, it must remain centered on the Savior and the fundamentals of the gospel. President Ballard gave the following counsel regarding testimonies:

> My experience throughout the Church leads me to worry that too many of our members' testimonies linger on "I am thankful" and "I love," and too few are able to say with humble but sincere clarity, "I know." As a result, our meetings sometimes lack the testimony-rich, spiritual underpinnings that stir the soul and have meaningful, positive impact on the lives of all those who hear them. Our testimony meetings need to be more centered on the Savior, the doctrines of the gospel, the blessings of the Restoration, and the teachings of the scriptures. We need to replace stories, travelogues, and lectures with pure testimonies.[3]

4 And now continue your journey. Assemble yourselves upon the land of Zion; and hold a meeting and rejoice together, and offer a sacrament unto the Most High.

5 And then you may return to bear record, yea, even altogether, or two by two, as seemeth you good, it mattereth not unto me; only be faithful, and declare glad tidings unto the inhabitants of the earth, or among the congregations of the wicked.

6 Behold, I, the Lord, have brought you together that the promise might be fulfilled, that the faithful among you should be preserved and rejoice together in the land of Missouri. I, the Lord, promise the faithful and cannot lie.

7 I, the Lord, am willing, if any among you desire to ride upon horses, or upon mules, or in chariots, he shall receive this blessing, if he receive it from the hand of the Lord, with a thankful heart in all things.

8 These things remain with you to do according to judgment and the directions of the Spirit.

9 Behold, the kingdom is yours. And behold, and lo, I am with the faithful always. Even so. Amen.

The elders that were blessed in this revelation continued their journey to Independence together. John Murdock was still so ill that the other elders pooled their money to purchase a horse for him to ride on.[4] When the elders arrived in Zion, they held a sacrament meeting (see verse 4) as directed by the Lord. (The conference was misdated as August 2 in the Minute Book; it was likely held on August 24.) Hyrum Smith, again sharing his testimony, read a portion of Psalm 102, which reads in part, "When the Lord shall build up Zion, he shall appear in his glory. He will regard the prayer of the destitute, and not despise their prayer. This shall be written for the generation to come: and the people which shall be created shall praise the Lord" (Psalm 102:16–18). David Whitmer also shared his testimony with the assembled group, exhorting them to perform "acts of righteousness" and to "sacrifice all for Christ."[5]

William McLellin, who attended the sacrament meeting, noted in his journal that the purpose of the meeting was to "offer a sacrament to the Most High to fill the commandment which they had received at Chariton." McLellin also noted that the same day, he retired to a nearby grove to consider if he should be ordained to the priesthood. When his prayer ended, the question entered into his mind, "What is your motive?" In response to this, the Spirit whispered to his heart, "The glory of God, the salvation of my own soul, and the welfare of the human family." He then went to the meeting without telling anyone of his experience. When he was called upon by the leaders of the meeting, McLellin told them, "I was resigned to the will of God in the matter and I believed that God would make my duty known to them if they would inquire." Hyrum Smith immediately arose and said he had received a witness of the Spirit that McLellin should be ordained an elder. After a sustaining vote, Hyrum Smith and Edward Partridge then ordained McLellin an elder, and he was later called as one of the original members of the Quorum of the Twelve in this dispensation.[6]

End Notes

1. Joseph Smith, in History, 1838–1856, volume A-1 [23 December 1805–30 August 1834], 145, josephsmithpapers.org. See also "Historical Introduction," Revelation, 13 August 1831 [D&C 62], josephsmithpapers.org.
2. Joseph F. Smith, *Gospel Doctrine, 5th ed.* (1939), 364.
3. M. Russell Ballard, "Pure Testimony," *Ensign* or *Liahona*, Nov. 2004, 41.
4. See "John Murdock, 1792-1871," Book of Abraham Project, accessed Feb. 13, 2024, http://boap.org/LDS/Early-Saints/JMurdock.html.
5. Minute Book 2, 6–7, josephsmithpapers.org.
6. See William McLellin, *The Journals of William E. McLellin, 1831-1836*, ed. Jan Shipps and John Welch (Provo, UT: Brigham Young University Studies, 1994), 35.

$\mathcal{D}$octrine and $\mathcal{C}$ovenants Section 63

Signs Follow Those That Believe

$\mathcal{H}$istorical $\mathcal{C}$ontext

FROM JUNE 19 TO AUGUST 27, 1831, JOSEPH SMITH WAS AWAY FROM Kirtland, Ohio, as he traveled to and from Independence, Missouri, to identify the location of the city of Zion (see Doctrine and Covenants 57–62). Returning from his trip to Zion, Joseph faced several decisions. He later noted in his history, "Many things transpired upon this journey to strengthen our faith, and which displayed the goodness of God in such a marvelous manner." He also noted "that we could not help beholding the exertions of Satan to blind the eyes of the people so as to hide the true light that lights every man that comes into the world."[1] While the difficult expedition strengthened the faith of many, some of the elders who went on the trip complained and moved quickly toward apostasy. Meanwhile, some of the members in Kirtland had also fallen away. John Whitmer noted, "The

Elders had returned to their homes in Ohio, the churches needed much exhortation[;] in the absence of the Elders many apostatized."[2]

Another pressing issue arose now that the location of the city of Zion had been identified. Many Church members desired to leave for Zion right away, and Joseph and the other Church leaders faced the dilemma of finding the best way to organize the migration to Missouri. Joseph later recorded, "In these infant days of the church, there was a great anxiety to obtain the word of the Lord upon every subject that in any way concerned our salvation; and as 'the land of Zion' was now the most important temporal object in view, I inquired of the Lord for further information upon the gathering of the Saints and the purchase of the land and other matters, and received the following [Doctrine and Covenants 63]."[3]

$\mathcal{V}$erse-by-$\mathcal{V}$erse $\mathcal{C}$ommentary

1 Hearken, O ye people, and open your hearts and give ear from afar; and listen, you that call yourselves the people of the Lord, and hear the word of the Lord and his will concerning you.

2 Yea, verily, I say, hear the word of him whose anger is kindled against the wicked and rebellious;

3 Who willeth to take even them whom he will take, and preserveth in life them whom he will preserve;

4 Who buildeth up at his own will and pleasure; and destroyeth when he pleases, and is able to cast the soul down to hell.

5 Behold, I, the Lord, utter my voice, and it shall be obeyed.

6 Wherefore, verily I say, let the wicked take heed, and let the rebellious fear and tremble; and let the unbelieving hold their lips, for the day of wrath shall come upon them as a whirlwind, and all flesh shall know that I am God.

The first part of the revelation addresses the apostasy beginning to take root among the members of the Church in Kirtland. Among the elders who traveled with Joseph Smith during the journey to Missouri, there was some antagonism, most notably from Ezra Booth who soon apostatized (see Doctrine and Covenants 64:15–16; Doctrine and Covenants 71). The Lord expresses His anger against those who selfishly seek to take and to destroy for their own pleasure.

The anger the Lord expresses here is consistent with the Savior's early acts and revelations. On several occasions, the Savior condemned anger, especially when it was unfounded (see Matthew 5:22; 3 Nephi 11:30). On other occasions, the Lord expressed anger at unjust acts, unfair treatment, or sinful behavior. The Lord's anger is a righteous indignation at the acts of those around Him. During His mortal ministry, the Savior looked with anger on those who claimed that healing a man with a withered hand on the Sabbath was a sin (see Mark 3:1–5). In this revelation, the Lord's anger is turned upon those seeking to arouse contention among the Saints.

> 7 And he that seeketh signs shall see signs, but not unto salvation.
>
> 8 Verily, I say unto you, there are those among you who seek signs, and there have been such even from the beginning;
>
> 9 But, behold, faith cometh not by signs, but signs follow those that believe.
>
> 10 Yea, signs come by faith, not by the will of men, nor as they please, but by the will of God.
>
> 11 Yea, signs come by faith, unto mighty works, for without faith no man pleaseth God; and with whom God is angry he is not well pleased; wherefore, unto such he showeth no signs, only in wrath unto their condemnation.
>
> 12 Wherefore, I, the Lord, am not pleased with those among you who have sought after signs and wonders for faith, and not for the good of men unto my glory.

Here the Savior addresses Saints who have based their faith solely on signs and wonders instead of rooting it in the word of God and prayer. Again, it is likely that this is a reference to Ezra Booth, who was converted when he witnessed Joseph Smith heal the arthritic arm of Elsa Johnson (see commentary for Doctrine and Covenants 42:19–20).

Signs often have a positive impact on a person's faith, but they are primarily useful in strengthening faith that is already developing naturally. As a basis for a testimony, signs can be a sandy foundation to build upon. The Book of Mormon people experienced indisputable signs, such as a days and nights with no darkness that fell on precise dates, as foretold by Samuel the Lamanite (see Helaman 14:2–4). We would expect such a grand sign to be a life-changing event for the majority of the people. Yet in the small span of a few years, many "began to be less and less astonished at a sign or a wonder from heaven, insomuch that they began to be hard in their hearts, and blind in their minds, and began to disbelieve all which they had heard and seen" (3 Nephi 2:1).

> 13 Nevertheless, I give commandments, and many have turned away from my commandments and have not kept them.
>
> 14 There were among you adulterers and adulteresses; some of whom have turned away from you, and others remain with you that hereafter shall be revealed.
>
> 15 Let such beware and repent speedily, lest judgment shall come upon them as a snare, and their folly shall be made manifest, and their works shall follow them in the eyes of the people.
>
> 16 And verily I say unto you, as I have said before, he that looketh on a woman to lust after her, or if any shall commit adultery in their hearts, they shall not have the Spirit, but shall deny the faith and shall fear.

Both the Savior and Joseph Smith taught that excessive sign seeking is a symptom of greater spiritual problems. Jesus declared that "an evil and adulterous generation seeketh after a sign" (Matthew 12:39). Joseph Smith taught that "he who seeketh a sign is an adulterous person. & that principle is Eternal undeviating & firm as the pillars of heaven. for whenever you see a man seeking after a sign you may set it down that he is an adulterous man."[4]

In a later history Joseph Smith shared the following experience: "When I was preaching in Philadelphia, a Quaker called out for a sign, I told him to be still. After Sermon he again asked for a sign. I told the Congregation the man was an Adulterer, that a wicked and adulterous generation seeketh after a sign, and that the Lord had said to me in a Revelation that any man who wanted a sign was an Adulterous person 'it is true' cried one 'for I caught him in the very act,' which the man afterwards confessed when he was baptized."[5]

> 17 Wherefore, I, the Lord, have said that the fearful, and the unbelieving, and all liars, and whosoever loveth and maketh a

lie, and the whoremonger, and the sorcerer, shall have their part in that lake which burneth with fire and brimstone, which is the second death.

18 Verily I say, that they shall not have part in the first resurrection.

19 And now behold, I, the Lord, say unto you that ye are not justified, because these things are among you.

The list of sins given here is given again in Doctrine and Covenants 76:103–106 as characteristics of those who are consigned to the telestial kingdom. These people are described as being cast into "that lake which burneth with fire and brimstone" and experiencing the "second death," a phrase taken from Revelation 21:8. The description of the sufferings of the wicked as a "lake of fire and brimstone," or something close to it, appears in scriptures several times (see 2 Nephi 9:18; 28:23; Jacob 3:11; 6:10; Alma 12:17). It is worth noting that this is ultimately not just a list of sins but the states of unrepentant sinners. For example, the verses speak not just of liars but of those who "loveth and maketh a lie" (verse 17). Those who sincerely repent, even of these serious transgressions, can find redemption through Jesus Christ.

While this imagery conjures common depictions of the final fate of the wicked as filled with flame and doom, it does not denote that God is cruel or takes delight in tormenting the wicked. In an 1844 discourse, Joseph Smith taught that "a sinner has his own mind and is his own condemner; the torment of the mind of man is as exquisite as a lake burning with fire and brimstone."[6] Torment is the natural conclusion of sin, and God does not have to actively seek to torment those who engage in unrighteous behavior. Eventually, they become their own tormentors.

20 Nevertheless, he that endureth in faith and doeth my will, the same shall overcome, and shall receive an inheritance upon the earth when the day of transfiguration shall come;

In this verse, the Lord shifts direction from chastising the wicked to pointing the faithful toward the rewards planned for the righteous. The "day of transfiguration" refers to the day the earth "will be renewed and receive its paradisiacal glory" (Articles of Faith 1:10). The word *transfigured* leads us to draw comparisons to the three Nephite disciples who were "changed from this body of flesh into an immortal state, that they could behold the things of God" (3 Nephi 28:15). The Savior further explains this transfiguration, which occurs at the time of His return to earth in glory, in a revelation given to Joseph Smith in 1833.

In that revelation the Lord declares that "every corruptible thing, both of man, or of the beasts of the field . . . shall be consumed" (Doctrine and Covenants 101:24). He adds that "the enmity of all flesh . . . shall cease," "Satan will have no power," and "there shall be no sorrow because there is no death" (see Doctrine and Covenants 101:26–29). This period of millennial glory is only a prelude to the final fate of the earth and its righteous inhabitants, for the earth will eventually die and be quickened (resurrected) again, and "the righteous shall inherit it" (Doctrine and Covenants 88:26). The earth will eventually be the home of those who endure to the end and receive all that the Father hath.

> 21 When the earth shall be transfigured, even according to the pattern which was shown unto mine apostles upon the mount; of which account the fulness ye have not yet received.

This is likely a reference to the moment chronicled in the synoptic gospels when Peter, James, and John were taken to a mountain where they saw the Savior transfigured, and where they saw Moses along with Elijah (see Matthew 17:1–13; Mark 9:2–13; Luke 9:28–36). The Joseph Smith Translation adds that John the Baptist also appeared on the mount following his martyrdom at the hands of Herodias (see Joseph Smith Translation, Mark 9:3 [in Mark 9:4, footnote a]). It also reveals that Moses and Elijah spoke with the Savior "of his death, and also his resurrection, which he should accomplish at Jerusalem" (Joseph Smith Translation, Luke 9:31 [in Luke 9:31, footnote a]). In verse 21, the Savior refers to this transfiguration as the pattern for the transfiguration of the earth after the Savior's coming.

The transfiguration on the mount occurred when the three who accompanied the Savior saw him "transfigured before them: and his face did shine as the sun, and his rainment was white as the light" (Matthew 17:2). The Apostle John later declared that "we beheld his glory, the glory as of the only begotten of the Father, full of grace and truth" (John 1:14). Peter spoke of himself and his companions being "eyewitnesses of his majesty" and that Jesus "received from the Father honour and glory" (2 Peter 1:16–17). It is also possible that the invitation to Peter, James, and John on the mount was linked to the "more sure word of prophecy" (2 Peter 1:19) or to being sealed up unto eternal life (see Doctrine and Covenants 131:5).

While we do not know everything about what happened on the Mount of Transfiguration, it is clear that what was shown to Peter, James, and John was of great importance to the future of God's children and to the destiny of the earth itself.

22 And now, verily I say unto you, that as I said that I would make known my will unto you, behold I will make it known unto you, not by the way of commandment, for there are many who observe not to keep my commandments.

23 But unto him that keepeth my commandments I will give the mysteries of my kingdom, and the same shall be in him a well of living water, springing up unto everlasting life.

Obedience to the commandments is key to opening up our understanding of the mysteries of godliness, and we demonstrate our faith in God by serving Him and keeping His commandments. The prophet Alma taught, "It is given unto many to know the mysteries of God; nevertheless they are laid under a strict command that they shall not impart only according to the portion of his word which he doth grant unto the children of men, according to the heed and diligence which they give unto him" (Alma 12:9).

This relationship between God and His children is not transactional. We really have nothing to offer to God other than our will. Rather, it is interpersonal. As we grow in our confidence to keep the commandments and enter into a relationship of trust and acceptance of God's will, He is able to give us greater and greater power so that our confidence shall "wax strong in the presence of God" (Doctrine and Covenants 121:45).

24 And now, behold, this is the will of the Lord your God concerning his saints, that they should assemble themselves together unto the land of Zion, not in haste, lest there should be confusion, which bringeth pestilence.

25 Behold, the land of Zion—I, the Lord, hold it in mine own hands;

26 Nevertheless, I, the Lord, render unto Cæsar the things which are Cæsar's.

27 Wherefore, I the Lord will that you should purchase the lands, that you may have advantage of the world, that you may

have claim on the world, that they may not be stirred up unto anger.

28 For Satan putteth it into their hearts to anger against you, and to the shedding of blood.

29 Wherefore, the land of Zion shall not be obtained but by purchase or by blood, otherwise there is none inheritance for you.

30 And if by purchase, behold you are blessed;

31 And if by blood, as you are forbidden to shed blood, lo, your enemies are upon you, and ye shall be scourged from city to city, and from synagogue to synagogue, and but few shall stand to receive an inheritance.

Having both addressed the wicked among the Church and promised blessings to the faithful, the Lord now turns to the specifics of the gathering to the land of Zion. He again emphasizes that the land will not be gained through bloodshed, an admonition the Lord gave earlier (see Doctrine and Covenants 58:53) and will repeat again to the Saints later (see Doctrine and Covenants 105:5). Rather, the land is to be obtained by purchase through the consecrated efforts of the Saints (see Doctrine and Covenants 45:65). The Lord warns that Satan wanted the Saints to attempt to obtain the land by force instead of by peaceful means (see Doctrine and Covenants 63:28, 31).

It was also important for the Saints gathering to Zion to obtain the land through legal means. In a letter written in July 1833 to the "Elders stationed in Zion and the churches abroad," Church leaders counseled, "To suppose we can come up here and take possession of this land by the shedding of blood, would be setting at naught the law of the glorious Gospel, and also the word of our glorious Redeemer: and to suppose that we can take possession of this country, without making regular purchases of the same according to the laws of our nation, would be reproaching this great Republic, in which the most of us were born, and under whose auspices we all have protection."[7]

Church leaders also had to consider the speed of the migration to Zion. While the implementation of the law of consecration would help the Saints obtain Zion more quickly, Church members were counseled to first work, save, and obtain the financial means needed to gather to Zion. The same epistle referenced earlier also counseled, "We would advise in the first place that every disciple, if in his power, pay his just debts, so as to owe no man, and then if he has any property left, let him be careful of it; and he can help the poor, by consecrating some for their inheritances: for as yet, there has not been enough consecrated, to plant the poor in inheritance, according to the regulation of the Church and the desire of the faithful."[8] While the Saints' desire to gather to Zion was increasing, the Lord emphasized that the Saints should not run faster than they had strength (see Mosiah 4:27).

> 32 I, the Lord, am angry with the wicked; I am holding my Spirit from the inhabitants of the earth.
>
> 33 I have sworn in my wrath, and decreed wars upon the face of the earth, and the wicked shall slay the wicked, and fear shall come upon every man;
>
> 34 And the saints also shall hardly escape; nevertheless, I, the Lord, am with them, and will come down in heaven from the presence of my Father and consume the wicked with unquenchable fire.
>
> 35 And behold, this is not yet, but by and by.
>
> 36 Wherefore, seeing that I, the Lord, have decreed all these things upon the face of the earth, I will that my saints should be assembled upon the land of Zion;
>
> 37 And that every man should take righteousness in his hands and faithfulness upon his loins, and lift a warning voice unto the inhabitants of the earth; and declare both by word and by flight that desolation shall come upon the wicked.

The Lord gives another reason for the gathering to Zion: the coming wars to precede the Savior's return to the earth. In an earlier revelation, the Lord warned of "wars in foreign lands" and "wars in your own lands" (Doctrine and Covenants 45:63). A central part of the drive to gather to Zion and build the city was to create "a land of peace, a city of refuge, a place of safety for the saints of the Most High God" (Doctrine and Covenants 45:66). The gathering was intended to save the Saints from these physical tribulations.

However, the Lord warns in these verses that the "saints shall hardly escape" (verse 34). The righteous Saints who heed the Lord's warnings will largely escape the tribulations of the last days. But it is unavoidable that they will suffer and be affected by the destruction decreed upon the wicked. The safety promised by the Lord concerns exaltation and glory in the next world, not an escape from these tribulations. "It is a false idea that the Saints will escape all the judgments, whilst the wicked suffer; for all flesh is subject to suffer, and 'the righteous shall hardly escape;' . . . many of the righteous shall fall a prey to disease, to pestilence, etc., by reason of the weakness of the flesh, and yet be saved in the Kingdom of God."[9]

Throughout the history of the Church, the Lord has shown the Saints the wisdom in heeding the voice of His prophets. He has also shown that part of our mortal experience is being tested and tried by the misused agency of our brothers and sisters.

38 Wherefore, let my disciples in Kirtland arrange their temporal concerns, who dwell upon this farm.

39 Let my servant Titus Billings, who has the care thereof, dispose of the land, that he may be prepared in the coming spring to take his journey up unto the land of Zion, with those that dwell upon the face thereof, excepting those whom I shall reserve unto myself, that shall not go until I shall command them.

40 And let all the moneys which can be spared, it mattereth not unto me whether it be little or much, be sent up unto the land of Zion, unto them whom I have appointed to receive.

41 Behold, I, the Lord, will give unto my servant Joseph Smith, Jun., power that he shall be enabled to discern by the Spirit those who shall go up unto the land of Zion, and those of my disciples who shall tarry.

42 Let my servant Newel K. Whitney retain his store, or in other words, the store, yet for a little season.

43 Nevertheless, let him impart all the money which he can impart, to be sent up unto the land of Zion.

44 Behold, these things are in his own hands, let him do according to wisdom.

45 Verily I say, let him be ordained as an agent unto the disciples that shall tarry, and let him be ordained unto this power;

46 And now speedily visit the churches, expounding these things unto them, with my servant Oliver Cowdery. Behold, this is my will, obtaining moneys even as I have directed.

47 He that is faithful and endureth shall overcome the world.

48 He that sendeth up treasures unto the land of Zion shall receive an inheritance in this world, and his works shall follow him, and also a reward in the world to come.

The farm mentioned in this portion of the revelation (see verse 38) was owned by Isaac Morley and located near Kirtland. Titus Billings and other Church members joined Morley in creating a communal order that lived on the farm. Joseph Smith lived on the farm for a few months after he emigrated from New York to Ohio (see Doctrine and Covenants 41:7). Newel K. Whitney's store, also mentioned in the revelation (see verse 42), became the functional headquarters of the Church during this early period. For a time, Joseph Smith and his family lived on the second floor of the store, and many key sections of the Doctrine and Covenants were received there (see Doctrine and Covenants 84–98; 101). Newel K. Whitney's designation as an "agent" for the Church foreshadowed his call as the Church's second bishop (see Doctrine and Covenants 72:1–8).

The Lord asked all of the Church members in Kirtland to begin raising money to build the city of Zion in Missouri. Kirtland remained an important Church center and would eventually become the place where the first temple built by the Saints in this dispensation would rise. However, in the revelations Kirtland was designated as a "stake" (Doctrine and Covenants 96:1; Doctrine and Covenants 104:40), while Independence, Missouri, was designated as the "center place" of Zion (Doctrine and Covenants 57:3). Over the next eight years, both Church centers in Ohio and Missouri played a vital role in the growth of the movement. However, in the grand story of the Restoration, the center place and location of the city of Zion remains in Independence, Missouri.

49 Yea, and blessed are the dead that die in the Lord, from henceforth, when the Lord shall come, and old things shall pass away, and all things become new, they shall rise from the dead and shall not die after, and shall receive an inheritance before the Lord, in the holy city.

50 And he that liveth when the Lord shall come, and hath kept the faith, blessed is he; nevertheless, it is appointed to him to die at the age of man.

51 Wherefore, children shall grow up until they become old; old men shall die; but they shall not sleep in the dust, but they shall be changed in the twinkling of an eye.

52 Wherefore, for this cause preached the apostles unto the world the resurrection of the dead.

53 These things are the things that ye must look for; and, speaking after the manner of the Lord, they are now nigh at hand, and in a time to come, even in the day of the coming of the Son of Man.

54 And until that hour there will be foolish virgins among the wise; and at that hour cometh an entire separation of the righteous and the wicked; and in that day will I send mine angels to pluck out the wicked and cast them into unquenchable fire.

Just as the Lord pronounced blessings on the Church members who had already arrived in Zion (see Doctrine and Covenants 59:1–4), here He blesses the Saints in Ohio by pointing them toward the bright millennial future. The Lord speaks of the new way of life to be found after His coming, when death, scarcity, and wickedness will pass away and men and women will enter into a higher and holier state (see commentary for Doctrine and Covenants 101:31). The Lord reminds the Saints, who were faced with the complexities of the practical creation of Zion, to keep their focus on the ultimate goal of the work and to prepare the earth for the Millennium of peace following the Savior's return. Not speaking in terms of years, decades, or centuries, but "after the manner of the Lord," He confirms that the return of Jesus Christ to the earth is "nigh at hand."

The Lord also refers to the parable of the ten virgins (see Matthew 25:5–13). While the assumption has often been made that the ten virgins represent the world as a whole, latter-day prophets and the context of section 63 suggest that the parable is about the members of the Church. President Oaks taught, "The arithmetic of this parable is chilling. The ten virgins obviously represent members of Christ's Church, for all were invited to the wedding feast and all knew what was required to be admitted when the bridegroom came. But only half were ready when he came."[10] A theme throughout section 63 is the blessing of the Saints who are keeping the commandments and the stern warning to those who are engaged in adultery and lying (see Doctrine and Covenants 63:14–19).

> 55 And now behold, verily I say unto you, I, the Lord, am not pleased with my servant Sidney Rigdon; he exalted himself in his heart, and received not counsel, but grieved the Spirit;
>
> 56 Wherefore his writing is not acceptable unto the Lord, and he shall make another; and if the Lord receive it not, behold he standeth no longer in the office to which I have appointed him.
>
> 57 And again, verily I say unto you, those who desire in their hearts, in meekness, to warn sinners to repentance, let them be ordained unto this power.
>
> 58 For this is a day of warning, and not a day of many words. For I, the Lord, am not to be mocked in the last days.

The Lord had previously commanded Sidney Rigdon to write a description of the land of Zion to help emigrants know what to expect (see Doctrine and Covenants 58:50–51). Rather than the "description of the land of Zion" the Lord had commanded him to write, Sidney's first attempt resulted in a letter that was a quasi-scriptural warning of the calamities of the last days. Sidney wrote of "the things which he has decreed upon the nations even wasting and destruction until they are utterly destroyed, and the earth made desolate by reason of the wickedness of its inhabitants according as he has made known in times past by the prophets and apostles, that such calamities should befall the inhabitants of the earth in the last days, unless they should repent, and turn to the living God."[11]

Eventually, another description of the land of Zion was included in Joseph Smith's official history (see commentary for Doctrine and Covenants 58:44–52). This revised epistle seems to have been more effective at helping to raise funds to build Zion. John Whitmer recorded that "immediately after the commandment was given and the epistle written, Oliver Cowdery and Newel K. Whitney went from place to place; and from church to church preaching and expounding the scriptures and commandments and obtaining moneys of the disciples for the purpose of buying lands for the Saints according to commandments and the disciples truly opened their hearts, and thus there has been lands purchased, for the inheritance of the saints."[12]

By one estimate, the effort raised around three thousand dollars among the Saints for the building of Zion.[13]

> 59 Behold, I am from above, and my power lieth beneath. I am over all, and in all, and through all, and search all things, and the day cometh that all things shall be subject unto me.
>
> 60 Behold, I am Alpha and Omega, even Jesus Christ.
>
> 61 Wherefore, let all men beware how they take my name in their lips—
>
> 62 For behold, verily I say, that many there be who are under this condemnation, who use the name of the Lord, and use it in vain, having not authority.
>
> 63 Wherefore, let the church repent of their sins, and I, the Lord, will own them; otherwise they shall be cut off.
>
> 64 Remember that that which cometh from above is sacred, and must be spoken with care, and by constraint of the Spirit; and in this there is no condemnation, and ye receive the Spirit through prayer; wherefore, without this there remaineth condemnation.

Near the end of the revelation, the Lord warns the disciples to take care with sacred things, particularly the name of the Savior. A later revelation informed the Saints that the original name of the Melchizedek Priesthood, "the holy priesthood after the Order of the Son of God," was changed in common use out of "respect or reverence to the name of the Supreme Being, [and] to avoid too frequent repetition of the name" (Doctrine and Covenants 107:3–4).

If we are to avoid frequent repetition of the Lord's name, then why did the Savior give His name to The Church of Jesus Christ of Latter-day Saints and then lead the prophets to insist on the use of the correct name? In these verses the Lord warns specifically against those who lack authority using His name in vain (see verse 62). In Webster's 1828 dictionary, the word *vain* meant "empty; worthless; having no substance, value or importance." Certainly His name has meaning when taken as an identifier of the Lord's true Church, or when used in any ordinances of the gospel. However, when His name is used in vain by people without authority, by people who take it upon themselves without serious commitment, or by people who use it as a profanity, these people come under the Lord's condemnation.

65 Let my servants, Joseph Smith, Jun., and Sidney Rigdon, seek them a home, as they are taught through prayer by the Spirit.

66 These things remain to overcome through patience, that such may receive a more exceeding and eternal weight of glory, otherwise, a greater condemnation. Amen.

Up to this point, Joseph Smith had been staying in a home built on Isaac Morley's farm (see Doctrine and Covenants 41:7). After Isaac Morley arrived back from his mission to Missouri (see Doctrine and Covenants 52:23), he sold his farm in preparation to move to Missouri. In response to the Lord's request to provide a home for Joseph and Sidney, John Johnson offered to have them live at his home in Hiram, Ohio. While living there in the following months, Joseph received fifteen different sections of the Doctrine and Covenants, and Joseph and Emma's family endured some of the most harrowing events of their lives.

End Notes

1. Joseph Smith, in History, 1838–1856, volume A-1 [23 December 1805–30 August 1834], 146, josephsmithpapers.org.
2. John Whitmer, History, 1831–circa 1847, 33, josephsmithpapers.org.
3. Joseph Smith, in History, 1838–1856, volume A-1 [23 December 1805–30 August 1834], 146, josephsmithpapers.org. See also "Historical Introduction," Revelation, 30 August 1831 [D&C 63], josephsmithpapers.org.
4. Discourse, 2 July 1839, as Reported by Willard Richards, 15, josephsmithpapers.org.
5. Joseph Smith, in History, 1838–1856, volume D-1 [1 August 1842–1 July 1843], 1466, josephsmithpapers.org.
6. Discourse, 7 April 1844, as Reported by Thomas Bullock, 20, josephsmithpapers.org.
7. History, 1838–1856, volume A-1 [23 December 1805–30 August 1834], 322, josephsmithpapers.org.
8. History, 1838–1856, volume A-1 [23 December 1805–30 August 1834], 322, josephsmithpapers.org.
9. History, 1838–1856, volume C-1 [2 November 1838–31 July 1842], 968, josephsmithpapers.org.
10. Dallin H. Oaks, "Preparation for the Second Coming," *Ensign* or *Liahona*, May 2004, 8.
11. John Whitmer, History, 1831–circa 1847, 34, josephsmithpapers.org.
12. John Whitmer, History, 1831–circa 1847, 37, josephsmithpapers.org.
13. See Warren A. Jennings, *Zion Is Fled: The Expulsion of the Mormons from Jackson County, Missouri* (Gainesville, FL: University of Florida PhD dissertation, 1963), 104–105.

$\mathcal{D}$octrine and $\mathcal{C}$ovenants Section 64

Ye Ought to Forgive One Another

$\mathcal{H}$istorical $\mathcal{C}$ontext

THE WEEKS LEADING UP TO THE RECEPTION OF DOCTRINE AND COVENANTS 64 were difficult for Joseph Smith and other Church leaders. There had been contention among the missionaries during the journey back from Missouri, and when Joseph Smith arrived in Kirtland in late August, he found that several members of the Church in Kirtland had also wandered from the path. In the weeks following his return, the Church held several conferences in which those in apostasy were held accountable for their errors. According to the minutes of these meetings, several elders were "silenced," a form of ecclesiastical punishment following the guidelines set forth in Doctrine and Covenants 42:74–93. Records show that at least three elders were silenced during these deliberations.[1]

During this time Joseph Smith was also preparing to resume his translation of the Bible. In addition, other groups of Saints were preparing to depart for Missouri to assist in building the city of Zion. This revelation addresses those Saints by emphasizing the importance of Missouri as the future place of Zion. It also addresses some of the lingering feelings of anger and bitterness felt on the journey from Missouri and the actions taken to quell the apostasy among the Saints in Kirtland.[2]

Verse-by-Verse Commentary

1 Behold, thus saith the Lord your God unto you, O ye elders of my church, hearken ye and hear, and receive my will concerning you.

2 For verily I say unto you, I will that ye should overcome the world; wherefore I will have compassion upon you.

3 There are those among you who have sinned; but verily I say, for this once, for mine own glory, and for the salvation of souls, I have forgiven you your sins.

4 I will be merciful unto you, for I have given unto you the kingdom.

5 And the keys of the mysteries of the kingdom shall not be taken from my servant Joseph Smith, Jun., through the means I have appointed, while he liveth, inasmuch as he obeyeth mine ordinances.

The Lord reiterates earlier revelations which emphasized that Joseph Smith held the keys necessary to provide guidance and direction to the entire Church (see Doctrine and Covenants 28:7; 43:1–3). Each of these revelations also emphasized that Joseph's leadership was conditional, based on his worthiness and obedience to the commandments. It is understandable that while the Church was relatively small, and while Joseph Smith was struggling to lay the foundations of the Church, others saw his foibles and weaknesses on full display.

Latter-day Saints have never claimed infallibility in themselves or in their leaders. Indeed, in this revelation, Joseph Smith himself is singled out for his struggle to forgive others (see Doctrine and Covenants 64:7). At the same time, the Lord asks His disciples to heed the counsel given to the men and women placed in presiding roles, as long as they are keeping themselves worthy by obeying the Lord's commandments. In an 1844 discourse, Joseph Smith declared, "I never told you I was perfect—but there is no error in the revelations which I have taught—must I then be thrown away as a thing of naught? I enjoin for your consideration, add to your faith, virtue, love. . . . I testify that no man has power to reveal it, but myself, things in heaven, in earth and hell—and all shut your mouths for the future—I commend you all to God, that you may inherit all things."[3]

> 6 There are those who have sought occasion against him without cause;
>
> 7 Nevertheless, he has sinned; but verily I say unto you, I, the Lord, forgive sins unto those who confess their sins before me and ask forgiveness, who have not sinned unto death.
>
> 8 My disciples, in days of old, sought occasion against one another and forgave not one another in their hearts; and for this evil they were afflicted and sorely chastened.
>
> 9 Wherefore, I say unto you, that ye ought to forgive one another; for he that forgiveth not his brother his trespasses standeth condemned before the Lord; for there remaineth in him the greater sin.
>
> 10 I, the Lord, will forgive whom I will forgive, but of you it is required to forgive all men.
>
> 11 And ye ought to say in your hearts—let God judge between me and thee, and reward thee according to thy deeds.

The disciples of Jesus Christ in all ages have struggled to forgive each other and have sometimes hindered the work through their weaknesses. We do not know exactly which disciples "in days of old" the Lord is referring to here, but the New Testament records several incidents in which the Lord's disciples argued among themselves. In the Gospel of Mark, the Savior settled a dispute among His disciples who argued over "who should be the greatest" (Mark 9:34). His disciples also engaged in subversion over ordinances, covenants, and missionary assignments (see Acts 15:24, 39). Paul wrote that he "withstood [Peter] to the face" over the issue of circumcision (see Galatians 2:11).

In our dispensation the disciples have had disputes, and the Lord requires us to forgive. In this revelation, it is likely that the Lord is asking Joseph and the other Church leaders to forgive each other in relation to the difficulties surrounding their trip to Missouri. Joseph had a sharp disagreement with Bishop Edward Partridge (see commentary for Doctrine and Covenants 58:13–18) while they were in Independence, and bad feelings lingered among several of the missionaries involved in the journey. The Lord urges them to forgive each other and continue with their work.

Joseph Smith at times struggled to forgive others who had wronged him. In December 1835 he was involved in an altercation with his youngest brother, William. Joseph criticized a debating society that William had organized. Enraged, William physically assaulted Joseph, injuring him badly. Over the next two weeks the brothers sought to reconcile but kept bringing up hurt feelings and making the situation worse. Finally, on New Year's Day, Joseph Smith Sr. called a family meeting to help the two brothers reconcile. Joseph Smith Jr. later wrote in his journal that as Father Smith spoke, "the spirit of God rested down upon us in mighty power, and our hearts were melted. . . . Br. William made an humble confession and asked my forgiveness for the abuse he had offered me and wherein I had been out of the way I asked his forgiveness, and the spirit of confession and forgiveness was mutual among us all."[4]

12 And him that repenteth not of his sins, and confesseth them not, ye shall bring before the church, and do with him as the scripture saith unto you, either by commandment or by revelation.

13 And this ye shall do that God may be glorified—not because ye forgive not, having not compassion, but that ye may be justified in the eyes of the law, that ye may not offend him who is your lawgiver—

14 Verily I say, for this cause ye shall do these things.

15 Behold, I, the Lord, was angry with him who was my servant Ezra Booth, and also my servant Isaac Morley, for they kept not the law, neither the commandment;

16 They sought evil in their hearts, and I, the Lord, withheld my Spirit. They condemned for evil that thing in which there was no evil; nevertheless I have forgiven my servant Isaac Morley.

17 And also my servant Edward Partridge, behold, he hath sinned, and Satan seeketh to destroy his soul; but when these things are made known unto them, and they repent of the evil, they shall be forgiven.

While forgiveness is essential in discipleship, accountability is also important. It is possible to forgive others and release the anguish inside while still seeking for justice. In this case, the Lord asks for those who refused to repent to be brought before the Church to be held responsible for the difficulties they had caused. Of the three men named here, two of them, Isaac Morley and Edward Partridge, sought and received forgiveness. We do not know the precise nature of the difficulties with Isaac Morley and Ezra Booth, but the way in which they both responded to this correction is interesting.

Isaac Morley repented and began preparations to sell his farm and move his family to Missouri, where he suffered tribulation and persecution at the hand of mobs. At one point, he was one of six Latter-day Saint men who offered up his life for his friends. His family moved from Missouri to Illinois, then crossed the plains and helped settle the Sanpete Valley in Utah. Father Morley died as an honored patriarch among the Saints in Fairview, Utah, in 1865.[5] Ezra Booth, in contrast, only increased in bitterness toward the Church after his journey to Missouri. Within several months, Booth's anger led to violence against Joseph Smith. According to Elder George A. Smith, Booth's apostasy "culminated in collecting a mob who tarred and feathered Joseph Smith, and inflicted upon his family the loss of one of its members [Joseph Murdock Smith] at Hyrum, Portage county, Ohio."[6]

18 And now, verily I say that it is expedient in me that my servant Sidney Gilbert, after a few weeks, shall return upon his business, and to his agency in the land of Zion;

19 And that which he hath seen and heard may be made known unto my disciples, that they perish not. And for this cause have I spoken these things.

20 And again, I say unto you, that my servant Isaac Morley may not be tempted above that which he is able to bear, and counsel wrongfully to your hurt, I gave commandment that his farm should be sold.

21 I will not that my servant Frederick G. Williams should sell his farm, for I, the Lord, will to retain a strong hold in the land

of Kirtland, for the space of five years, in the which I will not overthrow the wicked, that thereby I may save some.

22 And after that day, I, the Lord, will not hold any guilty that shall go with an open heart up to the land of Zion; for I, the Lord, require the hearts of the children of men.

The Lord provides counsel to Sidney Gilbert, Isaac Morley, and Frederick G. Williams about their respective properties and the best way for them to build Zion. While Sidney and Isaac are asked to begin settling their affairs in Kirtland so they can join the effort to build the city of Zion in Missouri, Frederick G. Williams is commanded to keep his farm in order to "retain a stronghold in Kirtland, for the space of five years" (verse 21). This instruction further extends the idea that in the grand design of the expansion of the Lord's Church in the latter days, Missouri would be the center place, while Kirtland would serve as a stake of Zion.

The prophecy made here that Kirtland will serve as a stronghold for the Saints, but only for five years, is remarkably precise. Many of the most important events in the early Restoration took place in Kirtland during the five years following this revelation. The First Presidency and the Quorum of the Twelve, along with other vital priesthood quorums, were organized (see Doctrine and Covenants 107). Revelations on the nature of the Godhead and the future state of the earth were given (see Doctrine and Covenants 93; 101:22–40). Most importantly, Kirtland is where the first temple of the Church would rise, and in that temple the Savior, along with Moses, Elias, and Elijah, appeared and bestowed further priesthood keys on Joseph Smith and Oliver Cowdery (see Doctrine and Covenants 109–110). However, Kirtland was a way station on the path to Zion, not the final destination.

Five years following this revelation, signs of great trouble within the Church began to appear. In the fall of 1836 Church leaders drew up a plan to create a bank in Kirtland to assist the poor and needy in obtaining lands and other necessities. The Kirtland Safety Society opened a few months later and quickly fell into difficulty. A nationwide economic panic led to the closure of hundreds of banks throughout the United States, and the Kirtland Safety Society was forced to close its doors in November 1837. Many members of the Church were unable to reconcile Joseph Smith's role as a prophet with the losses they suffered. Many began to call for his removal as President of the Church, declaring him to be a fallen prophet. Joseph Smith was finally forced to flee Kirtland in fear of his life on January 12, 1838. The five-year span of prosperity in Kirtland set down by the Lord turned out to be remarkably accurate.[7]

> 23 Behold, now it is called today until the coming of the Son of Man, and verily it is a day of sacrifice, and a day for the tithing of my people; for he that is tithed shall not be burned at his coming.
>
> 24 For after today cometh the burning—this is speaking after the manner of the Lord—for verily I say, tomorrow all the proud and they that do wickedly shall be as stubble; and I will burn them up, for I am the Lord of Hosts; and I will not spare any that remain in Babylon.
>
> 25 Wherefore, if ye believe me, ye will labor while it is called today.

Brent L. Top, a former dean of religion at Brigham Young University, used the Lord's statement about the time of His coming to demonstrate the meaning of the Savior's words in Doctrine and Covenants 64:23–25. He asked his students if they wanted to know the exact day of the Savior's coming. He wrote:

> The students usually shake their heads no and say, "We don't know the exact day"—demonstrating that they have heard loud and clear and understood what I have been teaching them. Then I push them a little more. "I'm serious," I say. "I can tell you the exact day." They push back. "No, you can't. You've just been telling us that no one knows." To which I respond, "Oh, yes, I can. And I will show you in the scriptures. You can go home and call your parents. You can tell your roommates. You can post it on social media. You can write it in your journal. You can 'take it to the bank,' so to speak. I can tell you the exact day!" That gets their attention (even though some laugh and think I am joking)! Then we turn to the sixty-fourth section of the Doctrine and Covenants and read the Lord's own words:
>
> "Behold, now *it is called today until the coming of the Son of Man*, and verily it is a day of sacrifice, and a day for the tithing of my people; for he that is tithed shall not be burned at his coming.
>
> "For after today cometh the burning—this is speaking after the manner of the Lord—for verily I say, tomorrow all the proud and they that do wickedly shall be as stubble; and I will burn them up, for I am the

Lord of Hosts; and I will not spare any that remain in Babylon" (Doctrine and Covenants 64:23–24).[8]

The point Brother Top makes in this demonstration is the following (quoted from President Hinckley):

There is no point in speculating concerning the day and the hour. Let us rather live each day so that if the Lord does come while we are yet upon the earth we shall be worthy of that change which will occur as in the twinkling of an eye and under which we shall be changed from mortal to immortal beings. And if we should die before he comes, then—if our lives have conformed to his teachings—we shall arise in that resurrection morning and be partakers of the marvelous experiences designed for those who shall live and work with the Savior in that promised Millennium.[9]

26 And it is not meet that my servants, Newel K. Whitney and Sidney Gilbert, should sell their store and their possessions here; for this is not wisdom until the residue of the church, which remaineth in this place, shall go up unto the land of Zion.

27 Behold, it is said in my laws, or forbidden, to get in debt to thine enemies;

28 But behold, it is not said at any time that the Lord should not take when he please, and pay as seemeth him good.

29 Wherefore, as ye are agents, ye are on the Lord's errand; and whatever ye do according to the will of the Lord is the Lord's business.

30 And he hath set you to provide for his saints in these last days, that they may obtain an inheritance in the land of Zion.

31 And behold, I, the Lord, declare unto you, and my words are sure and shall not fail, that they shall obtain it.

32 But all things must come to pass in their time.

33 Wherefore, be not weary in well-doing, for ye are laying the foundation of a great work. And out of small things proceedeth that which is great.

Providing counsel to Newel K. Whitney and Sidney Gilbert, the Lord provides a simple reminder that it will take time to build Zion. The actions of the Saints at this time were planting seeds, many of which did not fully bloom in the Saints' lifetimes. Even today we still wait for the fulfillment of the Lord's promises made concerning Zion, the building up of the New Jerusalem, and a number of other events. Here the Lord simply affirms that His words will come to pass, although we operate on the timetable set by God and not by man. The Saints of the early Restoration laid the foundations for Zion, an effort requiring great sacrifices from them and their families. But the Lord reminds them that their sacrifices were seen and would bring them one step closer to the building of the Celestial City.

> 34 Behold, the Lord requireth the heart and a willing mind; and the willing and obedient shall eat the good of the land of Zion in these last days.

> 35 And the rebellious shall be cut off out of the land of Zion, and shall be sent away, and shall not inherit the land.

> 36 For, verily I say that the rebellious are not of the blood of Ephraim, wherefore they shall be plucked out.

The scriptures are filled with promises made to the descendants of Ephraim, the son of Joseph and the birthright child of Israel (see 1 Chronicles 5:1–2; Jeremiah 31:9). Moses gave a blessing to the children of Ephraim, saying, "His glory is like the firstling of his bullock, and his horns are like the horns of unicorns: with them he shall push the people together to the ends of the earth: and they are the ten thousands of Ephraim, and they are the thousands of Manasseh" (Deuteronomy 33:17). The Doctrine and Covenants in particular speaks of the blessings given to the descendants of Ephraim. The Lord identified the Book of Mormon as the "record of the stick of Ephraim" (Doctrine and Covenants 27:5). A revelation given shortly after this one spoke of the other tribes of Israel bringing "forth their rich treasures unto the children of Ephraim, my servants" (Doctrine and Covenants 133:30).

Though Ephraim is considered the birthright tribe of the house of Israel, the Lord does not refer to the descendants of Ephraim as rulers but rather as servants. In Doctrine and Covenants 64 the Lord says that "the rebellious are not of the blood of Ephraim and will be plucked out" (verse 36). Many who come into the Church are literal descendants of Ephraim and the other tribes while many are not. The Lord does not distinguish between the two groups in the way He provides blessings to His children. The promises made to the fathers are important, but in the end, what the Lord requires of His servants is "the heart and a willing mind" (verse 34).

37 Behold, I, the Lord, have made my church in these last days like unto a judge sitting on a hill, or in a high place, to judge the nations.

38 For it shall come to pass that the inhabitants of Zion shall judge all things pertaining to Zion.

39 And liars and hypocrites shall be proved by them, and they who are not apostles and prophets shall be known.

40 And even the bishop, who is a judge, and his counselors, if they are not faithful in their stewardships shall be condemned, and others shall be planted in their stead.

In several places in scripture, the Lord gives the Saints the charge to assist in carrying out judgment upon the world. Speaking to the Nephite disciples, the Lord declared, "And know ye that ye shall be judges of this people, according to the judgment which I shall give unto you, which shall be just. Therefore, what manner of men ought ye to be? Verily I say unto you, even as I am" (3 Nephi 27:27). Urging the Saints to resolve their own differences rather than looking to outside sources, Paul wrote, "Know ye not that we shall judge the world?" and "Know ye not that we shall judge angels?" (1 Corinthians 6:2–3). In both of these cases, the Savior and Paul used the promise of a future judgment to motivate the Saints to live a virtuous life so that they can assist the Savior in judging the world without hypocrisy.

Ultimately, the Savior is the judge of all men and women (see 2 Nephi 9:41). The Saints are called to assist in acting as His servants on earth to determine worthiness before sacred ordinances such as baptisms, sealings, and other covenants can be extended. In all things the Savior seeks a fair judgment for all people based on their circumstances, light, and knowledge. The Prophet Joseph Smith taught, "It has been the design of Jehovah, from the commencement of the World, and is his purpose now, to regulate the affairs of the World in his own time; to stand as head of the universe and take the reins of government into his own hand. When that is done judgement will be administered in righteousness: anarchy and confusion will be destroyed, and 'nations will learn war no more.'"[10]

41 For, behold, I say unto you that Zion shall flourish, and the glory of the Lord shall be upon her;

42 And she shall be an ensign unto the people, and there shall come unto her out of every nation under heaven.

43 And the day shall come when the nations of the earth shall tremble because of her, and shall fear because of her terrible ones. The Lord hath spoken it. Amen.

The assurance given by the Lord in this revelation is that Zion will flourish. While trials and persecutions lay ahead of the Saints, the ending of the story is a happy one. The concept of Zion would expand beyond its beginning as a city built in Missouri to provide a home for the Saints, to a recognition of Zion as a people spread throughout the globe (see Doctrine and Covenants 97:11). Zion flourishes whenever a new temple is dedicated, a new stake is created, or a new member is baptized. Decades after this prophecy was given to Joseph Smith, his nephew President Joseph F. Smith remarked on its fulfillment:

> Zion is, indeed, flourishing on the hills, and it is rejoicing on the mountains, and we also who compose it are gathering and assembling together unto the place appointed. I now ask this congregation if they cannot see that this prediction (which was made many years before the idea prevailed at all among this people that we should ever migrate and gather out to these mountain valleys) has been and is being literally fulfilled? If there were no other prophecy uttered by Joseph Smith, fulfillment of which could be pointed to, this alone would be sufficient to entitle him to claim of being a true prophet.[11]

More than a century removed from President Joseph F. Smith's comments on the prophecy of Zion flourishing, we see its even greater fulfillment. Millions more Saints have made covenants, a handful of temples has grown to hundreds of dedicated houses of the Lord, and the members of the Church of the Lamb, though relatively few in number, are "armed with righteousness and with the power of God in great glory" (1 Nephi 14:14).

End Notes

1. See Minutes, 1 September 1831, 5; Minutes, 6 September 1831, 6, josephsmithpapers. org.

2. See "Historical Introduction," Revelation, 11 September 1831 [D&C 64], josephsmithpapers.org.

3. Discourse, 12 May 1844, as Reported by Thomas Bullock, 2, josephsmithpapers.org.

4. Journal, 1835–1836, 96, josephsmithpapers.org.

5. See Susan Easton Black, *Who's Who in the Doctrine & Covenants* (Salt Lake City, UT: Bookcraft, 1997), 198–200.

6. George A. Smith, in *Journal of Discourses,* 11:5.

7. See Mark Staker, *Hearken, O Ye People: The Historical Setting of Joseph Smith's Ohio Revelations* (Sandy, UT: Greg Kofford Books, 2010), 463–549.

8. Brent L. Top, *Watch and Be Ready: Preparing Spiritually for the Second Coming of Christ* (Salt Lake City, UT: Deseret Book, 2018), ebook.

9. Gordon B. Hinckley, "We Need Not Fear His Coming" (Brigham Young University devotional, Mar. 25, 1979), 4, speeches.byu.edu.

10. Joseph Smith, in History, 1838–1856, volume C-1 [2 November 1838–31 July 1842], 34, josephsmithpapers.org.

11. Joseph F. Smith, *Gospel Doctrine, 5th ed.* (1939), 486–487.

$\mathcal{D}$octrine and $\mathcal{C}$ovenants
Section 65
The Keys of the Kingdom

$\mathcal{H}$istorical $\mathcal{C}$ontext

THE REVELATION RECORDED IN DOCTRINE AND COVENANTS 65 WAS RE-
ceived on Sunday, October 30, 1831, at the John Johnson home in Hiram,
Ohio. William E. McLellin, a new convert who may have been present when
the revelation was received, recalled a Church service held in the Johnson
home the day the revelation was given. He wrote:

> This day the brethren and sisters collected at Bro. John Johnson's. And
> the brethren called on me to preach. But it seemed to me as if I could
> not. Here was the church who had been instructed by the first elders in
> the church. Here was Brothers John [Johnson], Sidney [Rigdon], Oliver
> [Cowdery], and Joseph [Smith] and it did not seem to me as if I could
> instruct them or even entertain the congregation, but with confidence
> along in Enoch's God I arose and addressed them about one hour and a
> half. And it was not I but the spirit and power of God which was in me

and it did seem to me before I finished as though it was not I or that I had got into another region where all was light and glory.[1]

Sometime during the day, Joseph Smith received this revelation. William McLellin made his own copy of the revelation and said that it related to Matthew 6:10, a part of the Lord's Prayer, which reads, "Thy kingdom come. Thy will be done on earth, as it is in heaven." While Joseph Smith was working on a translation of the Bible at this time, he appears to have translated this passage sometime earlier. However, the revelation does speak about the coming kingdom of God and the keys given to govern it. Joseph Smith also described the passage as a "revelation on prayer," which fits with McLellin's description.[2]

Prior to the 2013 edition of the Doctrine and Covenants, the exact date of this revelation was not known. Revelation Book 1 dates it as being received on October 30, 1831, meaning it was actually received the day after Doctrine and Covenants 66.[3]

Verse-by-Verse Commentary

1 Hearken, and lo, a voice as of one sent down from on high, who is mighty and powerful, whose going forth is unto the ends of the earth, yea, whose voice is unto men—Prepare ye the way of the Lord, make his paths straight.

2 The keys of the kingdom of God are committed unto man on the earth, and from thence shall the gospel roll forth unto the ends of the earth, as the stone which is cut out of the mountain without hands shall roll forth, until it has filled the whole earth.

This brief revelation makes two important connections to earlier dispensations. First, Joseph Smith is told that he has been given the "keys of the kingdom," a reference to a similar incident in the New Testament in which Peter was told he would receive "the keys of the kingdom of heaven" (Matthew 16:19). A revelation given just a few months later in March 1832 confirmed that Joseph was given the "keys of the kingdom which belong always to the Presidency of the High Priesthood" (Doctrine and Covenants 81:2). In a history written in the summer of 1832, Joseph Smith also wrote of "the keys of the Kingdom of God" being conferred upon him.[4]

Second, this revelation declares that a prophecy made by the prophet Daniel is about to be fulfilled in the Restoration of the kingdom of God in the latter days through the work of Joseph Smith and others. This prophecy of Daniel came when King Nebuchadnezzar, the ruler of Babylon, had a dream that greatly troubled him. In the dream, Nebuchadnezzar saw a "great image" with a head made of gold, breast and arms made of silver, a belly and thighs made of brass, legs of iron, and feet of iron and clay. Then the king saw a stone "cut out without hands" that "smote the image upon his feet that were iron and clay, and brake them to pieces," destroying the rest of the image. The stone grew in size to become "a great mountain and filled the whole earth" (Daniel 2:31–35).

In interpretation of this dream, Daniel explained to the king that the image represented different kingdoms of the earth. The head of gold represented Nebuchadnezzar's kingdom, while the parts of the statue made of silver, brass, iron, and clay represented inferior kingdoms that were to follow. As for the stone that destroyed the image, Daniel declared that in the days of the kingdoms of iron and clay "shall the God of heaven set up a kingdom, which shall never be destroyed: and the kingdom shall not be left to other people, but it shall break in pieces and consume all these kingdoms, and it shall stand forever" (Daniel 2:37–44). This stone is the restored gospel.

While Daniel only makes known the identity of the golden head as the Babylonian Empire, Elder Orson Pratt interpreted the dream to include successive empires. He taught that the silver breast and arms represented the Medo-Persian Empire and that the belly of brass represented the Macedonian Empire built by Alexander the Great. The legs of iron represented the Roman Empire, which was eventually split into two divisions and in turn was succeeded by the feet of clay and iron, representing the European kingdoms that ruled over much of the earth when the Restoration of the gospel began. Lastly, Elder Pratt taught that the "kingdom or stone cut out of the mountain without hands is a power superior to that of carnal weapons—the power of truth, for the kingdom of God cannot be organized on the earth without truth being sent down from heaven, without authority being given from the Most High."[5]

> 3 Yea, a voice crying—Prepare ye the way of the Lord, prepare ye the supper of the Lamb, make ready for the Bridegroom.
>
> 4 Pray unto the Lord, call upon his holy name, make known his wonderful works among the people.

5 Call upon the Lord, that his kingdom may go forth upon the earth, that the inhabitants thereof may receive it, and be prepared for the days to come, in the which the Son of Man shall come down in heaven, clothed in the brightness of his glory, to meet the kingdom of God which is set up on the earth.

6 Wherefore, may the kingdom of God go forth, that the kingdom of heaven may come, that thou, O God, mayest be glorified in heaven so on earth, that thine enemies may be subdued; for thine is the honor, power and glory, forever and ever. Amen.

The final verses of this revelation connect the coming of the kingdom of God to two New Testament passages, the parable of the ten virgins (see Matthew 25:1–13) and the Lord's Prayer (see Matthew 6:9–13). Making reference to these two passages, the Lord invites His disciples not only to pray for His coming but to "make known his wonderful works among the people" (verse 4). In issuing this invitation, the Savior invites us to be active participants in preparing the world for His coming. The Saints are not to sit back and wait for a rapture to remove them from the ills of the world but to actively work to build the kingdom and end the ills of the world.

The Savior will rule over the earth when He comes, but in the meantime the Church is instructed to do all it can to bring forth the kingdom of God on the earth. In many ways the Church is the mother of the coming kingdom. This connection was made literal through a passage Joseph Smith was directed to restore in the book of Revelation. In the original reading of the passage, John sees a woman in childbirth who was assailed by a dragon attempting to consume her child. The dragon represents Satan and his followers. The Joseph Smith Translation clarifies that "the woman . . . was the church of God, who had been delivered of her pains and brought forth the kingdom of God and his Christ" (Joseph Smith Translation, Revelation 12:7 [in Revelation 12:1, footnote a]). Therefore, the best thing a person can do to bring about the coming kingdom of God is to serve, support, and uplift the Church, the mother of the coming kingdom.

End Notes

1. William McLellin, *The Journals of William E. McLellin, 1831-1836*, ed. Jan Shipps and John Welch (Provo, UT: Brigham Young University Studies, 1994), 46–47.

2. See History, 1838–1856, volume A-1 [23 December 1805–30 August 1834], 155, josephsmithpapers.org.

3. See "Historical Introduction," Revelation, 30 October 1831 [D&C 65], josephsmithpapers.org.

4. See Joseph Smith—History, circa Summer 1832, 1, josephsmithpapers.org.

5. Orson Pratt, in *Journal of Discourses*, 15:72.

Doctrine and Covenants
Section 66
Keep These Sayings

Historical Context

WILLIAM E. McLELLIN WAS A NEW CONVERT FROM PARIS, ILLINOIS, WHEN he first met Joseph Smith at a conference held on October 25–26, 1831, in Orange, Ohio. At the conference, William was ordained to the high priesthood. Afterward William accompanied the Prophet to Hiram, Ohio, to the home of John and Elsa Johnson. He later wrote that after he arrived at the Johnson home, he "went before the Lord in secret, and on my knees asked him to reveal the answer to five questions through his Prophet."[1]

McLellin never recorded exactly what his five questions were, but from the answers given in the revelation, it is possible to put together a speculative list of the questions he brought before the Lord. His first question was likely close to "How does the Church I have just joined, organized by Joseph Smith, fit into the religious world?" (answered in Doctrine and Covenants 66:2). Question two may have been "What is my spiritual standing?" (answered in

253

Doctrine and Covenants 66:3). His next question may have been "What is my role in the Church? What am I to do now?" (answered in Doctrine and Covenants 66:5–8). He may have also asked, "I have seen the power to heal exercised by Church members; will I be able to have this power?" (answered in Doctrine and Covenants 66:9). His final question may have been "How can I escape the temptations of adultery and sin I have struggled with since the death of my wife?" (answered in Doctrine and Covenants 66:10–12).[2]

While we do not know precisely what McLellin's five questions were, the contents of the revelation reveal much about the struggles this new convert was wrestling with. In his journal, William wrote down his own copy of the revelation, prefacing it by writing, "This day the Lord condescended to hear my prayer and give me a revelation of his will, through the prophet or seer [Joseph]."[3] The revelation, now Doctrine and Covenants 66, answered McLellin's questions to his "full and entire satisfaction."[4] After recording the revelation, McLellin wrote in his journal, "This revelation [gave] great joy to my heart because some important questions were answered which had dwelt upon my mind with anxiety yet with uncertainty."[5]

*V*erse-by-*V*erse *C*ommentary

1 Behold, thus saith the Lord unto my servant William E. McLellin—Blessed are you, inasmuch as you have turned away from your iniquities, and have received my truths, saith the Lord your Redeemer, the Savior of the world, even of as many as believe on my name.

2 Verily I say unto you, blessed are you for receiving mine everlasting covenant, even the fulness of my gospel, sent forth unto the children of men, that they might have life and be made partakers of the glories which are to be revealed in the last days, as it was written by the prophets and apostles in days of old.

3 Verily I say unto you, my servant William, that you are clean, but not all; repent, therefore, of those things which are not pleasing in my sight, saith the Lord, for the Lord will show them unto you.

4 And now, verily, I, the Lord, will show unto you what I will concerning you, or what is my will concerning you.

The Lord begins his message to William by noting that William had already received the truth of the gospel. McLellin was baptized a few months prior to this revelation, in August 1831. On the day of his baptism he recorded the following in his journal:

> I rose early and betook myself to earnest prayer to God to direct me into truth; and from all the light that I could gain by examinations searches and researches I was bound as an honest man to acknowledge the truth and validity of the Book of Mormon and also that I had found the people of the Lord—the Living Church of Christ. Consequently as soon as we took breakfast I told Elder H. Smith that I wanted him to baptize me because I wanted to live among a people who were based upon pure principles and actuated by the Spirit of the Living God.[6]

The Lord addresses William's worthiness in what seems to be a direct response to feelings and doubts that had crept into William's heart after his baptism. McLellin wrote, "The enemy of all righteousness made a mighty struggle to persuade me that I was deceived until it seemed to me that horror would overwhelm me. I did not doubt the truth of the things which I had embraced, but my fears were respecting my own salvation." After these doubts came, William was visited by Newel Knight, who "came and by the Spirit of God was enabled to tell me the very secrets of my heart and in a degree chase darkness from my mind."[7] It appears that by the time William met Joseph Smith, he was once again in need of assurance of his salvation and in need of guidance in repenting of his sins.

5 Behold, verily I say unto you, that it is my will that you should proclaim my gospel from land to land, and from city to city, yea, in those regions round about where it has not been proclaimed.

6 Tarry not many days in this place; go not up unto the land of Zion as yet; but inasmuch as you can send, send; otherwise, think not of thy property.

7 Go unto the eastern lands, bear testimony in every place, unto every people and in their synagogues, reasoning with the people.

8 Let my servant Samuel H. Smith go with you, and forsake him not, and give him thine instructions; and he that is faithful shall be made strong in every place; and I, the Lord, will go with you.

9 Lay your hands upon the sick, and they shall recover. Return not till I, the Lord, shall send you. Be patient in affliction. Ask, and ye shall receive; knock, and it shall be opened unto you.

William was called to proclaim the gospel and was also given the promise that he would have the power to heal the sick. He was commanded to travel with Samuel H. Smith, the Prophet's brother. Prior to this revelation, McLellin had already preached with another Smith brother, Hyrum, and had seen the power of healing. When McLellin became sick, he asked Hyrum Smith for a blessing. He recorded in his journal, "We immediately bowed before the Lord and with all the faith which we had, we opened our hearts to him." Hyrum Smith laid hands on McLellin, who later wrote that it was "marvelous for me to relate that I was instantly healed."[8]

A few days later McLellin gave a sermon to a group of preachers on the coming forth of the Book of Mormon and on spiritual gifts. Afterward he was approached by a man called "Father Wood," who told him that his granddaughter was very sick. Without hesitation, McLellin and Hyrum Smith set out to the family's home, two miles away. He wrote, "The family seemed quite believing, and we all bowed before the great Jehovah and implored his mercy upon the child, we then arose and Brother Hyrum and I laid our hands upon it, and in a few minutes the little child got down from its mother's lap and began to play upon the floor. This caused them to rejoice and the old gentleman got down and prayed mightily, then arose and said that he believed that the Lord was there."[9]

Only a few days before this revelation was given, McLellin had injured his ankle and asked Joseph Smith about healing. McLellin recorded that in response, Joseph "turned to me and asked me if I believed in my heart that God through his instrumentality would heal it. I answered that I believed he would. He laid his hands on it and it was healed." William then accompanied Joseph to Hiram, Ohio, where this revelation was given.[10]

10 Seek not to be cumbered. Forsake all unrighteousness. Commit not adultery—a temptation with which thou hast been troubled.

11 Keep these sayings, for they are true and faithful; and thou shalt magnify thine office, and push many people to Zion with songs of everlasting joy upon their heads.

12 Continue in these things even unto the end, and you shall have a crown of eternal life at the right hand of my Father, who is full of grace and truth.

13 Verily, thus saith the Lord your God, your Redeemer, even Jesus Christ. Amen.

The last portion of this revelation must have been especially piercing for William to hear. We do not know the exact nature of his temptation to commit adultery. His wife, Cynthia Ann, whom he had married only two years earlier in 1829, had died sometime before the summer of 1831. In an entry in William's journal dated August 1, 1831, he wrote of visiting the grave of "my departed and dear companion Cinthia [sic] Ann and there they seemed to mourn with me for the loss of my dearest friend and her blessed little infant."[11] McLellin's journal entry may hint that Cynthia died in childbirth. He later spoke of spending "many lonesome and sorrowful hours" after her death. It appears that William and Cynthia enjoyed a warm and affectionate marriage, and the temptation to commit adultery came from his loneliness after her death and not any unhappiness with his spouse.[12]

It must have been encouraging for William to hear that in spite of his temptations, he was promised a "crown of eternal life" provided he endured faithful to the end. In a copy of the revelation he recorded himself, there is an addendum, which reads, "A revelation given to Wm. E. McLellin, a true descendant from joseph who was sold into Egypt down through the loins of Ephraim his son."[13] This addition to the revelation may have been part of the original record or may have been added by William himself. John Whitmer did not include these last two lines when he recorded the revelation in Revelation Book 1.[14] At any rate, so soon after the Lord had declared that "the rebellious are not of the blood of Ephraim" (Doctrine and Covenants 64:35), it must have been encouraging for William to know that he was of the blood of this birthright tribe of Israel.

William E. McLellin was a gifted preacher who was eventually called to serve as a member of the original Quorum of the Twelve Apostles called in this dispensation in 1835. Unfortunately, his service in the Twelve was short-lived because he was excommunicated in 1838. He explained that his apostasy centered on a loss of confidence in the Presidency of the Church, and "consequently he left off praying and keeping the commandments of God, and went his own way, and indulged himself in his lustful desires."[15] William never lost his testimony of the Book of Mormon or of the inspiration he saw in his early days in the Church, but he never fully returned to the Church either.

End Notes

1. William E. McLellin, *The Ensign of Liberty of the Church of Christ*, vol. 1, no. 4 (Jan. 1848), 61.

2. See William McLellin, *The Journals of William E. McLellin, 1831-1836*, ed. Jan Shipps and John Welch (Provo, UT: Brigham Young University Studies, 1994), 249–250.

3. McLellin, *The Journals of William E. McLellin*, 45.

4. Matthew C. Godfrey, "William McLellin's Five Questions," in *Revelations in Context* (2016).

5. McLellin, *The Journals of William E. McLellin*, 45. See also "Historical Introduction," Revelation, 30 October 1831 [D&C 66], josephsmithpapers.org.

6. McLellin, *The Journals of William E. McLellin*, 33–34.

7. McLellin, *The Journals of William E. McLellin*, 34.

8. McLellin, *The Journals of William E. McLellin*, 40.

9. McLellin, *The Journals of William E. McLellin*, 43.

10. See McLellin, *The Journals of William E. McLellin*, 45.

11. McLellin, *The Journals of William E. McLellin*, 30.

12. See Revelation, 29 October 1831 [D&C 66], 10, footnote 13, josephsmithpapers. org.

13. Revelation, 29 October 1831 [D&C 66], 10, josephsmithpapers.org.

14. See Revelation Book 1, 112, josephsmithpapers.org.

15. Journal, March–September 1838, 40, josephsmithpapers.org.

$\mathcal{D}$octrine and $\mathcal{C}$ovenants Section 67

That Which Is Righteous Cometh Down from Above

$\mathcal{H}$istorical $\mathcal{C}$ontext

ON NOVEMBER 1–2, 1831, A CONFERENCE WAS HELD AT THE JOHN JOHNSON home in Hiram, Ohio. The central question of the conference was that of publishing the revelations received by Joseph Smith. Many of the revelations had circulated privately among the Saints, but public access to the revelations was becoming a pressing question. The month before, Ezra Booth had published a series of letters in the *Ohio Star* claiming that certain commandments given to Joseph Smith were "concealed from the world." Booth made a number of outlandish claims about the revelations, including a charge that one of them commanded "that the Church shall build [Joseph Smith] an elegant house and give him 1,000 dollars."[1] No known revelation makes such a claim, and Joseph Smith and others may have felt the need to publish the revelations in the interest of transparency and to refute Booth's claims of abuse.

The conference provided an outpouring of revelation. During the first three days of November, four new revelations were received. Doctrine and Covenants 68 was received first, providing direction to four elders of the Church and counsel and guidance to the members of the Church in Zion. Doctrine and Covenants 1 and 133, now constituting the preface and the appendix of the book, were received during this time as well. Several of the elders attending the conference were asked to provide their witness that the revelations were true. The elders signed a document stating that they were "willing to bear testimony to all the world of mankind to every creature upon all the face of all the Earth upon the Islands of the Sea that god hath born record to our souls through the Holy Ghost shed forth upon us that these commandments are given by inspiration of God & are profitable for all men & are verily true."[2]

Sometime during the conference, Joseph Smith received Doctrine and Covenants 67, which addressed some of the fears the elders had concerning the revelations. The Lord declared that the elders had expressed concerns over imperfections in Joseph Smith and the language used in the revelations. One of the revelations given earlier in the conference had taught that the revelations came unto the Lord's "servants in their weakness, after the manner of their language, that they might come to understanding" (Doctrine and Covenants 1:24). In his own history Joseph Smith noted that "after this revelation [Doctrine and Covenants 1] was received some conversation was had concerning Revelations and language, and I received the following [Doctrine and Covenants 67]."[3]

Verse-by-Verse Commentary

1 Behold and hearken, O ye elders of my church, who have assembled yourselves together, whose prayers I have heard, and whose hearts I know, and whose desires have come up before me.

2 Behold and lo, mine eyes are upon you, and the heavens and the earth are in mine hands, and the riches of eternity are mine to give.

3 Ye endeavored to believe that ye should receive the blessing which was offered unto you; but behold, verily I say unto you

there were fears in your hearts, and verily this is the reason that ye did not receive.

4 And now I, the Lord, give unto you a testimony of the truth of these commandments which are lying before you.

5 Your eyes have been upon my servant Joseph Smith, Jun., and his language you have known, and his imperfections you have known; and you have sought in your hearts knowledge that you might express beyond his language; this you also know.

The Lord asked witnesses to bear record of the truthfulness of the Book of Mormon; similarly, Joseph Smith asked the elders present to share their testimony of the divine origins of the revelations. Oliver Cowdery and David Whitmer, two of the Three Witnesses of the Book of Mormon, were present at the conference. It is possible that the elders present expected spiritual manifestations similar to the dramatic experience these witnesses of the Book of Mormon experienced. The Lord in response told them that because "there were fears in [their] hearts" (verse 3), they did not receive. The revelation also hints at this desire, saying that the elders present "are not able to abide the presence of God now, neither the ministering of angels" (verse 13), perhaps alluding to the earlier experience of the Three Witnesses of the Book of Mormon.

In response to concerns expressed over the language found in the revelations, the Lord reminded the elders that Joseph Smith, like any other prophet, was an imperfect messenger with limitations on his own language. The revelation serves as a simple reminder that though the Savior is perfect, He works through imperfect people. Prophets, apostles, and all manner of leaders in the Church are flawed people doing the best they can to accomplish the Lord's work.

President Holland counseled Church members to "be kind regarding human frailty—your own as well as that of those who serve with you in a Church led by volunteer, mortal men and women. Except in the case of His only perfect Begotten Son, imperfect people are all God has ever had to work with. That must be terribly frustrating to Him, but He deals with it. So should we."[4]

6 Now, seek ye out of the Book of Commandments, even the least that is among them, and appoint him that is the most wise among you;

7 Or, if there be any among you that shall make one like unto it, then ye are justified in saying that ye do not know that they are true;

8 But if ye cannot make one like unto it, ye are under condemnation if ye do not bear record that they are true.

9 For ye know that there is no unrighteousness in them, and that which is righteous cometh down from above, from the Father of lights.

In response to the concerns raised over the revelations, the Lord challenged the elders at the conference to "appoint him that is most wise among you" to attempt to duplicate any of the revelations. William E. McLellin, a newly baptized schoolteacher from Paris, Tennessee, accepted the challenge to produce his own revelation. Joseph Smith later wrote:

Wm. E. McLellin, as the wisest man in his own estimation, having more learning than sense, endeavored to write a commandment like unto one of the least of the Lord's, but failed; it was an awful responsibility to write in the name of the Lord. The elders, and all present, that witnessed this vain attempt of a man to imitate the language of Jesus Christ, renewed their faith in the fulness of the gospel and in the truth of the commandments and revelations which the Lord had given to the church through my instrumentality; and the elders signified a willingness to bear testimony of their truth to all the world.[5]

While McLellin later became a bitter enemy of Joseph Smith, he should not be judged too harshly for his actions taken here. McLellin was a convert to the Church of only a few months and had met Joseph Smith a week prior to this meeting. A revelation given around this same time placed him among "the faithful elders of my church" (Doctrine and Covenants 68:7). He would eventually become a member of the first Quorum of the Twelve Apostles. Though McLellin's skepticism eventually eroded his testimony and his standing in the Church, those events came several years later. At this point in time, and in part because of this experience, McLellin was among the elders who felt honored "to have this privilege of bearing this testimony [of the revelations] unto the world."[6]

10 And again, verily I say unto you that it is your privilege, and a promise I give unto you that have been ordained unto this ministry, that inasmuch as you strip yourselves from jealousies

and fears, and humble yourselves before me, for ye are not sufficiently humble, the veil shall be rent and you shall see me and know that I am—not with the carnal neither natural mind, but with the spiritual.

11 For no man has seen God at any time in the flesh, except quickened by the Spirit of God.

12 Neither can any natural man abide the presence of God, neither after the carnal mind.

13 Ye are not able to abide the presence of God now, neither the ministering of angels; wherefore, continue in patience until ye are perfected.

14 Let not your minds turn back; and when ye are worthy, in mine own due time, ye shall see and know that which was conferred upon you by the hands of my servant Joseph Smith, Jun. Amen.

In exhorting the elders to greater faith, the Lord also corrects a common misunderstanding that it is impossible for a mortal person to see God in the flesh (see verse 11). The familiar quotation from the Gospel of John that "no man hath seen God at any time" was corrected in Joseph Smith's translation to read, "And no man hath seen God at any time, except he hath borne record of the Son; for except it is through him no man can be saved" (Joseph Smith Translation, John 1:19 [in John 1:18, footnote c]). Another New Testament passage that reads "[He] only hath immortality, dwelling in the light which no man can approach unto; whom no man hath seen, nor can see; to whom be honour and power everlasting" (1 Timothy 6:16) was changed in the Prophet's translation to read, "Whom no man hath seen, nor can he see, unto whom no man can approach, only he who hath the light and the hope of immortality dwelling in him" (Joseph Smith Translation, 1 Timothy 6:16 [in 1 Timothy 6:15, footnote a]). In one last example, the text of 1 John 4:12, which says that "no man hath seen God at any time," was changed to read, "No man hath seen God at any time, except them who believe" (Joseph Smith Translation, 1 John 4:12 [in 1 John 4:12, footnote a]).

The message of all of these corrections in the Joseph Smith Translation is clearly presented in Doctrine and Covenants 67. Here the Lord declares, "For no man has seen God at any time in the flesh, except quickened by the Spirit of God. Neither can any natural man abide the presence of God, neither after the carnal mind" (verses 11–12). It is possible for mortal people to survive in the presence of God if they are transfigured to abide the glory of God. God is more than capable of bringing about a change in the physical bodies of His servants, provided they are sufficiently humble and demonstrate the necessary faith to see God.

End Notes

1. Ezra Booth, "Mormonism—No. II," *Ohio Star* (Ravenna), Oct. 20, 1831.
2. Testimony, circa 2 November 1831, 121, josephsmithpapers.org.
3. Joseph Smith, in History, 1838–1856, volume A-1 [23 December 1805–30 August 1834], 161, josephsmithpapers.org. See also "Historical Introduction," Revelation, circa 2 November 1831 [D&C 67], josephsmithpapers.org.
4. Jeffrey R. Holland, "Lord, I Believe," *Ensign* or *Liahona*, May 2013, 94.
5. Joseph Smith, in History, 1838–1856, volume A-1 [23 December 1805–30 August 1834], 162, josephsmithpapers.org.
6. Testimony, circa 2 November 1831, 121, josephsmithpapers.org.

Doctrine and Covenants Section 68

Whatsoever They Shall Speak When Moved upon by the Holy Ghost Shall Be Scripture

Historical Context

DOCTRINE AND COVENANTS 68 WAS RECEIVED DURING THE NOVEMBER 1–2, 1831, conference in Hiram, Ohio, where the decision was made to publish Joseph Smith's revelations. During the conference, four elders, Orson Hyde, Luke Johnson, Lyman Johnson, and William E. McLellin, approached Joseph Smith and asked for a revelation to know the Lord's will for them. Joseph later wrote in his history, "As the following Elders were desirous to know the mind of the Lord concerning themselves, I enquired and received [Doctrine and Covenants 68]."[1] The first part of the revelation, consisting of verses 1–12, is addressed to these four elders.

The second part of the revelation, consisting of verses 13–35, is addressed to the Church generally. This part of the revelation provides valuable information about the office of bishop and gives instruction to the members of the Church about parenting, living the gospel, and prayer. Though this section clearly consists of two separate revelations, every form of the written revelation we know of displays both parts as one. In 1835 additional instructions and clarifications were added to the original 1831 revelation. These additions first appeared in *The Evening and the Morning Star,* a Church-owned newspaper, in June 1835. The publication of the revelation was in line with procedures established at the conference in 1831 that determined to print the revelations. In the conference minutes, the elders present resolved that "Brother Joseph Smith Jr. correct those errors or mistakes which he may discover by the Holy Spirit."[2] The new additions provided some clarifications about how bishops could be called and described the creation of the First Presidency as a governing council in the Church. The restoration of the council of the First Presidency took place a few months after the original revelation was received.[3]

Verse-by-Verse Commentary

1 My servant, Orson Hyde, was called by his ordination to proclaim the everlasting gospel, by the Spirit of the living God, from people to people, and from land to land, in the congregations of the wicked, in their synagogues, reasoning with and expounding all scriptures unto them.

2 And, behold, and lo, this is an ensample unto all those who were ordained unto this priesthood, whose mission is appointed unto them to go forth—

3 And this is the ensample unto them, that they shall speak as they are moved upon by the Holy Ghost.

4 And whatsoever they shall speak when moved upon by the Holy Ghost shall be scripture, shall be the will of the Lord, shall be the mind of the Lord, shall be the word of the Lord, shall be the voice of the Lord, and the power of God unto salvation.

5 Behold, this is the promise of the Lord unto you, O ye my servants.

Orson Hyde, Luke Johnson, Lyman Johnson, and William E. McLellin were all relatively new converts when the Lord spoke these words to them. Later all four of these elders received a call to serve as members of the original Quorum of the Twelve Apostles in this dispensation, but at the time this revelation was given, they were simply elders sent forth to preach. The oldest among the four, Orson Hyde, was twenty-six when this revelation was given. Yet in spite of their youth and relative inexperience, the Lord told these elders that they had the power to speak scripture when moved upon by the Holy Ghost.

The Lord's definition of scripture given in this passage is the most expansive and useful explanation provided in all of the standard works. Scripture is the mind of the Lord, the will of the Lord, the word of the Lord, the voice of the Lord, and the power of God unto salvation (see verse 4). It can be declared by people in the highest positions within the Church or by those in the lowest positions. It can be given by anyone regardless of their gender, ethnicity, or personal background. Anyone who speaks through the Holy Ghost and with the mind, will, word, and voice of the Lord can give scripture.

However, in providing such a broad definition of scripture, we must also be thoughtful and careful. Not everyone who claims to have received scripture actually has. To measure the validity of proposed scripture, we use the scriptural canon. The Bible Dictionary in the Latter-day Saint edition of the King James Version of the Bible defines *canon* as "a word of Greek origin, originally meaning 'a rod for testing straightness,' now used to denote the authoritative collection of the sacred books used by the true believers in Christ." Whenever anyone claims to have received new scripture, it must be measured and compared to the already established canon consisting of the Holy Bible, the Book of Mormon, the Doctrine and Covenants, and the Pearl of Great Price, as well as the Spirit.

For instance, when Hiram Page claimed to have received new scripture through the medium of a seer stone (see Doctrine and Covenants 28), Joseph Smith immediately became concerned because Page's revelations "were entirely at variance with the order of Gods house, as laid down in the new Testament, as well as in our late revelations."[4] The revelations received through Page's seer stone did not align with the established canon and therefore were not scripture. Part of the reason members of the Church are asked to continually study the standard works is to help them recognize false scripture when it emerges.

New scripture comes to the Church every day. Whether spoken by prophets and apostles or ministering brothers and sisters, it is given wherever and whenever it is needed. While the canon keeps us from being deceived, we must also recognize the generosity of God in speaking to His children and the multitude of heavenly messengers constantly influencing us.

> 6 Wherefore, be of good cheer, and do not fear, for I the Lord am with you, and will stand by you; and ye shall bear record of me, even Jesus Christ, that I am the Son of the living God, that I was, that I am, and that I am to come.
>
> 7 This is the word of the Lord unto you, my servant Orson Hyde, and also unto my servant Luke Johnson, and unto my servant Lyman Johnson, and unto my servant William E. McLellin, and unto all the faithful elders of my church—
>
> 8 Go ye into all the world, preach the gospel to every creature, acting in the authority which I have given you, baptizing in the name of the Father, and of the Son, and of the Holy Ghost.
>
> 9 And he that believeth and is baptized shall be saved, and he that believeth not shall be damned.
>
> 10 And he that believeth shall be blest with signs following, even as it is written.
>
> 11 And unto you it shall be given to know the signs of the times, and the signs of the coming of the Son of Man;
>
> 12 And of as many as the Father shall bear record, to you shall be given power to seal them up unto eternal life. Amen.

In proclaiming that His servants have the power to declare scripture, the Lord also empowers them to go forth with His authority to declare His words. In a revelation received only a few weeks earlier, the Lord had warned against too much zeal in seeking out signs (see Doctrine and Covenants 64:7–12). Here He counsels His servants that if they are focused on carrying out their duties and bringing people unto Christ, they will be "blest with signs" (verse 10). This confirms to the reader that signs are meant to strengthen existing faith, not to create faith from nothing. Signs are granted to those who already demonstrate their faith through their works.

The Lord even promises here that those who serve diligently will know the signs of the Second Coming. These signs have been sought by disciples in all ages of the world. The Lord reminds us that knowledge about the Savior's return is best obtained when we focus our efforts and energies on blessing others. Fixating too much on the details surrounding the Second Coming can ironically cause us to be less prepared for His coming.

13 And now, concerning the items in addition to the covenants and commandments, they are these—

14 There remain hereafter, in the due time of the Lord, other bishops to be set apart unto the church, to minister even according to the first;

15 Wherefore they shall be high priests who are worthy, and they shall be appointed by the First Presidency of the Melchizedek Priesthood, except they be literal descendants of Aaron.

16 And if they be literal descendants of Aaron they have a legal right to the bishopric, if they are the firstborn among the sons of Aaron;

17 For the firstborn holds the right of the presidency over this priesthood, and the keys or authority of the same.

18 No man has a legal right to this office, to hold the keys of this priesthood, except he be a literal descendant and the firstborn of Aaron.

19 But, as a high priest of the Melchizedek Priesthood has authority to officiate in all the lesser offices he may officiate in the office of bishop when no literal descendant of Aaron can be found, provided he is called and set apart and ordained unto this power, under the hands of the First Presidency of the Melchizedek Priesthood.

20 And a literal descendant of Aaron, also, must be designated by this Presidency, and found worthy, and anointed, and ordained under the hands of this Presidency, otherwise they are not legally authorized to officiate in their priesthood.

21 But, by virtue of the decree concerning their right of the priesthood descending from father to son, they may claim their anointing if at any time they can prove their lineage, or do ascertain it by revelation from the Lord under the hands of the above named Presidency.

The remainder of the revelation addresses the qualifications for a bishop to serve in the Church. At this time, there was only one bishop in the Church, Edward Partridge, though the Lord told the Church that "other bishops" would soon be set apart to carry out similar duties. The Lord specifies that bishops must be high priests and must be worthy to serve in this calling. The revelation mentions that literal descendants of Aaron have a legal right to the bishopric, but there are also several qualifying factors.

First, if a literal descendant of Aaron was identified, he would only have the right to serve in the position of bishop, as head of the Aaronic Priesthood. When most members of the Church think of a bishop, they think of the head of their local ward, who is appointed as a bishop (or the head of the Aaronic Priesthood) and also as the presiding high priest in the ward. A legal descendant of Aaron would have the right to serve as bishop but not as presiding high priest. Second, a person could not claim on his own to be a literal descendant of Aaron with a legal right to the bishopric. The revelation explains that the person would have to be identified, found worthy, and anointed by the First Presidency of the Melchizedek Priesthood. The individual could not identify himself as a literal firstborn son of Aaron through a patriarchal blessing or by his own revelation. God's house is a house of order, and in this instance, the First Presidency would have to receive revelation to identify a literal descendant of Aaron.

This particular revelation helps us to see Joseph's understanding, like ours, as a gradual and sometimes messy process. For example, the original text of the revelation read "a conference of high priests" in verse 19 instead of the First Presidency. This was a reference to the leadership of the Church during this time period. After the First Presidency was organized in 1833, verses 15 and 22–23 were changed to reflect the proper order of operations in the Church.[5]

One additional example will further illustrate the complexity of revelation. Although Joseph received a few revelations regarding the Aaronic Priesthood and descendants of Aaron in November of 1831 (one in early November and one on November 11), he also received information about the Aaronic Priesthood in the spring of 1835 in conjunction with a revelation to the newly organized Quorum of the Twelve Apostles and their call to serve a mission. At this time, God saw fit to teach Joseph more about the Aaronic Priesthood. The revelations Joseph received during these three periods are somewhat mixed together in our current Doctrine and Covenants. Some of section 107 was received in 1835 and some in 1831. In addition, some of section 68 was received in 1835 and some was received in 1831. This shows that Joseph learned line upon line, precept by precept, and may be more similar to how we experience personal revelation today.[6]

Many promises are made in the scriptures, particularly in the Doctrine and Covenants, to the descendants of Aaron and the tribe of Levi (see Doctrine and Covenants 13; 68:15–20; 84:18, 27–35; 107:13–17, 69–76). At the same time, promises made to our ancestors are weighed against the Lord's requirement of worthiness to serve in the work. While the Savior's words here hint at a larger role of the descendants of Aaron in the latter-day work, these promises still await their fulfillment. John the Baptist told Joseph Smith and Oliver Cowdery that the priesthood would never be taken again "until the sons of Levi do offer again an offering unto the Lord in righteousness" (Doctrine and Covenants 13:1). Joseph Smith and Malachi taught that the Lord "shall purify the sons of Levi, and purge them as gold and silver, that they may offer unto the Lord an offering in righteousness" (Doctrine and Covenants 128:24). No doubt the sons of Levi, including the descendants of Aaron, will play an important part in the Lord's work before His coming.

> 22 And again, no bishop or high priest who shall be set apart for this ministry shall be tried or condemned for any crime, save it be before the First Presidency of the church;
>
> 23 And inasmuch as he is found guilty before this Presidency, by testimony that cannot be impeached, he shall be condemned;
>
> 24 And if he repent he shall be forgiven, according to the covenants and commandments of the church.

This passage refers only to the members of the Presiding Bishopric. High priests who are set apart to serve as bishops typically serve under the direction of a stake president. If they commit a serious sin or transgression, they are held accountable before the presiding high priests of the stake, specifically the stake presidency. Since the members of the Presiding Bishopric of the Church serve without a geographical area of stewardship, they are accountable to the presidency of the Melchizedek Priesthood generally, or the First Presidency.

An 1835 revelation to Joseph Smith clarified this point of stewardship: "The most difficult cases of the church, inasmuch as there is not satisfaction upon the decision of the bishop or judges, it shall be handed over and carried up unto the council of the church, before the Presidency of the High Priesthood. . . . And after this decision it shall be had in remembrance no more before the Lord; for this is the highest council of the church of God, and a final decision upon controversies in spiritual matters" (Doctrine and Covenants 107:78, 80).

> 25 And again, inasmuch as parents have children in Zion, or in any of her stakes which are organized, that teach them not to understand the doctrine of repentance, faith in Christ the Son of the living God, and of baptism and the gift of the Holy Ghost by the laying on of the hands, when eight years old, the sin be upon the heads of the parents.
>
> 26 For this shall be a law unto the inhabitants of Zion, or in any of her stakes which are organized.
>
> 27 And their children shall be baptized for the remission of their sins when eight years old, and receive the laying on of the hands.
>
> 28 And they shall also teach their children to pray, and to walk uprightly before the Lord.

After addressing the role of bishops, the revelation speaks to the most fundamental unit of the Church, the family. The Family Proclamation teaches that "parents have a sacred duty to rear their children in love and righteousness, to provide for their physical and spiritual needs, and to teach them to love and serve one another, observe the commandments of God, and be law-abiding citizens wherever they live. Husbands and wives—mothers and fathers—will be held accountable before God for the discharge of these obligations."[7]

In this passage, one of the responsibilities given to parents is to teach their children and ensure that their children are baptized at eight years old, the age commonly referred to as the age of accountability. The earliest known reference to this teaching was given in the Joseph Smith Translation of Genesis. In the passage the Lord tells Abraham, "I will establish a covenant of circumcision with thee, and it shall be my covenant between me and thee, and thy seed after thee, in their generations; that thou mayest know forever that children are not accountable before me until they are eight years old" (Joseph Smith Translation, Genesis 17:11 [in Genesis 17:7, footnote a]).

While the age of eight is given as the general age of accountability and is the earliest a person can enter into the baptismal covenant with the Lord, sin and accountability must be understood in a more complex way. A revelation given to Joseph Smith in September 1830 teaches that "little children are redeemed from the foundation of the world through mine Only Begotten; Wherefore, they cannot sin, for power is not given unto Satan to tempt little children, until they begin to become accountable before me" (Doctrine and Covenants 29:46–47). For most people, accountability does not come suddenly at the age of eight but gradually develops as they are taught right from wrong. Parents should not wait until children are eight years old to begin teaching them the dangers of sin and how to follow the commandments. Also, parents are not freed from their obligations when their children become accountable for their own actions. In a reciprocal relationship, parents guide and help children throughout their lives, while raising and nurturing children helps their parents learn the divine art of godhood.

29 And the inhabitants of Zion shall also observe the Sabbath day to keep it holy.

30 And the inhabitants of Zion also shall remember their labors, inasmuch as they are appointed to labor, in all faithfulness; for the idler shall be had in remembrance before the Lord.

31 Now, I, the Lord, am not well pleased with the inhabitants of Zion, for there are idlers among them; and their children are also growing up in wickedness; they also seek not earnestly the riches of eternity, but their eyes are full of greediness.

32 These things ought not to be, and must be done away from among them; wherefore, let my servant Oliver Cowdery carry these sayings unto the land of Zion.

33 And a commandment I give unto them—that he that observeth not his prayers before the Lord in the season thereof, let him be had in remembrance before the judge of my people.

34 These sayings are true and faithful; wherefore, transgress them not, neither take therefrom.

35 Behold, I am Alpha and Omega, and I come quickly. Amen.

At the end of the revelation, the Lord reiterates His earlier expectations of the Saints living in Zion to keep the commandments and be diligent in their duties. The members of the Church living in Missouri were held to a higher standard when it came to the law of consecration. But this passage also emphasizes how integral healthy families are to the successful imple-mentation of the principles of consecration. Both idlers and parents who neglect to teach their children about the dangers of greed are mentioned in the same verse by the Lord. Alongside the charity and generosity necessary to build Zion, the value of self-reliance was to be enshrined in the hearts of the people.

The principles of self-reliance as part of the law of consecration continue to be valued among the Saints in our day. President Monson taught, "Let us be self-reliant and independent. Salvation can be obtained on no other principle."[8] In this greatest work of gathering Israel and building Zion, we must not be idle.

President Ballard implored the Saints to be innovative, stating the following:

> As we work to magnify our callings, we should seek the inspiration of the Spirit to solve problems in ways that will best help the people we serve. We have handbooks of instruction, and their guidelines should be followed. But within that framework are substantial opportunities to think, to be creative, and to make use of individual talents. The instruction to mag-nify our callings is not a command to embellish and complicate them. To innovate does not necessarily mean to expand; very often it means to simplify. . . .
>
> Being innovative also means that we do not have to be told everything we should do. The Lord said, "It is not meet that I should command in all things; for he that is compelled in all things, the same is a slothful and not a wise servant" (Doctrine and Covenants 58:26). We trust you, brothers and sisters, to use inspiration. We trust that you will do so within the framework of Church policies and principles. We trust that you will be wise in counseling together to help build faith and testimony in the lives of those whom you serve.[9]

End Notes

1. Joseph Smith, in History, 1838–1856, volume A-1 [23 December 1805–30 August 1834], 163, josephsmithpapers.org.

2. Minutes, 8 November 1831, 16, josephsmithpapers.org.

3. See "Historical Introduction," Revelation, 1 November 1831–A [D&C 68], josephsmithpapers.org. See also "Historical Introduction," Revelation, circa June 1835 [D&C 68], josephsmithpapers.org.

4. History, 1838–1856, volume A-1 [23 December 1805–30 August 1834], 54, josephsmithpapers.org.

5. See Revelation, 1 November 1831-A [D&C 68], 114, josephsmithpapers.org.

6. See "Historical Introduction," circa June 1835 [D&C 68], josephsmithpapers.org. See also Instruction on Priesthood, between circa 1 March and circa 4 May 1835 [D&C 107], josephsmithpapers.org.

7. "The Family: A Proclamation to the World," Gospel Library.

8. Thomas S. Monson, "Guiding Principles of Personal and Family Welfare," *Ensign*, Sept. 1986, 3.

9. M. Russell Ballard, "O Be Wise," *Ensign* or *Liahona*, Nov. 2017, 18–19.

Doctrine and Covenants Section 69

For the Rising Generations

Historical Context

AFTER THE NOVEMBER 1–2, 1831, CONFERENCE TO PUBLISH THE REVELA-
tions was completed, this revelation assigned John Whitmer to travel to
Missouri with Oliver Cowdery, who was earlier commanded to arrange
for the printing of the revelations (see Doctrine and Covenants 68:32).
William W. Phelps was already setting up a printing office in Independence,
Missouri, and Church leaders planned to print and produce the first bound
copies of Joseph Smith's revelations there. Whitmer was assigned to travel
with Oliver Cowdery as part of his assignment as Church Historian (see
Doctrine and Covenants 47).

Whitmer later recorded in his own history, "About this time it was in
contemplation for Oliver Cowdery to go to Zion and carry with him the
Revelation and Commandments, and I also received a revelation to go with
him. We left Ohio, on the 20th of Nov, 1831 and arrived in Zion, Mo. Jan.

5, 1832. When we arrived in Zion we found the saints in as good situation as we could reasonably expect."[1] In the following months, work continued in Missouri on the publication of the revelations. At the same time, storm clouds were gathering over the Saints in Missouri, and the shadow of mob violence was growing. John Whitmer noted in his history that a few weeks after his arrival in Independence, "the enemies held a counsel in Independence, Jackson County, Mo., how they might destroy the saints but did not succeed at this time."[2]

Verse-by-Verse Commentary

1 Hearken unto me, saith the Lord your God, for my servant Oliver Cowdery's sake. It is not wisdom in me that he should be entrusted with the commandments and the moneys which he shall carry unto the land of Zion, except one go with him who will be true and faithful.

2 Wherefore, I, the Lord, will that my servant, John Whitmer, should go with my servant Oliver Cowdery;

3 And also that he shall continue in writing and making a history of all the important things which he shall observe and know concerning my church;

4 And also that he receive counsel and assistance from my servant Oliver Cowdery and others.

5 And also, my servants who are abroad in the earth should send forth the accounts of their stewardships to the land of Zion;

John Whitmer, one of the eight witnesses of the Book of Mormon, had been called by revelation as Church Historian a few months earlier (see Doctrine and Covenants 47). While John initially doubted his ability to fill the role, he made an invaluable contribution to the history of the Church. John began writing a history at this time, but his most esteemed contributions came in the collection of documents he prepared. Beginning with his call in March 1831, the documentary record of the Church, including minutes, letters, and other items, grew in size and in depth. Most of the revelations being transported to Missouri had been recorded in John Whitmer's handwriting, and nearly all of the earliest copies of the revelations come from copies John made.

The Lord makes an important addition here to the historical work of the Church by adding that, in addition to the work of the Church Historian, the "servants who are abroad in the earth" should also send accounts of their stewardships (Doctrine and Covenants 69:5). The historical enterprise of the Church includes everyone who participates in this great work. The history of a small organization, branch, or ward might seem insignificant in the grand scheme of things, but each history is a valuable part of the larger story of the Restoration.

> 6 For the land of Zion shall be a seat and a place to receive and do all these things.
>
> 7 Nevertheless, let my servant John Whitmer travel many times from place to place, and from church to church, that he may the more easily obtain knowledge—
>
> 8 Preaching and expounding, writing, copying, selecting, and obtaining all things which shall be for the good of the church, and for the rising generations that shall grow up on the land of Zion, to possess it from generation to generation, forever and ever. Amen.

The Lord here affirms once again that the land of Zion will eventually become the geographical center of the Church. This thread is carefully woven throughout the Doctrine and Covenants. In commanding that the revelations be printed in Missouri, the Lord is emphasizing the importance of Zion and its development for the work of the Church in the latter days.

Although the Lord accepts Zion as the center place, He also commands John Whitmer to travel from "place to place, and from church to church" (verse 7) to record and preserve the history of the Church. The history of the Church must include not only the stories of those who are at its headquarters; the Saints who live in smaller units and more scattered places need to have their experiences and stories told as well. In John Whitmer's day, this included the different branches of the Church. In our day, it is important to remember that the story of the Church has not only unfolded in Fayette, Kirtland, and Nauvoo but is still unfolding around the world. The history of the Church in places like Dubai, United Arab Emirates; Shanghai, China; Tarawa, Kiribati; and Bengaluru, India, are just as important to our story as the experiences of these early Saints. Figuratively speaking, it is always 1830 in the Church somewhere, and future histories must include these new stories of the spread of the gospel.[3]

End Notes

1. John Whitmer, History, 1831–circa 1847, 38, josephsmithpapers.org.

2. John Whitmer, History, 1831–circa 1847, 38, josephsmithpapers.org.

3. See "Historical Introduction," Revelation, 11 November 1831–A [D&C 69], josephsmithpapers.org.

$\mathcal{D}$octrine and $\mathcal{C}$ovenants
Section 70
Heirs According to the Law of the Kingdom

$\mathcal{H}$istorical $\mathcal{C}$ontext

ONCE THE SAINTS DECIDED TO PUBLISH THE REVELATIONS, ANOTHER CON-
ference was held on November 12, 1831, at the John Johnson home to work
out the details of how to proceed. The minutes of the conference show that
the elders present "voted that Joseph Smith jr. be appointed to dedicate and
consecrate these brethren and the sacred writings and all they have entrusted
to their care, to the Lord: done accordingly." The minutes also record that
the members present declared the revelations to be "the foundation of the
Church & the salvation of the world and the keys of the mysteries of the
kingdom, and the riches of eternity to the church." They also declared that
the revelations were "prized by this conference to be worth to the Church
the riches of the whole Earth, speaking temporally."[1]

While writing his own history several years later, Joseph Smith reflected
on "the great benefits to the world, which result from the Book of Mormon

and the Revelations, which the Lord has seen fit, in his infinite wisdom, to grant unto us for our salvation, and for the salvation of all that will believe."[2] Joseph also said that the revelation came "in answer to an enquiry," though we do not know precisely the nature of that original question.[3] To facilitate the publication of the revelations, the Lord directed the elders present to form an adaptation of the earlier principles given on the law of consecration. This small group of people sacrificed and pooled their resources to help publish the revelations. The group later became known as the Literary Firm. The Literary Firm played a key role not only in the printing of Joseph Smith's revelations but also in the publication of Joseph Smith's translation of the Bible, the first Church hymnal, a Church almanac, children's literature, and various Church newspapers.[4]

Verse-by-Verse Commentary

1 Behold, and hearken, O ye inhabitants of Zion, and all ye people of my church who are afar off, and hear the word of the Lord which I give unto my servant Joseph Smith, Jun., and also unto my servant Martin Harris, and also unto my servant Oliver Cowdery, and also unto my servant John Whitmer, and also unto my servant Sidney Rigdon, and also unto my servant William W. Phelps, by the way of commandment unto them.

2 For I give unto them a commandment; wherefore hearken and hear, for thus saith the Lord unto them—

3 I, the Lord, have appointed them, and ordained them to be stewards over the revelations and commandments which I have given unto them, and which I shall hereafter give unto them;

4 And an account of this stewardship will I require of them in the day of judgment.

5 Wherefore, I have appointed unto them, and this is their business in the church of God, to manage them and the concerns thereof, yea, the benefits thereof.

6 Wherefore, a commandment I give unto them, that they shall not give these things unto the church, neither unto the world;

The elders mentioned in this revelation were given a sacred charge to oversee the printing of the revelations. Most of the men involved in this endeavor were with Joseph Smith from the beginning, though Sidney Rigdon and William W. Phelps were newer to the work. Joseph Smith, eager to recognize those involved in the work, declared during the November 12 conference:

> Brother Oliver has labored with me from the beginning in writing, etc., Brother Martin Harris has labored with me from the beginning, and Brothers John and Sidney also for a considerable time, and as these sacred writings are now going to the Church for their benefit, that we may have claim on the church for recompence—if this conference think these things worth prizing to be had on record to show hereafter—I feel that it will be according to the mind of the Spirit for by it these things were put into my heart which I know to be the Spirit of truth.[5]

While Joseph Smith believed that the elders involved in the compilation and printing of the sacred writings were entitled to compensation for their time and labor, the rest of the revelation shows that their recompense would feed directly into the law of consecration to benefit the poor and the needy in the Church. Church leaders did not ask the members of the Church to enter into any kind of economic arrangement that they themselves had not entered into. Like King Benjamin, the leaders of the Church were asked to serve side by side with the members, laboring together to help the poor and bring the words of the Lord to more people (see Mosiah 2:14).

> 7 Nevertheless, inasmuch as they receive more than is needful for their necessities and their wants, it shall be given into my storehouse;
>
> 8 And the benefits shall be consecrated unto the inhabitants of Zion, and unto their generations, inasmuch as they become heirs according to the laws of the kingdom.
>
> 9 Behold, this is what the Lord requires of every man in his stewardship, even as I, the Lord, have appointed or shall hereafter appoint unto any man.
>
> 10 And behold, none are exempt from this law who belong to the church of the living God;

11 Yea, neither the bishop, neither the agent who keepeth the Lord's storehouse, neither he who is appointed in a stewardship over temporal things.

12 He who is appointed to administer spiritual things, the same is worthy of his hire, even as those who are appointed to a stewardship to administer in temporal things;

13 Yea, even more abundantly, which abundance is multiplied unto them through the manifestations of the Spirit.

The law referred to in verse 10 is the law of the Church, particularly the law of consecration, revealed earlier in Doctrine and Covenants 42:30–42. This revelation demonstrates that, although the principles of the law of consecration are eternal, the implementation of the law is adaptable given the circumstances. Joseph Smith and the elders mentioned in this revelation were organized into a smaller consecrated group and given the charge to oversee the publication of the revelations and other Church literary projects. Entering into consecration was an expectation for everyone who chose to move to Missouri, as would be emphasized in a later revelation (see Doctrine and Covenants 72:17–18).

The elders who were asked to join the Literary Firm followed an adaptation of the law of consecration. They sacrificed their time and property to ensure the printing of the revelations, and in turn, the needs of their families were met through the money raised from the sale of the revelations. Once the needs of these families were met, the surplus was returned to the Church for use in the bishops' storehouse and to help others in the Church meet their needs. This is among the earliest examples in the history of the Church that show that the principles of consecration set forth in the scriptures can and should be adapted to meet the current conditions and needs of the Church. The task for Church leaders in any dispensation is to take those same principles and adapt them to the circumstances they live in.

14 Nevertheless, in your temporal things you shall be equal, and this not grudgingly, otherwise the abundance of the manifestations of the Spirit shall be withheld.

15 Now, this commandment I give unto my servants for their benefit while they remain, for a manifestation of my blessings upon their heads, and for a reward of their diligence and for their security;

16 For food and for raiment; for an inheritance; for houses and for lands, in whatsoever circumstances I, the Lord, shall place them, and whithersoever I, the Lord, shall send them.

17 For they have been faithful over many things, and have done well inasmuch as they have not sinned.

18 Behold, I, the Lord, am merciful and will bless them, and they shall enter into the joy of these things. Even so. Amen.

The Literary Firm continued to operate until 1836. Initially the conference called for printing ten thousand copies of the revelations.[6] That number was reduced to three thousand. W. W. Phelps purchased a printing press in Cincinnati, Ohio, and he was able to begin setting up the printing operation in Independence, Missouri, by December 1831. The next year, the Literary Firm began publishing *The Evening and the Morning Star,* a Church newspaper. By December 1832 the first copies of the revelations, titled the *Book of Commandments,* went to press. On July 20, 1833, a mob destroyed the Church press in Independence. Only a few copies of the printing were saved, and fewer than five hundred copies of the *Book of Commandments* were ultimately salvaged.

Undeterred by persecution, the Literary Firm set up shop in Kirtland, Ohio, and began work on a new and updated version of the *Book of Commandments,* which was eventually titled the *Doctrine and Covenants.* The press in Kirtland also continued to produce *The Evening and the Morning Star,* along with the *Latter-day Saints Messenger and Advocate,* and a political paper, the *Northern Times.* The press in Kirtland was also responsible for the first Latter-day Saint hymnbook, published in 1835.[7] These early papers are invaluable sources for the teachings of early Church leaders and for the preservation of the revelations given to Joseph Smith. Although persecutions and the high cost of printing kept the Literary Firm hovering just above insolvency, the group managed to preserve and publish some of the most important documents of this crucial formative period of the Church.[8]

End Notes

1. Minutes, 12 November 1831, 18, josephsmithpapers.org.
2. Joseph Smith, in History, 1838–1856, volume A-1 [23 December 1805–30 August 1834], 173, josephsmithpapers.org.
3. See History, 1838–1856, volume A-1 [23 December 1805–30 August 1834], 173, josephsmithpapers.org.
4. See Lyndon W. Cook, *The Revelations of the Prophet Joseph Smith: A Historical and Biographical Commentary of the Doctrine and Covenants* (Salt Lake City, UT: Deseret Book, 1985), 113. See also "Historical Introduction," Revelation, 12 November 1831 [D&C 70], josephsmithpapers.org.
5. Minute Book 2, 18, josephsmithpapers.org.
6. See Minutes, 1–2 November 1831, 15, josephsmithpapers.org.
7. See Collection of Sacred Hymns, 1835, josephsmithpapers.org.
8. See Cook, *The Revelations of the Prophet Joseph Smith*, 112–117.

$\mathcal{D}$octrine and $\mathcal{C}$ovenants Section 71

No Weapon That Is Formed against You Shall Prosper

$\mathcal{H}$istorical $\mathcal{C}$ontext

WHILE WORK ON PUBLISHING THE REVELATIONS MOVED FORWARD, HOSTIL-ity to the Church was rising as well. Two former elders of the Church, Ezra Booth and Symonds Rider, had begun to stir up opposition to the work. In the *Ohio Star* (a newspaper in nearby Ravenna, Ohio), Ezra Booth published a series of letters criticizing the Church. Booth developed this negative opinion of the Church after he was called to travel to Missouri to help locate the place for the city of Zion (see Doctrine and Covenants 52:23). He was unimpressed with the appearance of Independence, Missouri, and caused contention among the missionaries during the journey home. Shortly after he returned to Ohio, he began to push against the Church. In one of his letters to the *Ohio Star*, Booth claimed that "a journey of one thousand miles to the west, has taught me more abundantly, than I should have learned from any other source . . . the imbecility of human nature, and especially my own weakness." He called on members of the Church to "look at [Mormonism] with their own eyes, and no longer suffer these strangers to blind your eyes, and daub you over with their untampered mortar."[1]

A few months before Booth began publishing his letters, Symonds Rider became disaffected with the Church as well. He gave a copy of a revelation titled "The Laws of the Church of Christ" (Doctrine and Covenants 42) to the *Western Courier,* another newspaper in Ravenna, Ohio. Rider claimed that Church leaders had been "commanded not to communicate it to the world, nor even to their followers, until they become strong in the faith."[2] Rider believed that the revelation, which contained instructions on how to live the law of consecration, was part of a plot "to take their property from them and place it under the control of Joseph Smith the prophet."[3]

On December 1, 1831, Joseph Smith received a revelation in response to this new opposition. In this revelation, Joseph Smith and Sidney Rigdon were commanded to preach the gospel in the regions around where they lived in order to fight the falsehoods being spread by the enemies of the Church.[4]

$\mathcal{V}$erse-by-$\mathcal{V}$erse $\mathcal{C}$ommentary

1 Behold, thus saith the Lord unto you my servants Joseph Smith, Jun., and Sidney Rigdon, that the time has verily come that it is necessary and expedient in me that you should open your mouths in proclaiming my gospel, the things of the kingdom, expounding the mysteries thereof out of the scriptures, according to that portion of Spirit and power which shall be given unto you, even as I will.

2 Verily I say unto you, proclaim unto the world in the regions round about, and in the church also, for the space of a season, even until it shall be made known unto you.

3 Verily this is a mission for a season, which I give unto you.

4 Wherefore, labor ye in my vineyard. Call upon the inhabitants of the earth, and bear record, and prepare the way for the commandments and revelations which are to come.

Joseph and Sidney were called on this mission largely to refute the false-hoods being spread by Ezra Booth and Symonds Rider. While Booth's apostasy is thoroughly explained in the letters he wrote to the *Ohio Star*, the reasons why Symonds Rider became antagonistic toward the Church are less clear. One possible reason for his leaving may be that, according to a popular rumor, Rider's name was misspelled in his mission call, and this mistake led to his apostasy. This story can be traced back to Reverend Burke A. Hinsdale, a friend of Rider, who declared, "His [Symonds Rider's] commission came, and he found his name was misspelled. Was the Holy Spirit so fallible as to fail even in orthography?" But upon closer examination, the reasons for Rider's dissension are undoubtedly more complex.

One evidence for Rider's reasons being more complex is that a copy of the revelation exists in Symonds Rider's own handwriting, and in this copy, he misspells his own name as "Simonds." Members of the Campbellite Church that Rider was part of commonly misspelled his name as "Simonds" as well. Furthermore, Rider may have used different spellings for his name at different times, and he himself never mentions the misspelling in his own writings. Given these and other factors, it is unlikely that the misspelling was a major factor in his decision to apostatize.[5] Such a factor would be ironic because, in the current Doctrine and Covenants (2013), the spelling of Rider's name does not match the spelling on his headstone, where the name is written as "Symonds Ryder." In the Doctrine and Covenants, the name is spelled as "Simonds Ryder" (Doctrine and Covenants 52:37). In materials produced for the Joseph Smith Papers project, the name is spelled "Symonds Rider."[6] All of these attempts are best guesses based on the multiple ways in which Rider appears to have spelled his own name.

A more likely reason for Rider's discord was his concern over the law of consecration, which was revealed in February 1831 (see Doctrine and Covenants 42:30–42). While other elders of the Church departed on missions in the spring of 1831, Rider remained behind in Ohio, fixated on the law of consecration. He later gave a copy of the law (see Doctrine and Covenants 42) to the *Western Courier*. In an account provided by Reverend Hinsdale, Rider wrote to a friend, saying, "When they [Joseph Smith and other Church leaders] went to Missouri to lay the foundation of the splendid city of Zion, and also of the temple, they left their papers behind. This gave their new converts an opportunity to become acquainted with the internal arrangement of their church, which revealed to them the horrid fact that a plot was laid to take their property from them and place it under the control of Joseph Smith the prophet."[7]

Whatever his reasons for leaving the Church, Rider became one of the most bitter enemies of Joseph Smith. Simmering throughout the winter of 1831–32, his rancor reached its peak on March 24, 1832, when Rider and Booth led a mob attack on the John Johnson home where Joseph Smith was staying. The Prophet and Sidney Rigdon were badly beaten and tarred and feathered by the mob. Symonds Rider was never brought to justice for this action and remained an elder in the Campbellite Church until his death in 1870.

> 5 Now, behold this is wisdom; whoso readeth, let him understand and receive also;
>
> 6 For unto him that receiveth it shall be given more abundantly, even power.
>
> 7 Wherefore, confound your enemies; call upon them to meet you both in public and in private; and inasmuch as ye are faithful their shame shall be made manifest.
>
> 8 Wherefore, let them bring forth their strong reasons against the Lord.
>
> 9 Verily, thus saith the Lord unto you—there is no weapon that is formed against you shall prosper;
>
> 10 And if any man lift his voice against you he shall be confounded in mine own due time.
>
> 11 Wherefore, keep my commandments; they are true and faithful. Even so. Amen.

At times, Church members must turn the other cheek toward their enemies, but at other times, they must respond and correct falsehoods told about their faith. In this revelation, the Lord instructed Joseph and Sidney to "confound your enemies; call upon them to meet you both in public and in private" (verse 7). Following the instructions in this revelation, Sidney Rigdon paid the *Ohio Star* to insert a notice in the newspaper challenging Ezra Booth and Symonds Rider to a public debate over their accusations. Sidney announced his intention to preach in the brick schoolhouse in Ravenna on Christmas Day and invited Booth and Rider to meet him there to contest his claims. Neither of them accepted Sidney's challenge.[8]

The meeting held in Ravenna on Christmas Day, 1831, was only one of many meetings held during this time to dispel the falsehoods spread by Booth and Rider. Joseph Smith's later history states:

> From this time until the 8th or 10th of January 1832 myself and Elder [Sidney] Rigdon continued to preach in Shalersville, Ravenna, and other places, setting forth the truth; vindicating the cause of our Redeemer; shewing that the day of vengeance was coming upon this generation like a thief in the night: that prejudice, blindness, and darkness, filled the minds of many, and caused them to persecute the true church, and reject the true light: by which means we did much towards allaying the excited feelings which were growing out of the scandalous letters then being published in the "Ohio Star," at Ravenna, by the before mentioned apostate Ezra Booth.[9]

Joseph and Sidney answered the anti-Mormons (as they were then called) of their day, but how do we respond to those who seek to tear down the faith of others in our day? Elder Lawrence E. Corbridge, a member of the Quorum of the Seventy, spoke once about how one of his assignments as a General Authority was to read many of the publications written to attack the faith of Church members. He noted the endless array of questions raised by those who seek to destroy faith and then offered this counsel:

> Begin by answering the primary questions. There are primary questions and there are secondary questions. Answer the primary questions first. Not all questions are equal and not all truths are equal. The primary questions are the most important. Everything else is subordinate. There are only a few primary questions. I will mention four of them.
>   1. Is there a God who is our Father?
>   2. Is Jesus Christ the Son of God, the Savior of the world?
>   3. Was Joseph Smith a prophet?
>   4. Is The Church of Jesus Christ of Latter-day Saints the kingdom of God on the earth?
>   By contrast, the secondary questions are unending. They include questions about Church history, polygamy, people of African descent and the priesthood, women and the priesthood, how the Book of Mormon was translated, the Pearl of Great Price, DNA and the Book of Mormon, gay marriage, the different accounts of the First Vision, and on and on.
>   If you answer the primary questions, the secondary questions get answered too, or they pale in significance and you can deal with things

you understand and things you don't and things you agree with and things you don't without jumping ship altogether.[10]

End Notes

1. Ezra Booth, letters I and VII, cited in Eber Howe, *Mormonism Unvailed* (1834).
2. "Secret Bye Laws of the Mormonites," *Western Courier* (Ravenna, OH), Sept. 1, 1831.
3. "Symonds Rider, Hiram, OH, to A. S. Hayden, 1 February 1868," in Amos S. Hayden, *Early History of the Disciples in the Western Reserve: With Biographical Sketches of the Principle Agents in their Religious Movement* (Whitefish, MT: Kessinger Publishing, 2009), 221.
4. See History, 1838–1856, volume A-1 [23 December 1805–30 August 1834], 175, josephsmithpapers.org. See also "Historical Introduction," Revelation, 1 December 1831 [D&C 71], josephsmithpapers.org.
5. See Mark Staker, *Hearken, O Ye People: The Historical Setting of Joseph Smith's Ohio Revelations* (Sandy, UT: Greg Kofford Books, 2010), 294–95.
6. See "Historical Introduction," Revelation 1 December 1831 [D&C 71], josephsmithpapers.org. I have used the spelling favored by the Joseph Smith Papers project in this commentary.
7. Quoted in Susan Easton Black, *Who's Who in the Doctrine & Covenants* (Salt Lake City, UT: Bookcraft, 1997), 257.
8. See Staker, *Hearken, O Ye People,* 301.
9. Joseph Smith, in History, 1838–1856, volume A-1 [23 December 1805–30 August 1834], 179, josephsmithpapers.org.
10. Lawrence E. Corbridge, "Stand Forever" (Brigham Young University devotional, Jan. 27, 2019), 2–3, speeches.byu.edu.

$\mathcal{D}$octrine and $\mathcal{C}$ovenants Section 72

The Bishop in Zion

$\mathcal{H}$istorical $\mathcal{C}$ontext

DOCTRINE AND COVENANTS 72 CONSISTS OF THE THREE REVELATIONS GIV-
en on December 4, 1831. At this time, Joseph Smith gathered with other
leaders in Kirtland to discuss several issues concerning the Church. We do
not have the exact minutes of their conversation, but Joseph Smith recorded
the circumstances of the meeting in a later history. He wrote:

> Knowing now the mind of the Lord, that the time had come that the
> gospel should be proclaimed in power and demonstration to the world,
> from the scriptures, reasoning with men as in days of old, I took a journey
> to Kirtland, in company with Elder Sidney Rigdon, on the 3rd day of
> December to fulfil the above Revelation. On the 4th. several of the Elders
> and members assembled together to learn their duty and for edification,
> and, after some time had been spent in conversing about our temporal and
> Spiritual welfare, I received the following [Doctrine and Covenants 72].[1]

In the revelation, Newel K. Whitney was called to serve as the second bishop in the Church (see verses 1–8). The second part of the revelation explained Bishop Whitney's duties as the bishop of the Church in Ohio (see verses 9–23). The final part of the revelation provided guidance to Bishop Whitney on how to issue recommends to Church members who were given the opportunity to travel to Missouri and assist in building the city of Zion (see verses 24–26).[2]

Verse-by-Verse Commentary

1 Hearken, and listen to the voice of the Lord, O ye who have assembled yourselves together, who are the high priests of my church, to whom the kingdom and power have been given.

2 For verily thus saith the Lord, it is expedient in me for a bishop to be appointed unto you, or of you, unto the church in this part of the Lord's vineyard.

3 And verily in this thing ye have done wisely, for it is required of the Lord, at the hand of every steward, to render an account of his stewardship, both in time and in eternity.

4 For he who is faithful and wise in time is accounted worthy to inherit the mansions prepared for him of my Father.

5 Verily I say unto you, the elders of the church in this part of my vineyard shall render an account of their stewardship unto the bishop, who shall be appointed of me in this part of my vineyard.

6 These things shall be had on record, to be handed over unto the bishop in Zion.

7 And the duty of the bishop shall be made known by the commandments which have been given, and the voice of the conference.

8 And now, verily I say unto you, my servant Newel K. Whitney is the man who shall be appointed and ordained unto this power. This is the will of the Lord your God, your Redeemer. Even so. Amen.

Prior to this revelation, there was only one bishop in the Church, Edward Partridge (see Doctrine and Covenants 41:9). Bishop Partridge traveled to Missouri with Joseph Smith and was instructed to relocate there with his family (see Doctrine and Covenants 58:14). To assist the Saints in Kirtland, a new bishop was needed. Newel K. Whitney, who was earlier called to act as an agent for the Church (see Doctrine and Covenants 63:42–45), was called to serve as the bishop for the Kirtland area. These two leaders acted as regional bishops, with Bishop Partridge watching over the Church in Missouri and Bishop Whitney watching over the Church in Ohio.

Speaking generally to all Church members, the revelation declares that an accounting of each member's stewardship shall one day be required before the Lord. But every person's stewardship is not the same. Church leaders who are asked to preside over an area of geographical stewardship are called local and area authorities. Church leaders with no specific geographical stewardship are called General Authorities. Fathers and mothers hold a joint stewardship over their families, acting as co-presiding officers. Elder L. Tom Perry taught, "Since the beginning, God has instructed mankind that marriage should unite husband and wife together in unity. Therefore, there is not a president or a vice president in a family. The couple works together eternally for the good of the family. They are united together in word, in deed, and in action as they lead, guide, and direct their family unit. They are on equal footing."[3]

Again, regardless of age, callings, or marital status, everyone has a stewardship. Elder Wirthlin taught:

> Each of you has an eternal calling from which no Church officer has authority to release you. This is a calling given you by our Heavenly Father Himself. In this eternal calling, as with all other callings, you have a stewardship, and 'it is required of the Lord, at the hand of every steward, to render an account of his stewardship, both in time and in eternity' (Doctrine and Covenants 72:3). This most important stewardship is the glorious responsibility your Father in Heaven has given you to watch over and care for your own soul.[4]

9 The word of the Lord, in addition to the law which has been given, making known the duty of the bishop who has been ordained unto the church in this part of the vineyard, which is verily this—

10 To keep the Lord's storehouse; to receive the funds of the church in this part of the vineyard;

11 To take an account of the elders as before has been commanded; and to administer to their wants, who shall pay for that which they receive, inasmuch as they have wherewith to pay;

12 That this also may be consecrated to the good of the church, to the poor and needy.

13 And he who hath not wherewith to pay, an account shall be taken and handed over to the bishop of Zion, who shall pay the debt out of that which the Lord shall put into his hands.

14 And the labors of the faithful who labor in spiritual things, in administering the gospel and the things of the kingdom unto the church, and unto the world, shall answer the debt unto the bishop in Zion;

15 Thus it cometh out of the church, for according to the law every man that cometh up to Zion must lay all things before the bishop in Zion.

The responsibilities of the bishop are further explained here. Included among them is the responsibility to watch over the Lord's storehouse and look after the poor and the needy of the Church. This was especially fitting for Bishop Whitney, whose store, "N. K. Whitney & Co.," effectively functioned as the bishops' storehouse in Kirtland and the first such storehouse in the Church. The Church was small enough during this time that having two bishops facilitate the law of consecration and the temporal needs of the Church was sufficient.

As the role of bishop evolved within the Church, more bishops continued to be called to meet the needs of the growing membership. By 1842 the city of Nauvoo was organized into municipal "wards," and each ward was assigned a bishop who would watch over the temporal needs of the Saints in their respective location. Later, after the main body of the Church emigrated to the western United States, bishops were called to preside over wards in larger settlements, such as Salt Lake City, and in smaller settlements. During this time, the role of bishop was elevated to include the function of also acting as the presiding high priest of each ward, giving the bishops and their counselors responsibilities for the temporal and spiritual needs of the members in their wards.[5]

Today, just like in Bishop Whitney's day, bishops are called to teach the doctrine and principles relating to welfare and self-reliance and to direct the welfare work of the ward council. Bishops are told directly to "seek out the poor and provide assistance to those in need."[6] As welfare needs have increased, other officers of the Church have been directed to assist the bishops. President Eyring counseled, "It is the duty of the bishop to find and provide help to those who still need assistance after all they and their families can do. I found that the Lord sends the Holy Ghost to make it possible to 'seek, and ye shall find' in caring for the poor as He does in finding truth. But I also learned to involve the Relief Society president in the search. She may get the revelation before you do."[7]

16 And now, verily I say unto you, that as every elder in this part of the vineyard must give an account of his stewardship unto the bishop in this part of the vineyard—

17 A certificate from the judge or bishop in this part of the vineyard, unto the bishop in Zion, rendereth every man acceptable, and answereth all things, for an inheritance, and to be received as a wise steward and as a faithful laborer;

18 Otherwise he shall not be accepted of the bishop of Zion.

19 And now, verily I say unto you, let every elder who shall give an account unto the bishop of the church in this part of the vineyard be recommended by the church or churches, in which he labors, that he may render himself and his accounts approved in all things.

20 And again, let my servants who are appointed as stewards over the literary concerns of my church have claim for assistance upon the bishop or bishops in all things—

21 That the revelations may be published, and go forth unto the ends of the earth; that they also may obtain funds which shall benefit the church in all things;

22 That they also may render themselves approved in all things, and be accounted as wise stewards.

23 And now, behold, this shall be an ensample for all the extensive branches of my church, in whatsoever land they shall be established. And now I make an end of my sayings. Amen.

24 A few words in addition to the laws of the kingdom, respecting the members of the church—they that are appointed by the Holy Spirit to go up unto Zion, and they who are privileged to go up unto Zion—

25 Let them carry up unto the bishop a certificate from three elders of the church, or a certificate from the bishop;

26 Otherwise he who shall go up unto the land of Zion shall not be accounted as a wise steward. This is also an ensample. Amen.

The final part of the revelation emphasizes the role of the bishop as a judge in Israel. Part of the bishops' responsibilities, they were told, would be to provide certificates for worthy Church members who act as wise stewards over their own responsibilities. However, because there were only two bishops in the Church at the time, the Lord directed that these certificates could also be signed by three elders in good standing with the Church (see verse 25). Members were required to obtain a certificate of this kind before they were allowed to emigrate to Missouri to assist in building the city of Zion.

These certificates are the earliest forerunners of present-day temple recommends. At the time of this revelation, no temples had yet been built by the Church, and many years would pass before the full blessings of the temple would be revealed. But being found worthy to travel to Zion and to be declared a wise and faithful steward by a bishop of the Church carried its own blessings. The certificates and recommends issued by Church leaders then and now signify more than worthiness to travel to Zion or to enter the temple. In the ultimate sense, they certify our worthiness to enter the kingdom of God.

President Howard W. Hunter expressed the importance of a certification from a Church leader when he said, "Truly, the Lord desires that His people be a temple-motivated people. It would be the deepest desire of my heart to have every member of the Church be temple worthy. I would hope that every adult member would be worthy of—and carry—a current temple recommend, even if proximity to a temple does not allow immediate or frequent use of it."[8]

End Notes

1. Joseph Smith, in History, 1838–1856, volume A-1 [23 December 1805–30 August 1834], 176, josephsmithpapers.org.

2. See "Historical Introduction," Revelation, 4 December 1831–A [D&C 72:1–8], josephsmithpapers.org. See also "Historical Introduction," Revelation, 4 December 1831–A [D&C 72:9–23], josephsmithpapers.org; "Historical Introduction," Revelation, 4 December 1831–A [D&C 72:24–26], josephsmithpapers.org.

3. L. Tom Perry, "Fatherhood, an Eternal Calling," *Ensign* or *Liahona*, May 2004, 71.

4. Joseph B. Wirthlin, "True to the Truth," *Ensign*, May 1997, 16.

5. See William G. Hartley, "Bishop, History of the Office," in *My Fellow Servants: Essays on the History of the Priesthood* (Brigham City, UT: Brigham Distributing, 2010), 117–19.

6. *General Handbook: Serving in The Church of Jesus Christ of Latter-day Saints*, 6.4, Gospel Library.

7. Henry B. Eyring, "Opportunities to Do Good," *Ensign* or *Liahona*, May 2011, 25.

8. Howard W. Hunter, "The Great Symbol of Our Membership," *Ensign*, October 1994, 5.

Doctrine and Covenants Section 73

Continue the Work of Translation

Historical Context

IN A REVELATION RECEIVED IN DECEMBER 1831 (SEE DOCTRINE AND
Covenants 71), the Lord commanded Joseph Smith and Sidney Rigdon
to counter the work of disaffected members like Ezra Booth and Symonds
Rider. Assisted by several elders of the Church, Joseph and Sidney were
largely successful in dispelling the spread of such falsehoods. Booth and
Rider had declined Sidney Rigdon's invitation to, in a public meeting, de-
fend their claims. After working to quell such opposition, Joseph and Sidney
then received a revelation commanding them to return to their work of
translating the Bible. Joseph Smith gave the following account of events in
his 1838 history, writing:

> Myself and Elder [Sidney] Rigdon continued to preach in Shalersville,
> Ravenna, and other places, setting forth the truth; vindicating the cause
> of our Redeemer; shewing that the day of vengeance was coming upon

this generation like a thief in the night: that prejudice, blindness, and darkness, filled the minds of many, and caused them to persecute the true church, and reject the true light: by which means we did much towards allaying the excited feelings which were growing out of the scandalous letters then being published in the "Ohio Star," at Ravenna, by the before mentioned apostate Ezra Booth. On the 10th of January I received the following [Doctrine and Covenants 73].[1]

$\mathcal{V}$erse-by-$\mathcal{V}$erse $\mathcal{C}$ommentary

1 For verily, thus saith the Lord, it is expedient in me that they should continue preaching the gospel, and in exhortation to the churches in the regions round about, until conference;

2 And then, behold, it shall be made known unto them, by the voice of the conference, their several missions.

3 Now, verily I say unto you my servants, Joseph Smith, Jun., and Sidney Rigdon, saith the Lord, it is expedient to translate again;

4 And, inasmuch as it is practicable, to preach in the regions round about until conference; and after that it is expedient to continue the work of translation until it be finished.

5 And let this be a pattern unto the elders until further knowledge, even as it is written.

6 Now I give no more unto you at this time. Gird up your loins and be sober. Even so. Amen.

After a month of preaching throughout the region, Joseph and Sidney had much success thwarting the work of Ezra Booth, Symonds Rider, and others seeking to injure the work of the Church. When Ezra Booth refused to publicly debate Sidney Rigdon, the *Ohio Star* ceased publishing his letters criticizing the Church. With their work accomplished, Joseph and Sidney were commanded to return to their translation of the Bible. A few weeks after returning to this task, Joseph and Sidney read John 5:29, and doing so led to their vision of the three degrees of glory (see Doctrine and Covenants 76:15–19). The eighteen months following this revelation were filled with many revelations and other special events. During this time, twenty-three revelations were received (which are now found in Doctrine and Covenants 73–96). Among these are some of the most doctrinally important revelations given in this dispensation, including Doctrine and Covenants 76, 84, 88, and 93.

While answering their enemies was important for Joseph Smith and the other leaders of the Church, studying the scriptures brought the most fruitful moments of the Restoration. Translating the Bible helped the Prophet and his associates look deeply at every word and ponder the meanings. Such pondering opened the door to further revelation and instruction. Speaking of the Bible, Joseph Smith later said that we "can mark the power of Omnipotence inscribed upon the heavens, can also see His own hand-writing in the sacred volume; and he who reads it oftenest will like it best, and he who is acquainted with it, will know the hand wherever he can see it."[2]

Joseph did not see the Bible as a dead collection of writings but as a portal to living revelation. One reminiscence records him saying, "You may hug up to yourselves the Bible, but, except through faith in it you get revelation for yourself, the Bible will profit you but little."[3]

End Notes

1. Joseph Smith, in History, 1838–1856, volume A-1 [23 December 1805–30 August 1834], 179, josephsmithpapers.org. See also "Historical Introduction," to Revelation, 4 December 1831–A [D&C 72:1–8]; Revelation, 4 December 1831–A [D&C 72:9–23]; and Revelation, 4 December 1831–A [D&C 72:24–26], josephsmithpapers.org.
2. Letter to the Church, circa March 1834, 142, josephsmithpapers.org.
3. David Osborn's recollection of an 1837 statement, published in the *Juvenile Instructor,* *Mar.* 15, 1892. See *The Teachings of Joseph Smith,* ed. Larry E. Dahl, and Donald Q. Cannon (Salt Lake City, UT: Bookcraft, 1997), 73.

$\mathcal{D}$octrine and $\mathcal{C}$ovenants Section 74

Now They Are Holy

$\mathcal{H}$istorical $\mathcal{C}$ontext

DOCTRINE AND COVENANTS 74 PROVIDES AN EXPLANATION OF SCRIPTURE, specifically 1 Corinthians 7:14. This biblical passage was often used to justify infant baptism, a practice condemned in the Book of Mormon (see Moroni 8:9). The placement of Doctrine and Covenants 74 makes it seem as though it was received in early 1832 when Joseph Smith was working on translating the New Testament; however, this revelation likely came much earlier, probably in the spring of 1830. When John Whitmer, the Church Historian, copied the revelation into Revelation Book 1, he dated it "1830" and gave it the title "Explanation of Scripture."[1] This revelation was not included in the 1833 Book of Commandments, and when it was inserted into the 1835 Doctrine and Covenants, no date was provided.[2]

When Joseph Smith began his history in 1838, the editors of that work mistakenly assumed that this revelation was given around the time that

Joseph Smith recommenced his work on translating the New Testament, in early 1832.[3] However, by 1832, John Whitmer had already copied the revelation into Revelation Book 1, which he took with him when he departed for Missouri in late 1831. While we do not know the exact date of the revelation, John Whitmer's original dating suggests it was given in New York before Joseph Smith was commanded to move to Ohio (Doctrine and Covenants 37). The Lord likely revealed this scripture in response to discussions that members were having with new converts about infant baptism.[4] The updated information about the origins of the revelation first appeared in the 2013 edition of the Doctrine and Covenants.[5]

Verse-by-Verse Commentary

1 For the unbelieving husband is sanctified by the wife, and the unbelieving wife is sanctified by the husband; else were your children unclean, but now are they holy.

2 Now, in the days of the apostles the law of circumcision was had among all the Jews who believed not the gospel of Jesus Christ.

3 And it came to pass that there arose a great contention among the people concerning the law of circumcision, for the unbelieving husband was desirous that his children should be circumcised and become subject to the law of Moses, which law was fulfilled.

4 And it came to pass that the children, being brought up in subjection to the law of Moses, gave heed to the traditions of their fathers and believed not the gospel of Christ, wherein they became unholy.

5 Wherefore, for this cause the apostle wrote unto the church, giving unto them a commandment, not of the Lord, but of himself, that a believer should not be united to an unbeliever; except the law of Moses should be done away among them,

This revelation deals with a passage from the New Testament that can be difficult for modern readers to understand. In context, Paul is commenting on the issue of whether a woman who is married to a nonbeliever should continue in the marriage. Paul felt that the believing partner should not initiate a divorce, but if the unbelieving partner desired to end the marriage, the believer should not feel bound to remain in the union. Paul's reasoning for this was summarized as "For how do you know, wife, that you will not save your husband? Or how do you know, husband, that you will not save your wife?"[6]

The issue of a mixed-faith marriage becomes especially delicate when children are introduced. Paul's use of the word *unclean* in 1 Corinthians 7 refers to the children not being brought up in a proper relationship with the Lord. According to Paul, a sanctifying relationship with God is more likely to develop among children with a believing parent in the home because regardless of the beliefs of one's spouse, the principles of a happy family life are the same: "Successful marriages and families are established and maintained on principles of faith, prayer, repentance, forgiveness, respect, love, compassion, work, and wholesome recreational activities."[7]

However, Paul also recognized that, though the principles of a happy family are the same, believers need to establish boundaries regarding who they will marry. For example, bringing up a child within the law of Moses and the law of Christ was not possible, for the laws were often contradictory. Therefore, Paul counseled that Christian believers should not marry Jewish believers unless they agreed not to force their children to live the law of Moses. The revelation notes that this counsel from Paul came "not of the Lord, but of himself" (Doctrine and Covenants 74:5). This does not mean that Paul was contradicting the will of the Lord, but rather that he was providing counsel of his own accord. Still, it is wise for Church members who are in mixed-faith marriages to discuss and set clear expectations with their spouses about the religious upbringing of their children. Lack of communication on this matter can be the source of much heartache for those in mixed-faith marriages.

> 6 That their children might remain without circumcision; and that the tradition might be done away, which saith that little children are unholy; for it was had among the Jews;
>
> 7 But little children are holy, being sanctified through the atonement of Jesus Christ; and this is what the scriptures mean.

Paul's teachings in this passage in Corinthians were often used to support the doctrine of infant baptism. According to one modern theologian, "With the exception of the Scripture passage where Jesus blesses little children no passage has been laid under more laborious contribution to serve the cause of infant baptism than this one [1 Corinthians 7:14]."[8] The teaching that young children who had not yet reached the age of accountability (see Doctrine and Covenants 68:27) should be baptized is strongly refuted in scripture. The Book of Mormon prophet Mormon called infant baptism a "gross error" and declared that "it is solemn mockery before God, that ye should baptize little children" (Moroni 8:6, 9).

Around the time this revelation was likely received, the Lord instructed the Church that children should be blessed in the Church but that "no one can be received into the church of Christ unless he has arrived unto the years of accountability before God, and is capable of repentance" (Doctrine and Covenants 20:70–71). Joseph Smith maintained this teaching throughout his life. In an 1842 discourse he declared, "The doctrine of Baptizing children, or sprinkling them, or they must welter in hell is a doctrine not true, not supported in Holy writ, and is not consistent with the character of God. All children are redeemed by the blood of Jesus Christ, and the moment that children leave this world they are taken to the bosom of Abraham."[9]

End Notes

1. Revelation Book 1, 60, josephsmithpapers.org.
2. See Doctrine and Covenants, 1835, Section LXXIII, 202, josephsmithpapers.org.
3. See History, 1838–1856, volume A-1 [23 December 1805–30 August 1834], 178, josephsmithpapers.org.
4. See "Historical Introduction," Explanation of Scripture, 1830 [D&C 74], footnote 5, josephsmithpapers.org.
5. See "Historical Introduction," Explanation of Scripture, 1830 [D&C 74]
6. Thomas A. Wayment, "1 Corinthians 7:14," in *The New Testament: A Translation for Latter-day Saints* (Salt Lake City, UT: Deseret Book, 2018).
7. Family Proclamation, 1995, paragraph 7.
8. Paul K. Jewett, *Infant Baptism and the Covenant of Grace* (Grand Rapids, MI: Wm. B. Eerdmans-Lightning Source, 1978), 122, quoted in Explanation of Scripture, 1830 [D&C 74], footnote 1, josephsmithpapers.org.
9. *Times and Seasons,* 15 April 1842, 751, josephsmithpapers.org.

End Notes

Doctrine and Covenants Section 75

Let Every Man Be Diligent in All Things

Historical Context

ON JANUARY 25, 1832, A GENERAL CONFERENCE OF THE CHURCH WAS HELD near Amherst, Ohio. The conference was attended by "between 70 and 80 official characters" from various locations.[1] At the conference, several important events took place. First, Orson Pratt was appointed as president of the elders. Next, Joseph Smith was ordained as the "President of the High Priesthood," heeding the instructions given in revelation a few months prior that "one be appointed of the high priesthood to preside over the priesthood of the Church."[2]

There are no known minutes of this conference, but a later account in Joseph Smith's history recorded, "At this conference much harmony prevailed, and considerable business was done to advance the kingdom and promulgate the gospel to the inhabitants of the surrounding Country. The Elders seemed anxious for me to enquire of the Lord, that they might know his will, or learn what would be most pleasing to him, for them to do, in order to bring men to a sense of their condition: for, as it was written, all men had gone out of the way, so that none doth good; no, not one. I enquired and received the following [Doctrine and Covenants 75].”[3]

This section, section 75, is made up of two separate revelations given at the conference, comprising verses 1–22 and 23–36. A copy of the of revelations kept by Newel K. Whitney and written in Sidney Rigdon's handwriting records it as two different revelations. Another collection of revelations kept by Samuel Smith and Orson Hyde, however, includes only the first revelation.[4] In Revelation Book 1, Church Historian John Whitmer recorded both as separate revelations given on the same day.[5] When the revelations were published in the 1835 Doctrine and Covenants, they were combined into one section and have been combined as such ever since.[6]

At least one of the revelations was received in the presence of the entire conference. Orson Pratt said that the revelation was received "in the presence of the whole assembly."[7] Another attendee of the conference, Edson Barney, said that Sidney Rigdon wrote the revelation as it was dictated by Joseph Smith.[8] This was one of many occasions during which groups of people witnessed Joseph Smith receiving a revelation (see commentary for Doctrine and Covenants 50).[9]

Verse-by-Verse Commentary

1 Verily, verily, I say unto you, I who speak even by the voice of my Spirit, even Alpha and Omega, your Lord and your God—

2 Hearken, O ye who have given your names to go forth to proclaim my gospel, and to prune my vineyard.

3 Behold, I say unto you that it is my will that you should go forth and not tarry, neither be idle but labor with your might—

4 Lifting up your voices as with the sound of a trump, proclaiming the truth according to the revelations and commandments which I have given you.

5 And thus, if ye are faithful ye shall be laden with many sheaves, and crowned with honor, and glory, and immortality, and eternal life.

These scriptures reiterate that it is important to labor diligently to preach the gospel. They further emphasize the importance of "proclaiming the truth according to the revelations and commandments which I have given unto you" (verse 4). Such an emphasis on the commandments and revelations given in our time highlights the importance of sharing what is unique about our message. There is much to be gained from building on common beliefs with other faiths, but we also need to emphasize why we are different from those of other faiths.

One key difference between our faith and other faiths is the Restoration of the gospel of Jesus Christ. During a meeting held in Philadelphia, Pennsylvania, in January 1840, Parley P. Pratt recorded an experience that underlines the importance of emphasizing the Restoration in our teaching. According to Elder Pratt:

> A very large church was opened for him [Joseph Smith] to preach in, and about three thousand people assembled to hear him. Brother Rigdon spoke first, and dwelt on the Gospel, illustrating his doctrine by the Bible. When he was through, Brother Joseph arose like a lion about to roar; and being full of the Holy Ghost, spoke in great power, bearing testimony of the visions he had seen, the ministering of angels which he had enjoyed; and how he had found the plates of the Book of Mormon, and translated them by the gift and power of God. He commenced by saying: "If nobody else had the courage to testify of so glorious a message from Heaven, and of the finding of so glorious a record, he felt to do it in justice to the people, and leave the event with God.[10]

Elder Pratt added, "The entire congregation were astounded; electrified, as it were, and overwhelmed with the sense of the truth and power by which he spoke, and the wonders which he related. A lasting impression was made; many souls were gathered into the fold."[11]

As illustrated in the way Joseph Smith taught the congregation in Philadelphia, we have an obligation to bear witness of the Restoration of Christ's gospel. Outreach and understanding toward other faiths will always be an important part of our work, but we also have a solemn charge to boldly proclaim the Restoration of the gospel of Jesus Christ in the latter days through the Prophet Joseph Smith.

> 6 Therefore, verily I say unto my servant William E. McLellin, I revoke the commission which I gave unto him to go unto the eastern countries;

7 And I give unto him a new commission and a new commandment, in the which I, the Lord, chasten him for the murmurings of his heart;

8 And he sinned; nevertheless, I forgive him and say unto him again, Go ye into the south countries.

9 And let my servant Luke Johnson go with him, and proclaim the things which I have commanded them—

10 Calling on the name of the Lord for the Comforter, which shall teach them all things that are expedient for them—

11 Praying always that they faint not; and inasmuch as they do this, I will be with them even unto the end.

12 Behold, this is the will of the Lord your God concerning you. Even so. Amen.

The second part of this revelation is directed toward William E. McLellin, who had previously been called to serve a mission with Samuel Smith (see Doctrine and Covenants 68:7–8). The pair left to preach in eastern Ohio on November 16, 1831. On December 15, McLellin fell ill with a violent cold that confined him to bed. The elders' mission was cut short, and McLellin returned to Hiram, Ohio, on December 29, just forty-four days after his mission began. When Samuel Smith wrote about this brief term in the mission field, he commented, "We went a short distance, but because of disobedience, our way was hedged up before us."[12] Samuel never elaborated on what the nature of the disobedience was, but in this revelation, McLellin was rebuked for "the murmurings of his heart" (verse 7). He was then assigned to a new field of labor with Luke Johnson instead of with Samuel Smith.

Brother McLellin was not cut off from the Lord because of his disobedience or illness. In fact, during the time between returning from his first mission and receiving this revelation, he had an extraordinary experience. Years after this time, Brother McLellin told Orson Pratt that on January 18, 1832, about a week before Doctrine and Covenants section 75 was given, he found himself alone with Joseph Smith in the translating room of the Johnson home. William asked Joseph to inquire of the Lord regarding an important matter, and Joseph replied, "Do you inquire of God [?] . . . I will pray for you that you may obtain." William complied with the Prophet's instructions, later recalling, "I did receive and I wrote it. And when I read it to him [Joseph Smith] he shed tears of joy and said to me, 'Brother William, that is the mind of the will of God, and as much a revelation as I ever received in my life. You have written it by the spirit of inspiration.'"[13] William later reflected:

> I was never vain enough to suppose that "I was planted in Joseph's stead," nor that it was my duty or privilege to receive by revelation laws or regulations for the whole church. I knew better. But at that time I saw, heard, and felt what I wrote. There and then I learned a principle, and was put in possession of a power that I shall never forget. I learned to know the voice of the Spirit of God clothed in words. And if I had heeded its voice from that day to this, I should have missed many—very many difficulties through which I have passed.[14]

Serving as a coda to William's earlier experience when he was challenged by the Lord to write scripture but failed, this episode shows the tender mercy of God toward His children. Even a troubled soul like William McLellin was inspired to learn that the Lord knew him and his desires (see commentary for Doctrine and Covenants 67).

> 13 And again, verily thus saith the Lord, let my servant Orson Hyde and my servant Samuel H. Smith take their journey into the eastern countries, and proclaim the things which I have commanded them; and inasmuch as they are faithful, lo, I will be with them even unto the end.
>
> 14 And again, verily I say unto my servant Lyman Johnson, and unto my servant Orson Pratt, they shall also take their journey into the eastern countries; and behold, and lo, I am with them also, even unto the end.
>
> 15 And again, I say unto my servant Asa Dodds, and unto my servant Calves Wilson, that they also shall take their journey unto the western countries, and proclaim my gospel, even as I have commanded them.
>
> 16 And he who is faithful shall overcome all things, and shall be lifted up at the last day.
>
> 17 And again, I say unto my servant Major N. Ashley, and my servant Burr Riggs, let them take their journey also into the south country.

18 Yea, let all those take their journey, as I have commanded them, going from house to house, and from village to village, and from city to city.

19 And in whatsoever house ye enter, and they receive you, leave your blessing upon that house.

20 And in whatsoever house ye enter, and they receive you not, ye shall depart speedily from that house, and shake off the dust of your feet as a testimony against them.

21 And you shall be filled with joy and gladness; and know this, that in the day of judgment you shall be judges of that house, and condemn them;

22 And it shall be more tolerable for the heathen in the day of judgment, than for that house; therefore, gird up your loins and be faithful, and ye shall overcome all things, and be lifted up at the last day. Even so. Amen.

In these commandments to various elders, the Lord again emphasizes the elders' different roles in acting as judges of the people and instructs them to shake the dust off their feet as a testimony against those who reject them (see Doctrine and Covenants 24:15–16). Along with this, He also instructs the elders to bless the homes that they enter. Those commissioned by the Church have an obligation to teach, judge, *and* bless the homes they visit.

An experience shared by William F. Cahoon illustrates how these duties are carried out. When he was just seventeen years old, Cahoon was called as a teacher and asked to visit the homes of the Saints. The family of Joseph Smith was among those he was asked to visit. After receiving this young man warmly into his home, Joseph said, "Brother William, I submit myself and my family into your hands . . . ask all the questions you feel like." William later recalled, "By this time my fears and trembling had ceased and I said, 'Brother Joseph are you trying to live your religion?' He answered 'Yes.' I then said 'Do you pray in your family?' He said 'Yes.' 'Do you teach your family the principles of the gospel?' He replied 'Yes, I am trying to do it.' 'Do you ask a blessing on your food?' He answered 'Yes.' 'Are you trying to live in peace and harmony with all your family?' He said that he was."

William then turned to Emma Smith and said, "'Sister Emma, are you trying to live your religion? Do you teach your children to obey their parents? Do you try to teach them to pray?' To all these questions she answered

'Yes, I am trying to do so.' I then turned to Joseph and said, 'I am now through with my questions as a teacher; and now if you have any instructions to give, I shall be happy to receive them.' He said 'God bless you, Brother William; and if you are humble and faithful, you shall have power to settle all difficulties that may come before you in the capacity of a teacher.' I then left my parting blessing upon him and his family, as a teacher, and took my departure."[15]

23 And again, thus saith the Lord unto you, O ye elders of my church, who have given your names that you might know his will concerning you—

24 Behold, I say unto you, that it is the duty of the church to assist in supporting the families of those, and also to support the families of those who are called and must needs be sent unto the world to proclaim the gospel unto the world.

25 Wherefore, I, the Lord, give unto you this commandment, that ye obtain places for your families, inasmuch as your brethren are willing to open their hearts.

26 And let all such as can obtain places for their families, and support of the church for them, not fail to go into the world, whether to the east or to the west, or to the north, or to the south.

27 Let them ask and they shall receive, knock and it shall be opened unto them, and be made known from on high, even by the Comforter, whither they shall go.

28 And again, verily I say unto you, that every man who is obliged to provide for his own family, let him provide, and he shall in nowise lose his crown; and let him labor in the church.

29 Let every man be diligent in all things. And the idler shall not have place in the church, except he repent and mend his ways.

30 Wherefore, let my servant Simeon Carter and my servant Emer Harris be united in the ministry;

31 And also my servant Ezra Thayre and my servant Thomas B. Marsh;

32 Also my servant Hyrum Smith and my servant Reynolds Cahoon;

33 And also my servant Daniel Stanton and my servant Seymour Brunson;

34 And also my servant Sylvester Smith and my servant Gideon Carter;

35 And also my servant Ruggles Eames and my servant Stephen Burnett;

36 And also my servant Micah B. Welton and also my servant Eden Smith. Even so. Amen.

In the final instructions given here, the Lord directs the elders to ensure their families are taken care of before they depart on their missions. The Lord teaches that "every man is obliged to provide for his own family" (verse 28). Both ancient and modern prophets have taught that fathers must fulfill their duties to "provide the necessities of life and protection for their families."[16] Paul, writing to Timothy, declared, "But if any provide not for his own, and specially for those of his own house, he hath denied the faith, and is worse than an infidel" (1 Timothy 5:8).

In our time, Elder Christofferson has taught that "breadwinning is a consecrated activity." He added, "Providing for one's family, although it generally requires time away from the family, is not inconsistent with fatherhood—it is the essence of being a good father. 'Work and family are overlapping domains.' This, of course, does not justify a man who neglects his family for his career or, at the other extreme, one who will not exert himself and is content to shift his responsibility to others."[17]

End Notes

1. "Historical Introduction," Revelation, 25 January 1832–A [D&C 75:1–22], footnote 3, josephsmithpapers.org.

2. Revelation, 11 November 1831–B [D&C 107 (partial)], 122, josephsmithpapers.org.

3. Joseph Smith, in *History of the Church*, 1:242–43.

4. See Revelation, 25 January 1832–A [D&C 75:1–22], josephsmithpapers.org.

5. See Revelation Book 1, 131, josephsmithpapers.org.

6. See Doctrine and Covenants, 1835, Section LXXXVII, 221, josephsmithpapers.org.

7. "Historical Introduction," Revelation, 25 January 1832–A [D&C 75:1–22], footnote 12, josephsmithpapers.org.

8. See "Prophet Joseph's Birthday," Saint George Utah Stake, General Minutes, Dec. 23, 1880. It is possible that Barney's memory was faulty and that Frederick G. Williams initially inscribed the revelation.

9. See "Historical Introduction," Revelation, 25 January 1832–A [D&C 75:1–22] josephsmithpapers.org. See also "Historical Introduction," Revelation, 25 January 1832–A [D&C 75:23–36], josephsmithpapers.org.

10. Parley P. Pratt, *Autobiography of Parley P. Pratt (Revised and Enhanced)* (Salt Lake City, UT: Deseret Book, 2000), 298–299.

11. Parley P. Pratt, *Autobiography of Parley P. Pratt*, 362.

12. William McLellin, *The Journals of William E. McLellin, 1831-1836*, ed. Jan Shipps and John Welch (Provo, UT: Brigham Young University Studies, 1994), 300.

13. McLellin, *The Journals of William E. McLellin*, 301.

14. McLellin, *The Journals of William E. McLellin*, 301.

15. *Juvenile Instructor* 27 (15 August 1892): 492–93.

16. "The Family: A Proclamation to the World," Gospel Library.

17. D. Todd Christofferson, "Fathers," *Ensign* or *Liahona*, May 2016, 95.

$\mathcal{D}$octrine and $\mathcal{C}$ovenants
Section 76
He Lives!

$\mathcal{H}$istorical $\mathcal{C}$ontext

No REVELATION GIVEN IN THIS DISPENSATION MORE FULLY DEMONSTRATES the importance of Joseph Smith's translation of the Bible than does Doctrine and Covenants 76. One simple verse, John 5:29, sparked this panoramic vision of the afterlife and the final state of men and women. An introductory note in the earliest manuscript of the vision summarizes it as "concerning the church of the first born and concerning the economy of God and his vast creation throughout all eternity."[1] A later revelation defined the "church of the Firstborn" as "all those who are begotten through me [Jesus Christ]" and who "are partakers of the glory of the same" (Doctrine and Covenants 93:22). An 1828 dictionary defines *economy* as "primarily, the management, regulation and government of a family or the concerns of a household."[2] The aim of the vision is nothing less than to show the final fate of the righteous and to show how God governs and regulates His family.

Most of the information we know about how the vision was received comes from Philo Dibble, who was present while the vision was received in the John Johnson home. Elder Dibble relates "that Joseph and Sidney were in the spirit and saw the heavens open, there were other men in the room, perhaps twelve, among whom I was one during a part of the time—probably two-thirds of the time,—I saw the glory and felt the power but did not see the vision." Philo recorded that "Joseph would, at intervals, say: 'What do I see?' as one might say while looking out the window and beholding what all in the room could not see. Then he would relate what he had seen or what he was looking at. Then Sidney replied, 'I see the same.' Presently Sidney would say 'what do I see?' and would repeat what he had seen or was seeing, and Joseph would reply, 'I see the same.'"[3] Philo continued, saying:

> This manner of conversation was repeated at short intervals to the end of the vision, and during the whole time not a word was spoken by any other person. Not a sound nor motion made by anyone but Joseph and Sidney, and it seemed to me that they never moved a joint or limb during the time I was there, which I think was over an hour, and to the end of the vision. Joseph sat firmly and calmly all the time in the midst of a magnificent glory, but Sidney sat limp and pale, apparently as limber as a rag, observing which, Joseph remarked, smilingly, "Sidney is not used to it as I am."[4]

Philo may not have been present for the entirety of the vision experience, but he did note changes in Joseph Smith's appearance during the time of the vision. In another recollection he said, "I arrived at Father Johnson's just as Joseph and Sidney were coming out of the vision alluded to in the Book of Doctrine and Covenants, in which mention is made of the three degrees of glories. Joseph wore black clothes, but at this time seemed to be dressed in an element of glorious white, and his face shone as if it were transparent, but I did not see the same glory attending Sidney."[5]

At least four different times in the vision, Joseph Smith and Sidney Rigdon were commanded to write what they saw (see verses 28, 49, 80, 113). They recorded the vision shortly after receiving it and signed both of their names at the end. Sidney signed first, indicating that he was most likely the scribe; however, the earliest copy of the vision we have is in the handwriting of Frederick G. Williams. In his own history Joseph Smith introduced the vision by writing, "From sundry revelations which had been received, it was apparent that many important points, touching the Salvation of man, had been taken from the Bible, or lost before it was compiled. It appeared self-evident from what truths were left, that if God rewarded everyone according to the deeds done in the body, the term 'heaven,' as intended for the Saints eternal home, must include more kingdoms than one. Accordingly, on the 16th of February, 1832. while translating St John's Gospel, myself and Elder [Sidney] Rigdon Saw the following [Doctrine and Covenants 76]."[6]

Verse-by-Verse Commentary

1 Hear, O ye heavens, and give ear, O earth, and rejoice ye inhabitants thereof, for the Lord is God, and beside him there is no Savior.

2 Great is his wisdom, marvelous are his ways, and the extent of his doings none can find out.

3 His purposes fail not, neither are there any who can stay his hand.

4 From eternity to eternity he is the same, and his years never fail.

The 1832 vision given to Joseph Smith is centered first and foremost on Jesus Christ and His Resurrection. The vision begins by proclaiming that Christ is the only Savior of mankind and the only source of salvation for men and women. The same emphasis is found throughout all of the revelations of the Restoration, which enlarge and enlighten our understanding of the role of Jesus Christ as our Savior.

When it comes to understanding the doctrinal content of the vision itself, it helps to reference a commentary of sorts that Joseph Smith provided through an exchange with W. W. Phelps almost a decade after the vision was given. Phelps published a poem in the Church newspaper, the *Times and Seasons*, entitled "Vade Mecum" ("Go With Me"). Phelps's poem invited the Prophet to provide more details about the visions he saw of the eternal worlds. It read in part:

Go with me, will you go to the mansions above,
Where the bliss, and the knowledge, the light, and the love,
And the glory of God do eternally be?—
Death, the wages of sin, is not there. Go with me.[7]

In response to "Vade Mecum," another poem was published entitled "The Answer," which is a poetic version of the vision. There is some debate over who authored "The Answer."[8] It is likely that W. W. Phelps composed the poem in collaboration with Joseph Smith, who signed his name at the end of "The Answer." Because of Joseph Smith's involvement, "The Answer" effectively functions as a commentary on the 1832 vision; in many places it clarifies and expands certain doctrinal points made in the vision. For example, verse 4 of section 76, which originally reads "From eternity to eternity he is the same, and his years never fail," was expanded to read:

> His throne is the heavens, his life time is all
> Of eternity *now*, and eternity *then*;
> His union is power, and none stays his hand,—
> The Alpha, Omega, for ever: Amen.[9]

Throughout our exploration of the 1832 vision, we will refer back to Joseph Smith and W. W. Phelps's collaboration to provide a clearer understanding of the doctrines taught in section 76.

> 5 For thus saith the Lord—I, the Lord, am merciful and gracious unto those who fear me, and delight to honor those who serve me in righteousness and in truth unto the end.
>
> 6 Great shall be their reward and eternal shall be their glory.
>
> 7 And to them will I reveal all mysteries, yea, all the hidden mysteries of my kingdom from days of old, and for ages to come, will I make known unto them the good pleasure of my will concerning all things pertaining to my kingdom.
>
> 8 Yea, even the wonders of eternity shall they know, and things to come will I show them, even the things of many generations.
>
> 9 And their wisdom shall be great, and their understanding reach to heaven; and before them the wisdom of the wise shall perish, and the understanding of the prudent shall come to naught.
>
> 10 For by my Spirit will I enlighten them, and by my power will I make known unto them the secrets of my will—yea, even those things which eye has not seen, nor ear heard, nor yet entered into the heart of man.

In Joseph Smith's time, one of the definitions used for the word *mystery* was "any thing in the character or attributes of God, or in the economy of divine providence, which is not revealed to man."[10] Near the beginning and end of the vision, all men and women are invited to receive a testimony, and committed disciples are invited to receive their own revelation of the truths found within. Near the end of the vision, Joseph and Sidney wrote that the things they saw "are only to be seen and understood by the power of the Holy Spirit, which God bestows on those who love him, and purify themselves before him" (see Doctrine and Covenants 76:116).

This promise is extended to every person who chooses to qualify to know the mysteries of God. The poetic form of the vision makes this point even more clear:

> From the council in Kolob, to time on the earth.
> And for ages to come unto them I will show
> My pleasure & will, what my kingdom will do:
> Eternity's wonders they truly shall know.[11]

One very direct way God reveals His mysteries is by showing the different degrees of glory to those who qualify to make eternal covenants with God. In the ordinances of the temple endowment, which were fully revealed almost a decade after the 1832 vision was given, disciples who qualify for the blessings of the temple are also given a tour through the different degrees of glory and receive a broadened understanding of the work of God.

> 11 We, Joseph Smith, Jun., and Sidney Rigdon, being in the Spirit on the sixteenth day of February, in the year of our Lord one thousand eight hundred and thirty-two—
>
> 12 By the power of the Spirit our eyes were opened and our understandings were enlightened, so as to see and understand the things of God—
>
> 13 Even those things which were from the beginning before the world was, which were ordained of the Father, through his Only Begotten Son, who was in the bosom of the Father, even from the beginning;
>
> 14 Of whom we bear record; and the record which we bear is the fulness of the gospel of Jesus Christ, who is the Son, whom we saw and with whom we conversed in the heavenly vision.

15 For while we were doing the work of translation, which the Lord had appointed unto us, we came to the twenty-ninth verse of the fifth chapter of John, which was given unto us as follows—

16 Speaking of the resurrection of the dead, concerning those who shall hear the voice of the Son of Man:

17 And shall come forth; they who have done good, in the resurrection of the just; and they who have done evil, in the resurrection of the unjust.

The vision found in Doctrine and Covenants 76 is in reality a series of visions in which Joseph and Sidney were taken on a guided tour of eternity. Along the way, in their vision of the Father and the Son, they saw the highest potential of each man and woman personified (see verses 19–24). In the next vision, they were shown the fall of Lucifer and the depths of depravity to which a son of God can fall (see verses 25–29). They then witnessed the terrible fate of those who came to earth but then chose to follow Satan into a state of perdition or ruin (see verses 30–38; 43–49). From the depths of perdition they then ascended into the celestial kingdom, seeing the fate of the righteous and valiant sons and daughters of God with their accompanying glory (see verses 50–70, 92–96). Joseph and Sidney then saw the terrestrial glory, filled with the honorable but not valiant people of the world (see verses 71–80). Finally, they saw a vision of the telestial glory, where those who were neither valiant nor honorable dwell (see verses 81–86).

At the end of the vision, each of the three degrees of glory is further explained, and insight is given into how they are governed and administered (see verses 87–113). The vision then closes by reiterating the promise made at its opening, that all those who qualify can see and understand the same things that Joseph and Sidney saw (see verses 114–119). This panoramic view of the afterlife came from the two men pondering the meaning of John 5:29. All of this knowledge grew from a sincere question of the soul asked about a single verse of scripture.

18 Now this caused us to marvel, for it was given unto us of the Spirit.

19 And while we meditated upon these things, the Lord touched the eyes of our understandings and they were opened, and the glory of the Lord shone round about.

20 And we beheld the glory of the Son, on the right hand of the Father, and received of his fulness;

21 And saw the holy angels, and them who are sanctified before his throne, worshiping God, and the Lamb, who worship him forever and ever.

22 And now, after the many testimonies which have been given of him, this is the testimony, last of all, which we give of him: That he lives!

23 For we saw him, even on the right hand of God; and we heard the voice bearing record that he is the Only Begotten of the Father—

24 That by him, and through him, and of him, the worlds are and were created, and the inhabitants thereof are begotten sons and daughters unto God.

The first vision Joseph and Sidney received was of the Father, with the Son standing at His right hand. It is worth noting that this was the first time Joseph Smith recorded a vision he had of the Father and the Son. The first written account of Joseph's earliest vision of them, which took place in 1820, was written down in the summer of 1832, several months after this vision was recorded. The beautiful and profound testimony in section 76 of the living Christ remains one of the most frequently shared and emphasized testimonies of Joseph Smith and Sidney Rigdon. It forms a significant portion of "The Living Christ," another testimony published by the First Presidency and Quorum of the Twelve Apostles in 2000.[12]

This vision also adds to our understanding of the infinite nature of Christ's Atonement. It was revealed to Joseph Smith in 1830 that Jesus Christ, under the direction of the Father, created "worlds without number" (Moses 1:29–35). Here it is revealed that Christ is not only the Creator of those worlds but also their Redeemer. The revelation states that through Christ, the "worlds" are and were created and that "the inhabitants thereof are begotten sons and daughters unto God" (verse 24). The poetic version of the vision is even clearer on this point, stating:

By him, of him, and through him, the worlds were all made,
Even all that career in the heavens so broad,
Whose inhabitants, too, from the first to the last,
Are sav'd by the very same Saviour of ours;

And, of course, are begotten God's daughters and sons,
By the very same truths, and the very same pow'rs.[13]

This stanza of the poem suggests that not only is the Savior the same on the other worlds, but the "very same truths, and the very same pow'rs"—meaning the priesthood, the ordinances, and the covenants—are the same on the other worlds. Undoubtedly, the other worlds have their own witnesses of Jesus Christ, but the gospel, the good news of Christ, is universal throughout all the worlds.

> 25 And this we saw also, and bear record, that an angel of God who was in authority in the presence of God, who rebelled against the Only Begotten Son whom the Father loved and who was in the bosom of the Father, was thrust down from the presence of God and the Son,
>
> 26 And was called Perdition, for the heavens wept over him—he was Lucifer, a son of the morning.
>
> 27 And we beheld, and lo, he is fallen! is fallen, even a son of the morning!
>
> 28 And while we were yet in the Spirit, the Lord commanded us that we should write the vision; for we beheld Satan, that old serpent, even the devil, who rebelled against God, and sought to take the kingdom of our God and his Christ—
>
> 29 Wherefore, he maketh war with the saints of God, and encompasseth them round about.

The vision is a study in contrasts: The vision of the Father and the Son demonstrates the highest ideal that men and women can aspire to: the perfected Son of God. The next vision illustrates the depravities that God's children can descend to by showing the fall of Lucifer. The names used to refer to Satan in this passage are instructive as to what happened to him. The name Lucifer means the "shining one"[14] (Isaiah 14:12). He is here described as "an angel of God who was in authority in the presence of God, who rebelled against the Only Begotten Son whom the Father loved" (verse 25). After his fall, he was called Perdition, a Latin term that in Joseph Smith's time meant "entire loss or ruin; utter destruction."[15] We do not know what kind of authority Lucifer held when he was in the presence of God, nor do we know the precise meaning of "a son of the morning" (verse 26). The poetic version of the vision refers to him being "thrust down to woe from his Godified state."[16]

One of the great contributions of latter-day revelation is to shed more light on the origins and works of Satan. Joseph Smith had earlier learned while translating the book of Genesis that Satan is a son of God who rebelled against God (see Moses 4:1–4). According to this revelation, Satan sought to destroy the agency of humankind and literally became *Satan*, a term meaning in Hebrew "to oppose, obstruct, or accuse," or in Greek just simply "adversary."[17] Further information was given about Satan a few years later when Joseph Smith translated the book of Abraham, in which we learn that when God chose Jesus Christ as the central figure of the plan, Satan "was angry, and kept not his first estate; and, at that day, many followed after him" (Abraham 3:28).

While it is not pleasant to discuss Satan or his aims, the amount of space he is given in the vision suggests that it is important that we know about him. After celestial glory, which is described in twenty-nine verses of the vision, the fall of Satan and the sons of perdition are given more attention than any other group. Around seventeen verses of the vision center on these souls confirmed as perdition.

> 30 And we saw a vision of the sufferings of those with whom he made war and overcame, for thus came the voice of the Lord unto us:
>
> 31 Thus saith the Lord concerning all those who know my power, and have been made partakers thereof, and suffered themselves through the power of the devil to be overcome, and to deny the truth and defy my power—
>
> 32 They are they who are the sons of perdition, of whom I say that it had been better for them never to have been born;
>
> 33 For they are vessels of wrath, doomed to suffer the wrath of God, with the devil and his angels in eternity;
>
> 34 Concerning whom I have said there is no forgiveness in this world nor in the world to come—
>
> 35 Having denied the Holy Spirit after having received it, and having denied the Only Begotten Son of the Father, having crucified him unto themselves and put him to an open shame.

Following a vision of the original son of perdition, another vision opens to reveal the fate of those who kept their first estate but, after coming to earth, become sons of perdition. The sin against the Holy Ghost, which Alma speaks of as an "unpardonable" sin (Alma 39:6), is explained in greatest detail here. The text explains that these individuals deny not only the witness of the Holy Ghost but also the witness of the Son, "having crucified him unto themselves and put him to an open shame" (verse 35). The terrible fate of the sons of perdition rests upon the great knowledge that has been bestowed upon them and upon the responsibility that comes from having a sure witness of the truth and then denying it.

Joseph Smith explained in greater detail why the penalties placed upon the sons of perdition are so severe:

All sins shall be forgiven except the sin against the Holy Ghost; for Jesus will save all except the sons of perdition. What must a man do to commit the unpardonable sin? he must receive the Holy Ghost, have the heavens opened unto him, and know God, and then sin against him: after a man has sinned against the Holy Ghost there is no repentance for him; he has got to say that the sun does not shine while he sees it—he has got to deny Jesus Christ when the heavens have been opened unto him, and to deny the plan of salvation with his eyes open to the truth of it; and from that time he begins to be an enemy. This is the case with many apostates of The Church of Jesus Christ of Latter-day Saints. When a man begins to be an enemy to this work, he hunts me—he seeks to kill me, and never ceases to thirst for my blood. He gets the spirit of the Devil—the same spirit that they had who crucified the Lord of life—the same spirit that sins against the Holy Ghost. You cannot save such persons—you cannot bring them to repentance; they make open war like the Devil and awful is the consequence.[18]

36 These are they who shall go away into the lake of fire and brimstone, with the devil and his angels—

37 And the only ones on whom the second death shall have any power;

38 Yea, verily, the only ones who shall not be redeemed in the due time of the Lord, after the sufferings of his wrath.

39 For all the rest shall be brought forth by the resurrection of the dead, through the triumph and the glory of the Lamb, who

was slain, who was in the bosom of the Father before the worlds were made.

40 And this is the gospel, the glad tidings, which the voice out of the heavens bore record unto us—

41 That he came into the world, even Jesus, to be crucified for the world, and to bear the sins of the world, and to sanctify the world, and to cleanse it from all unrighteousness;

42 That through him all might be saved whom the Father had put into his power and made by him;

43 Who glorifies the Father, and saves all the works of his hands, except those sons of perdition who deny the Son after the Father has revealed him.

44 Wherefore, he saves all except them—they shall go away into everlasting punishment, which is endless punishment, which is eternal punishment, to reign with the devil and his angels in eternity, where their worm dieth not, and the fire is not quenched, which is their torment—

45 And the end thereof, neither the place thereof, nor their torment, no man knows;

46 Neither was it revealed, neither is, neither will be revealed unto man, except to them who are made partakers thereof;

47 Nevertheless, I, the Lord, show it by vision unto many, but straightway shut it up again;

48 Wherefore, the end, the width, the height, the depth, and the misery thereof, they understand not, neither any man except those who are ordained unto this condemnation.

49 And we heard the voice, saying: Write the vision, for lo, this is the end of the vision of the sufferings of the ungodly.

What is the ultimate fate of the sons of perdition? This passage of the vision confirms that they are "the only ones on whom the second death shall have any power; Yea, verily, the only ones who shall not be redeemed in the due time of the Lord" (verses 37–39). However, even sons of perdition receive blessings because of the atoning work of Jesus Christ. Paul and Alma both teach that the Resurrection is universal for all of God's children who kept their first estate and came to earth (see 1 Corinthians 15:22; Alma 11:41–45). A later revelation to Joseph Smith also confirmed that the sons of perdition will be resurrected (see Doctrine and Covenants 88:102). The poetic version of these verses of Doctrine and Covenants 76 reads:

> They are they, who must groan through the great second death,
> And are not redeemed in the time of the Lord;
> While all the rest are, through the triumph of Christ,
> Made partakers of grace, by the power of his word.[19]

"All the rest" described in the poem consist of the celestial, terrestrial, or telestial beings who are redeemed from the second death, or spiritual death. All except the sons of perdition will return to the presence of God, even if it is only a temporary return. Samuel the Lamanite proclaimed:

> For behold, he surely must die that salvation may come; yea, it behooveth him and becometh expedient that he dieth, to bring to pass the resurrection of the dead, that thereby men may be brought into the presence of the Lord.
>
> Yea, behold, this death bringeth to pass the resurrection, and redeemeth all mankind from the first death—that spiritual death; for all mankind, by the fall of Adam being cut off from the presence of the Lord, are considered as dead, both as to things temporal and to things spiritual.
>
> But behold, the resurrection of Christ redeemeth mankind, yea, even all mankind, and bringeth them back into the presence of the Lord. (Helaman 14:15–17)

> 50 And again we bear record—for we saw and heard, and this is the testimony of the gospel of Christ concerning them who shall come forth in the resurrection of the just—
>
> 51 They are they who received the testimony of Jesus, and believed on his name and were baptized after the manner of his burial, being buried in the water in his name, and this according to the commandment which he has given—
>
> 52 That by keeping the commandments they might be washed and cleansed from all their sins, and receive the Holy Spirit by the laying on of the hands of him who is ordained and sealed unto this power;

53 And who overcome by faith, and are sealed by the Holy Spirit of promise, which the Father sheds forth upon all those who are just and true.

The next vision presented is of the celestial people brought forth in the First Resurrection. Apparently, only part of what Joseph and Sidney learned about the celestial kingdom is revealed in this vision. Joseph Smith later said, "I could explain a hundred-fold more than I ever have, of the glories of the Kingdoms manifested to me in the vision, were I permitted, and were the people prepared to receive it, the Lord deals with this people as a tender parent with a child, communicating light and intelligence and the knowledge of his ways, as they can hear it."[20]

Many of the truths we now know about the celestial kingdom were revealed to the Prophet in subsequent revelations and were shared in his discourses. A primary example of this came when Joseph Smith revealed that in the celestial kingdom, there are "three heavens or degrees; and in order to obtain the highest, a man must enter into this order of the priesthood [meaning the new and everlasting covenant of marriage]" (Doctrine and Covenants 131:1–2). The only knowledge given thus far about the inhabitants of the lower degrees within the celestial kingdom is that they act as ministering angels to those who have obtained the fulness of the Father (see Doctrine and Covenants 132:15–19).

54 They are they who are the church of the Firstborn.

55 They are they into whose hands the Father has given all things—

56 They are they who are priests and kings, who have received of his fulness, and of his glory;

57 And are priests of the Most High, after the order of Melchizedek, which was after the order of Enoch, which was after the order of the Only Begotten Son.

58 Wherefore, as it is written, they are gods, even the sons of God—

59 Wherefore, all things are theirs, whether life or death, or things present, or things to come, all are theirs and they are Christ's, and Christ is God's.

60 And they shall overcome all things.

61 Wherefore, let no man glory in man, but rather let him glory in God, who shall subdue all enemies under his feet.

62 These shall dwell in the presence of God and his Christ forever and ever.

63 These are they whom he shall bring with him, when he shall come in the clouds of heaven to reign on the earth over his people.

64 These are they who shall have part in the first resurrection.

65 These are they who shall come forth in the resurrection of the just.

66 These are they who are come unto Mount Zion, and unto the city of the living God, the heavenly place, the holiest of all.

67 These are they who have come to an innumerable company of angels, to the general assembly and church of Enoch, and of the Firstborn.

68 These are they whose names are written in heaven, where God and Christ are the judge of all.

69 These are they who are just men made perfect through Jesus the mediator of the new covenant, who wrought out this perfect atonement through the shedding of his own blood.

70 These are they whose bodies are celestial, whose glory is that of the sun, even the glory of God, the highest of all, whose glory the sun of the firmament is written of as being typical.

The introductory text to the earliest copy of the vision declares that one of the vision's primary concerns is "the church of the Firstborn."[21] These verses provide the clearest description of what is required to enter into the Church of the Firstborn and the blessings given its members. The Church of the Firstborn is not the same organization as The Church of Jesus Christ of Latter-day Saints but rather a community of those who overcome all things and are "made perfect through Jesus the mediator of the new covenant" (verse 69). The poetic version of the vision describes this community as follows:

They're priests of the order of Melchisedek,
Like Jesus, (from whom is this highest reward,)

Receiving a fulness of glory and light;
As written: They're Gods; even sons of the Lord.
So all things are theirs; yea, of life, or of death;
Yea, whether things now, or to come, all are theirs,
And they are the Savior's, and he is the Lord's,
Having overcome all, as eternity's heirs.[22]

These heirs of eternity become so by entering into the ordinances and covenants of the gospel of Jesus Christ. The ordinance of baptism is given here as the gate to the celestial kingdom. This is consistent with what Joseph and Sidney would have known in 1832. Ordinances given later, such as the endowment and sealing ceremonies, unlocked more of the doors of eternity. The completion of ordinances alone, however, does not bring an assurance of salvation. A later revelation to Joseph Smith clarifies that "all covenants, contracts, bonds, obligations, oaths, vows, performances, connections, associations, or expectations, that are not made and entered into and sealed by the Holy Spirit of promise . . . are of no efficacy, virtue, or force in and after the resurrection from the dead" (Doctrine and Covenants 132:7). Only righteous living can bring the seal of the Holy Spirit, making these ordinances truly meaningful in time and eternity.

> 71 And again, we saw the terrestrial world, and behold and lo, these are they who are of the terrestrial, whose glory differs from that of the church of the Firstborn who have received the fulness of the Father, even as that of the moon differs from the sun in the firmament.
>
> 72 Behold, these are they who died without law;
>
> 73 And also they who are the spirits of men kept in prison, whom the Son visited, and preached the gospel unto them, that they might be judged according to men in the flesh;
>
> 74 Who received not the testimony of Jesus in the flesh, but afterwards received it.
>
> 75 These are they who are honorable men of the earth, who were blinded by the craftiness of men.
>
> 76 These are they who receive of his glory, but not of his fulness.
>
> 77 These are they who receive of the presence of the Son, but not of the fulness of the Father.

78 Wherefore, they are bodies terrestrial, and not bodies celestial, and differ in glory as the moon differs from the sun.

79 These are they who are not valiant in the testimony of Jesus; wherefore, they obtain not the crown over the kingdom of our God.

80 And now this is the end of the vision which we saw of the terrestrial, that the Lord commanded us to write while we were yet in the Spirit.

The next vision opened is of the terrestrial glory. In the terrestrial world are the honorable men and women of the earth who never accepted the fulness of the gospel. Those who "died without law" (verse 72) seem to be non-Christians who never had a chance to hear the gospel, or law, in this life. However, this statement needs some clarification: only non-Christians who never heard the gospel in this life and then reject it in the next life are bound for the terrestrial kingdom. A later revelation given to Joseph Smith clarifies that "all who have died without a knowledge of this gospel, who would have received it if they had been permitted to tarry, shall be heirs of the celestial kingdom of God" (Doctrine and Covenants 137:7).

In a similar fashion, the revelation makes a distinction between receiving the full knowledge of the gospel and receiving a more general testimony of Jesus Christ (see Doctrine and Covenants 76:82). The spirits in the terrestrial kingdom are those who received the testimony of Jesus after death but chose to reject the ordinances and covenants that would allow entrance into the celestial kingdom. This decision indicates that even if they knew about Jesus Christ during their mortal lives, the inhabitants of the terrestrial kingdom never fully received a testimony or were not valiant in their testimony of the Savior. The poetic version of the vision explains this idea further:

> They receiv'd not the truth of the Savior at first;
> But did, when they heard it in prison, again.
> Not valiant for truth, they obtain'd not the crown,
> But are of that glory that's typ'd by the moon;
> They are they, that come into the presence of Christ,
> But not to the fulness of God, on his throne.[23]

Though the root word of *terrestrial* is the Latin *terra*, meaning "earth," the terrestrial kingdom is considered to be more like the earth in its Edenic or paradisiacal state, similar to the way Paul described Adam as "earthy" in his created state (see 1 Corinthians 15:45, 47). During the Millennium after the Savior's return, the earth will be elevated to a terrestrial, or paradisiacal, state (see Articles of Faith 1:10). Taking this information into account, it is more correct to call the terrestrial kingdom a heaven than it is to call it a purgatory or a hell. After all, the inhabitants of the terrestrial kingdom enjoy the presence of the Son, a considerable blessing on any plane of existence (see verse 77).

> 81 And again, we saw the glory of the telestial, which glory is that of the lesser, even as the glory of the stars differs from that of the glory of the moon in the firmament.
>
> 82 These are they who received not the gospel of Christ, neither the testimony of Jesus.
>
> 83 These are they who deny not the Holy Spirit.
>
> 84 These are they who are thrust down to hell.
>
> 85 These are they who shall not be redeemed from the devil until the last resurrection, until the Lord, even Christ the Lamb, shall have finished his work.
>
> 86 These are they who receive not of his fulness in the eternal world, but of the Holy Spirit through the ministration of the terrestrial;
>
> 87 And the terrestrial through the ministration of the celestial.
>
> 88 And also the telestial receive it of the administering of angels who are appointed to minister for them, or who are appointed to be ministering spirits for them; for they shall be heirs of salvation.

The next vision consists of the telestial glory. The word *telestial* appears in scripture only in the Doctrine and Covenants, though Joseph Smith placed it into his translation of the Bible (see Joseph Smith Translation, 1 Corinthians 15:40 [in 1 Corinthians 15:40, footnote *a*]). The word itself was new to the English language when the vision was given, and even today it is defined in one dictionary as "the lowest of three Mormon degrees or kingdoms of glory attainable in heaven."[24] It is possible that the word is derived from the Greek prefix *tele*, which means "at a distance." This prefix is often used in words like *telephone*, which means "a faraway voice," or *television*, which means "distant viewing." We do not know if this is the correct etymology of the word, though the connotation is that the telestial glory is distant from God.[25]

The telestial glory consists of those "who received not the gospel of Christ, neither the testimony of Jesus" (verse 82). Those in the telestial kingdom refuse to even accept a basic testimony of Jesus. The poetic version of the vision further explains:

> These are they that receiv'd not the gospel of Christ,
> Or evidence, either, that he ever was;
> As the stars are all diff'rent in glory and light,
> So differs the glory of these by the laws.[26]

While it is true that every knee shall bow and every tongue confess that Jesus is the Christ (see Philippians 2:9–11; Doctrine and Covenants 76:11), this is not the same thing as every person gaining a testimony of Jesus. Telestial beings accept Christ only out of a practical recognition of power, not a confession of the power of Christ to save them.

While telestial beings are "thrust down to hell," it is comforting to know that hell is not a permanent state (see commentary for Doctrine and Covenants 19:4–12). Eventually, death and hell will give up those whom they hold captive (see 2 Nephi 9:12; Revelation 20:13). The inhabitants of the telestial kingdom will not be redeemed until the Second Resurrection (see verse 85), but they will be redeemed. A loving God has no interest in the eternal torment of His children. Punishment is meted out only to the degree that it will be required for their reformation and cleansing to "inherit" a degree of "salvation" and glory.

> 89 And thus we saw, in the heavenly vision, the glory of the telestial, which surpasses all understanding;
>
> 90 And no man knows it except him to whom God has revealed it.
>
> 91 And thus we saw the glory of the terrestrial which excels in all things the glory of the telestial, even in glory, and in power, and in might, and in dominion.
>
> 92 And thus we saw the glory of the celestial, which excels in all things—where God, even the Father, reigns upon his throne forever and ever;

93 Before whose throne all things bow in humble reverence, and give him glory forever and ever.

One of the vision's grand themes is the mercy of God. These verses state that even the glory of the telestial kingdom, the lowest and furthest from God, surpasses all understanding. The world we live in is often spoken of as telestial. Imagine this world, with all of its beauty and wonder, with no war, famine, hunger, disease, poverty, or death. And this is the place where those "who are liars, and sorcerers, and adulterers, and whoremongers" (Doctrine and Covenants 76:103) are destined to dwell!

The benevolence shown in the vision was a stumbling block for some of the early Saints. Brigham Young later recalled, "When God revealed to Joseph Smith and Sidney Rigdon that there was a place prepared for all, according to the light they had received and their rejection of evil and practice of good, it was a great trial to many, and some apostatized because God was not going to send to everlasting punishment heathens and infants, but had a place of salvation, in due time, for all, and would bless the honest and virtuous and truthful, whether they ever belonged to any church or not. It was a new doctrine to this generation, and many stumbled at it."[27] Brigham's brother Joseph was even more blunt is his assessment of the vision, declaring, "When I came to read the visions of the different glories of the eternal world, and of the sufferings of the wicked, I could not believe it at the first. Why the Lord was going to save everybody[!]"[28]

94 They who dwell in his presence are the church of the First-born; and they see as they are seen, and know as they are known, having received of his fulness and of his grace;

95 And he makes them equal in power, and in might, and in dominion.

96 And the glory of the celestial is one, even as the glory of the sun is one.

97 And the glory of the terrestrial is one, even as the glory of the moon is one.

The vision boldly proclaims that those who become part of the Church of the Firstborn will receive a fulness of the Savior's grace and become His, "equal in power, and in might, and in dominion" (verse 95), becoming "joint-heirs with Jesus Christ" (Romans 8:17). In an 1844 discourse, Joseph Smith exhorted the Saints, saying:

> You have got to learn how to be Gods yourselves, and to be Kings and Priests to God . . . heirs of God, and joint heirs with Jesus Christ. What is it? to inherit the same power, the same glory, and the same exaltation, until you arrive at the station of a God, and ascend the throne of eternal power the same as those who have gone before. What did Jesus do? Why I do the things I saw my Father do, when worlds came rolling into existence. My Father worked out his kingdom with fear and trembling, and I must do the same, and when I get my kingdom I shall present it to my Father, so that he may obtain kingdom upon kingdom, and it will exalt Him in glory. He will then take a higher exaltation, and I will take his place, and thereby become exalted myself.[29]

98 And the glory of the telestial is one, even as the glory of the stars is one; for as one star differs from another star in glory, even so differs one from another in glory in the telestial world;

99 For these are they who are of Paul, and of Apollos, and of Cephas.

100 These are they who say they are some of one and some of another—some of Christ and some of John, and some of Moses, and some of Elias, and some of Esaias, and some of Isaiah, and some of Enoch;

101 But received not the gospel, neither the testimony of Jesus, neither the prophets, neither the everlasting covenant.

102 Last of all, these all are they who will not be gathered with the saints, to be caught up unto the church of the Firstborn, and received into the cloud.

103 These are they who are liars, and sorcerers, and adulterers, and whoremongers, and whosoever loves and makes a lie.

104 These are they who suffer the wrath of God on earth.

105 These are they who suffer the vengeance of eternal fire.

106 These are they who are cast down to hell and suffer the wrath of Almighty God, until the fulness of times, when Christ shall have subdued all enemies under his feet, and shall have perfected his work;

The description of the vision returns here to the glory of the telestial. This portion of the vision highlights the emptiness of a life lived in opposition to God. It points out that the telestial "suffer the wrath of God *on earth*" (verse 104; emphasis added), confirming Alma's teaching that "wickedness never was happiness" (Alma 41:10). It also points out the sad truth that many who are outwardly religious are among the most involved in sin. The poetic version of the vision reads:

> These are they that came out for Apollos and Paul;
> For Cephas and Jesus, in all kinds of hope;
> For Enoch and Moses, and Peter, and John;
> For Luther and Calvin, and even the Pope.
> For they never received the gospel of Christ,
> Nor the prophetic spirit that came from the Lord;
> Nor the covenant neither, which Jacob once had;
> They went their own way, and they have their reward.[30]

This is not to say that those who find Christ through Apollos, Paul, Luther, Calvin, or the Pope are not true Christians. The warning is that those who glorify mortal messengers but do not build their faith on Jesus Christ are building on a sandy foundation (see Helaman 5:12). Devotion to a single person, ideology, or philosophy outside of the gospel of Jesus Christ does not bring salvation.

> 107 When he shall deliver up the kingdom, and present it unto the Father, spotless, saying: I have overcome and have trodden the wine-press alone, even the wine-press of the fierceness of the wrath of Almighty God.
>
> 108 Then shall he be crowned with the crown of his glory, to sit on the throne of his power to reign forever and ever.
>
> 109 But behold, and lo, we saw the glory and the inhabitants of the telestial world, that they were as innumerable as the stars in the firmament of heaven, or as the sand upon the seashore;
>
> 110 And heard the voice of the Lord saying: These all shall bow the knee, and every tongue shall confess to him who sits upon the throne forever and ever;
>
> 111 For they shall be judged according to their works, and every man shall receive according to his own works, his own dominion, in the mansions which are prepared;

112 And they shall be servants of the Most High; but where God and Christ dwell they cannot come, worlds without end.

The vision states that the inhabitants of the telestial world are "as innumerable as the stars in the firmament of heaven" (verse 109) and that "where God and Christ dwell they cannot come" (verse 112). In light of this phrase, the question is often asked, "Is there eventual advancement from one glory to another? Could a person who is sent to the telestial kingdom progress over time to the terrestrial kingdom and then on to the celestial?" Differing opinions have been held by different leaders of the Church, but it can be hazardous to set one Church leader against another. The question became so nettlesome in the twentieth century that Joseph L. Anderson, a secretary to the First Presidency, provided this standard response to the question: "The brethren direct me to say that the Church has never announced a definite doctrine upon this point. Some of the brethren have held the view that it was possible in the course of progression to advance from one glory to another, invoking the principle of eternal progression; others of the brethren have taken the opposite view. But as stated, the Church has never announced a definite doctrine on this point."[31]

Does this mean that a person who goes to the celestial glory is cut off from their loved ones who do not achieve the same glory? A celestial being is not cut off from any place in the universe. Can a celestial being visit a telestial kingdom? The Father and the Son, both resurrected celestial beings, visit our earth, a telestial kingdom, with great frequency. The best way for people to ensure that they will never be cut off from the presence of their loved ones is to strive to achieve celestial glory. One of the blessings of celestial glory is the power to visit and minister to any person in any part of the universe.

Finally, as we accept that we simply do not know the answer to the question of advancement between the kingdoms, it is perhaps best to trust in God's mercy. One of the vision's great messages is the scope of God's plan for His sons and daughters and the lengths to which He will go to extend mercy to all of them. Lorenzo Snow captured the grand mercy of this doctrine when he said:

God loves his offspring, the human family. His design is not simply to furnish happiness to the few here, called Latter-day Saints. The plan and scheme that he is now carrying out is for universal salvation; not only for the salvation of the Latter-day Saints, but for the salvation of every man and woman on the face of the earth, for those also in the spirit world, and for those who may hereafter come upon the face of the earth. It is for the salvation of every son and daughter of Adam. They are the offspring of the Almighty, he loves them all and his plans are for the salvation of the whole, and *he will bring all up into that position in which they will be as happy and as comfortable as they are willing to be.*[32]

113 This is the end of the vision which we saw, which we were commanded to write while we were yet in the Spirit.

114 But great and marvelous are the works of the Lord, and the mysteries of his kingdom which he showed unto us, which surpass all understanding in glory, and in might, and in dominion;

115 Which he commanded us we should not write while we were yet in the Spirit, and are not lawful for man to utter;

116 Neither is man capable to make them known, for they are only to be seen and understood by the power of the Holy Spirit, which God bestows on those who love him, and purify themselves before him;

117 To whom he grants this privilege of seeing and knowing for themselves;

118 That through the power and manifestation of the Spirit, while in the flesh, they may be able to bear his presence in the world of glory.

119 And to God and the Lamb be glory, and honor, and dominion forever and ever. Amen.

While others may have struggled to accept the vision's tenets, Joseph Smith recognized its wonder and power. When he recorded it in his later history, he offered this assessment of the vision:

Nothing could be more pleasing to the Saint, upon the order of the kingdom of the Lord, than the light which burst upon the world, through the foregoing vision. Every law, every commandment, every promise, every truth, and every point, touching the destiny of man, from Genesis to Revelation, where the purity of either remains unsullied from the wisdom of men, goes to shew the perfection of the theory, and witnesses the fact that that document is a transcript from the Records of the eternal world. The sublimity of the ideas; the purity of the language; the scope for action; the continued duration for completion, in order that the heirs of salvation, may confess the Lord and bow the knee; The rewards for faithfulness and the punishments for sins, are so much beyond the narrow mindedness of men, that every honest man is constrained to exclaim; It came from God.[33]

The vision forms the backbone of the Latter-day Saint understanding of the Resurrection and the eternal destiny of the sons and daughters of God. The vision emphasizes the centrality of Jesus Christ in our salvation and the expansive nature of the ways in which Christ offers salvation to all. The result is an assurance of better things to come. Brigham Young summarized its value when he said, "You cannot find a compass on earth that points so directly, as the Gospel plan of salvation. It has a place for everything, and puts everything in its place."[34]

End Notes

1. Vision, 16 February 1832 [D&C 76], 1, josephsmithpapers.org.
2. *An American Dictionary of the English Language*, s.v. "economy," accessed February 13, 2024, https://webstersdictionary1828.com/Dictionary/economy.
3. Philo Dibble, "Recollections of the Prophet Joseph Smith," *Juvenile Instructor* 27, no. 10 (May 15, 1892).
4. Dibble, "Recollections of the Prophet Joseph Smith."
5. Philo Dibble, "Philo Dibble's Narrative," in *Four Faith Promoting Classics: A String of Pearls, Fragments of Experience, Gems for the Young Folks, Early Scenes in Church History* (Salt Lake City, UT: Bookcraft, 1968), 74–96.
6. Joseph Smith, in History, 1838–1856, volume A-1 [23 December 1805–30 August 1834], 183, josephsmithpapers.org. See also "Historical Introduction," Vision, 16 February 1832 [D&C 76], josephsmithpapers.org.
7. Poem from William W. Phelps, between 1 and 20 January 1843, 82, josephsmithpapers.org.
8. See Bruce Van Orden, *We'll Sing and We'll Shout: The Life and Times of W. W. Phelps* (Salt Lake City, UT: Deseret Book, 2018), 394–95; Lawrence R. Flake, *Three Degrees of Glory: Joseph Smith's Insights on the Kingdoms of Heaven* (Salt Lake City, UT: Covenant Communications, 2000), 16–17.
9. Poem to William W. Phelps, between circa 1 and circa 15 February 1843, 82, josephsmithpapers.org.
10. *An American Dictionary of the English Language*, s.v. "mystery," accessed February 13, 2024, https://webstersdictionary1828.com/Dictionary/mystery.
11. Poem to William W. Phelps, between circa 1 and circa 15 February 1843, 82, stanza 7, josephsmithpapers.org.
12. See "The Living Christ: The Testimony of the Apostles," Gospel Library.
13. Poem to William W. Phelps, between circa 1 and circa 15 February 1843, 83, stanzas 19–20, josephsmithpapers.org.
14. Adele Berlin and Marc Zvi Brettler, ed., *The Jewish Study Bible: Second Edition* (New York: Oxford University Press, 2014), 794.
15. *An American Dictionary of the English Language*, s.v. "perdition," accessed February 13, 2024, https://webstersdictionary1828.com/Dictionary/perdition.
16. Poem to William W. Phelps, between circa 1 and circa 15 February 1843, 83, stanza 21, josephsmithpapers.org.
17. *Lexham Bible Dictionary* (Bellingham, WA: Lexham Press, 2016), s.v. "Satan."
18. Joseph Smith, in History, 1838–1856, volume E-1 [1 July 1843–30 April 1844], 1976, josephsmithpapers.org.

19. Poem to William W. Phelps, between circa 1 and circa 15 February 1843, 83, stanza 31, josephsmithpapers.org.

20. Joseph Smith, in History, 1838–1856, volume D-1 [1 August 1842–1 July 1843], 1556, josephsmithpapers.org.

21. Vision, 16 February 1832 [D&C 76], 1, josephsmithpapers.org.

22. Poem to William W. Phelps, between circa 1 and circa 15 February 1843, 83, stanza 45–46, josephsmithpapers.org.

23. Poem to William W. Phelps, between circa 1 and circa 15 February 1843, 83, stanzas 56–57, josephsmithpapers.org.

24. See *Merriam-Webster.com Dictionary*, s.v. "telestial glory," accessed February 14, 2024, https://www.merriam-webster.com/dictionary/telestial%20glory.

25. Stephen E. Robinson and H. Dean Garrett, *A Commentary on the Doctrine and Covenants* (Salt Lake City, UT: Deseret Book, 2000), 2:318.

26. Poem to William W. Phelps, between circa 1 and circa 15 February 1843, 83, stanza 59, josephsmithpapers.org.

27. Brigham Young, in *Journal of Discourses*, 16:42.

28. *Deseret News*, Mar. 18, 1857, 11.

29. Joseph Smith, in History, 1838–1856, volume E-1 [1 July 1843–30 April 1844], 1971, josephsmithpapers.org.

30. Poem to William W. Phelps, between circa 1 and circa 15 February 1843, 83, stanza 70–71, josephsmithpapers.org.

31. Letter from the Office of The First Presidency, March 5, 1952, and again on December 17, 1965, cited in George T. Boyd, "A Mormon Concept of Man," *Dialogue: A Journal of Mormon Thought* 3, no. 1 (Spring 1968): 72.

32. *The Teachings of Lorenzo Snow*, comp. Clyde J. Williams (1984), 91; emphasis added.

33. Joseph Smith, in History, 1838–1856, volume A-1 [23 December 1805–30 August 1834], 192, josephsmithpapers.org.

34. Brigham Young, in *Journal of Discourses*, 3:96.

Appendix

Below is a supplemental study aid that was partially quoted in the commentary for Doctrine and Covenants 76. It is the poetic version of the vision revealed to Joseph Smith and Sidney Rigdon.

FROM W[illiam] W. PHELPS TO JOSEPH SMITH: THE PROPHET.
Vade Mecum, (translated,) Go With Me.

Go with me, will you go to the saints that have died,—
To the next, better world, where the righteous reside;
Where the angels and spirits in harmony be
In the joys of a vast paradise? Go with me.

Go with me where the truth and the virtues prevail;
Where the union is one, and the years never fail;
Not a heart can conceive, nor a nat'ral eye see
What the Lord has prepar'd for the just. Go with me.

Go with me where there is no destruction or war;
Neither tyrants, or sland'rers, or nations ajar;
Where the system is perfect, and happiness free,
And the life is eternal with God. Go with me.

Go with me, will you go to the mansions above,
Where the bliss, and the knowledge, the light, and the love,
And the glory of God do eternally be?—
Death, the wages of sin, is not there. Go with me.

Nauvoo, Jan. 1843.[1]

THE ANSWER

to William W. Phelps, esq.

A Vision.

1. I will go, I will go, to the home of the Saints,
Where the virtue's the value, and life the reward;
But before I return to my former estate
I must fulfil the mission I had from the Lord.

2. Wherefore, hear, O ye heavens, and give ear O ye earth;
And rejoice ye inhabitants truly again;
For the Lord he is God, and his life never ends,
And besides him there ne'er was a Saviour of men.

3. His ways are a wonder; his wisdom is great;
The extent of his doings, there's none can unveil;
His purposes fail not; from age unto age
He still is the same, and his years never fail.

4. His throne is the heavens, his life time is all
Of eternity *now*, and eternity *then*;
His union is power, and none stays his hand,—
The Alpha, Omega, for ever: Amen.

5. For thus saith the Lord, in the spirit of truth,
I am merciful, gracious, and good unto those
That fear me, and live for the life that's to come;
My delight is to honor the saints with repose;

6. That serve me in righteousness true to the end;
Eternal's their glory, and great their reward;
I'll surely reveal all my myst'ries to them,—
The great hidden myst'ries in my kingdom stor'd—

7. From the council in Kolob, to time on the earth.
And for ages to come unto them I will show
My pleasure & will, what my kingdom will do:
Eternity's wonders they truly shall know.

8. Great things of the future I'll show unto them,
Yea, things of the vast generations to rise;
For their wisdom and glory shall be very great,
And their pure understanding extend to the skies:

9. And before them the wisdom of wise men shall cease,
And the nice understanding of prudent ones fail!
For the light of my spirit shall light mine elect,
And the truth is so mighty 't will ever prevail.

10. And the secrets and plans of my will I'll reveal;
The sanctified pleasures when earth is renew'd,
What the eye hath not seen, nor the ear hath yet heard;
Nor the heart of the natural man ever hath view'd.

11. I, Joseph, the prophet, in spirit beheld,
And the eyes of the inner man truly did see
Eternity sketch'd in a vision from God,
Of what was, and now is, and yet is to be.

12. Those things which the Father ordained of old,
Before the world was, or a system had run,—
Through Jesus the Maker and Savior of all;
The only begotten, (Messiah) his son.

13. Of whom I bear record, as all prophets have,
And the record I bear is the fulness,—yea even
The truth of the gospel of Jesus—*the Christ,*
With whom I convers'd, in the vision of heav'n.

14. For while in the act of translating his word,
Which the Lord in his grace had appointed to me,
I came to the gospel recorded by John,
Chapter fifth and the twenty ninth verse, which you'll see.
Which was given as follows:
Speaking of the resurrection of the dead,—
Concerning those who shall hear the voice of the son of man—
And shall come forth:—
They who have done good in the resurrection of the just.
And they who have done evil in the resurrection of the unjust.

15. I marvel'd at these resurrections, indeed!
For it came unto me by the spirit direct:—
And while I did meditate what it all meant,
The Lord touch'd the eyes of my own intellect:—

16. Hosanna forever! they open'd anon,
And the glory of God shone around where I was;
And there was the Son, at the Father's right hand,
In a fulness of glory, and holy applause.

17. I beheld round the throne, holy angels and hosts,
And sanctified beings from worlds that have been,
In holiness worshipping God and the Lamb,
Forever and ever, amen and amen!

18. And now after all of the proofs made of him,
By witnesses truly, by whom he was known,
This is mine, last of all, that he lives; yea he lives!
And sits at the right hand of God, on his throne.

19. And I heard a great voice, bearing record from heav'n,
He's the Saviour, and only begotten of God—
By him, of him, and through him, the worlds were all made,
Even all that career in the heavens so broad,

20. Whose inhabitants, too, from the first to the last,
Are sav'd by the very same Saviour of ours;
And, of course, are begotten God's daughters and sons,
By the very same truths, and the very same pow'rs.

21. And I saw and bear record of warfare in heav'n;
For an angel of light, in authority great,
Rebell'd against Jesus, and sought for his pow'r,
But was thrust down to woe from his Godified state.

22. And the heavens all wept, and the tears drop'd like dew,
That Lucifer, son of the morning had fell!
Yea, is fallen! is fall'n, and become, Oh, alas!
The son of Perdition; the devil of hell!

23. And while I was yet in the spirit of truth,
The commandment was: write ye the vision all out;
For Satan, old serpent, the devil's for war,—
And yet will encompass the saints round about.

24. And I saw, too, the suff'ring and mis'ry of those,
(Overcome by the devil, in warfare and fight,)
In hell-fire, and vengeance, the doom of the damn'd;
For the Lord said, the vision is further: so write.

25. For thus saith the Lord, now concerning all those
Who know of my power and partake of the same;
And suffer themselves, that they be overcome
By the power of Satan; despising my name:—

26. Defying my power, and denying the truth;—
They are they—of the world, or of men, most forlorn,
The Sons of Perdition, of whom, ah! I say,
'T were better for them had they never been born!

27. They're vessels of wrath, and dishonor to God,
Doom'd to suffer his wrath, in the regions of woe,
Through the terrific night of eternity's round,
With the devil and all of his angels below:

28. Of whom it is said, no forgiveness is giv'n,
In this world, alas! nor the world that's to come;
For they have denied the spirit of God,
After having receiv'd it: and mis'ry's their doom.

29. And denying the only begotten of God,—
And crucify him to themselves, as they do,
And openly put him to shame in their flesh,
By gospel they cannot repentance renew.

30. They are they, who must go to the great lake of fire,
Which burneth with brimstone, yet never consumes,
And dwell with the devil, and angels of his,
While eternity goes and eternity comes.

31. They are they, who must groan through the great second death,
And are not redeemed in the time of the Lord;
While all the rest are, through the triumph of Christ,
Made partakers of grace, by the power of his word.

32. The myst'ry of Godliness truly is great;—
The past, and the present, and what is to be;
And this is the gospel—glad tidings to all,
Which the voice from the heavens bore record to me:

33. That he came to the world in the middle of time,
To lay down his life for his friends and his foes,
And bear away sin as a mission of love;
And sanctify earth for a blessed repose.

34. 'Tis decreed, that he'll save all the work of his hands,
And sanctify them by his own precious blood;
And purify earth for the Sabbath of rest,
By the agent of fire, as it was by the flood.

35. The Savior will save all his Father did give,
Even all that he gave in the regions abroad,
Save the Sons of Perdition: They're lost; ever lost,
And can never return to the presence of God.

36 They are they, who must reign with the devil in hell,
In eternity now, and eternity then,
Where the worm dieth not, and the fire is not quench'd;—
And the punishment still, is eternal. Amen.

37. And which is the torment apostates receive,
But the end, or the place where the torment began,
Save to them who are made to partake of the same,
Was never, nor will be, revealed unto man.

38. Yet God shows by vision a glimpse of their fate,
And straightway he closes the scene that was shown:
So the width, or the depth, or the misery thereof,
Save to those that partake, is forever unknown.

39. And while I was pondering, the vision was closed;
And the voice said to me, write the vision: for lo!
'Tis the end of the scene of the sufferings of those,
Who remain filthy still in their anguish and woe.

40. And again I bear record of heavenly things,
Where virtue's the value, above all that's pric'd—
Of the truth of the gospel concerning the just,
That rise in the first resurrection of Christ.

41. Who receiv'd and believ'd, and repented likewise,
And then were baptis'd, as a man always was,
Who ask'd and receiv'd a remission of sin,
And honored the kingdom by keeping its laws.

42. Being buried in water, as Jesus had been,
And keeping the whole of his holy commands,
They received the gift of the spirit of truth,
By the ordinance truly of laying on hands.

43. For these overcome, by their faith and their works,
Being tried in their life-time, as purified gold,
And seal'd by the spirit of promise, to life,
By men called of God, as was Aaron of old.

44. They are they, of the church of the first born of God,—
And unto whose hands he committeth all things;
For they hold the keys of the kingdom of heav'n,
And reign with the Savior, as priests, and as kings.

45. They're priests of the order of Melchisedek,
Like Jesus, (from whom is this highest reward,)
Receiving a fulness of glory and light;
As written: They're Gods; even sons of the Lord.

46. So all things are theirs; yea, of life, or of death;
Yea, whether things now, or to come, all are theirs,
And they are the Savior's, and he is the Lord's,
Having overcome all, as eternity's heirs.

47. 'Tis wisdom that man never glory in man,
But give God the glory for all that he hath;
For the righteous will walk in the presence of God,
While the wicked are trod under foot in his wrath.

48. Yea, the righteous shall dwell in the presence of God,
And of Jesus, forever, from earth's second birth—
For when he comes down in the splendor of heav'n,
All these he'll bring with him, to reign on the earth.

49. These are they that arise in their bodies of flesh,
When the trump of the first resurrection shall sound;
These are they that come up to Mount Zion, in life,
Where the blessings and gifts of the spirit abound.

50. These are they that have come to the heavenly place;
To the numberless courses of angels above:
To the city of God; e'en the holiest of all,
And the home of the blessed, the fountain of love:

51. To the church of old Enoch, and of the first born:
And gen'ral assembly of ancient renown'd,
Whose names are all kept in the archives of heav'n,
As chosen and faithful, and fit to be crown'd.

52. These are they that are perfect through Jesus' own blood,
Whose bodies celestial are mention'd by Paul,
Where the sun is the typical glory thereof,
And God, and his Christ, are the true judge of all.

53. Again I beheld the terrestrial world,
In the order and glory of Jesus, go on;
'Twas not as the church of the first born of God,
But shone in its place, as the moon to the sun.

54. Behold, these are they that have died without law;
The heathen of ages that never had hope,
And those of the region and shadow of death,
The spirits in prison, that light has brought up.

55. To spirits in prison the Savior once preach'd,
And taught them the gospel, with powers afresh;
And then were the living baptiz'd for their dead,
That they might be judg'd as if men in the flesh.

56. These are they that are hon'rable men of the earth;
Who were blinded and dup'd by the cunning of men:
They receiv'd not the truth of the Savior at first;
But did, when they heard it in prison, again.

57. Not valiant for truth, they obtain'd not the crown,
But are of that glory that's typ'd by the moon;
They are they, that come into the presence of Christ,
But not to the fulness of God, on his throne.

58. Again I beheld the telestial, as third,
The lesser, or starry world, next in its place.
For the leaven must leaven three measures of meal,
And every knee bow that is subject to grace.

59. These are they that receiv'd not the gospel of Christ,
Or evidence, either, that he ever was;
As the stars are all diff'rent in glory and light,
So differs the glory of these by the laws.

60. These are they that deny not the spirit of God,
But are thrust down to hell, with the devil, for sins,
As hypocrites, liars, whoremongers, and thieves,
And stay 'till the last resurrection begins.

61. 'Till the Lamb shall have finish'd the work he begun;
Shall have trodden the wine press, in fury alone,
And overcome all by the pow'r of his might:
He conquers to conquer, and save all his own.

62. These are they that receive not a fulness of light,
From Christ, in eternity's world, where they are,
The terrestrial sends them the Comforter, though;
And minist'ring angels, to happify there.

63. And so the telestial is minister'd to,
By ministers from the terrestrial one,
As terrestrial is, from the celestial throne;
And the great, greater, greatest, seem's stars, moon, and sun.

64. And thus I beheld, in the vision of heav'n,
The telestial glory, dominion and bliss,
Surpassing the great understanding of men,—
Unknown, save reveal'd, in a world vain as this.

65. And lo, I beheld the terrestrial, too,
Which excels the telestial in glory and light,
In splendor, and knowledge, and wisdom, and joy,
In blessings, and graces, dominion and might.

66. I beheld the celestial, in glory sublime;
Which is the most excellent kingdom that is,—
Where God, e'en the Father, in harmony reigns;
Almighty, supreme, and eternal, in bliss.

67. Where the church of the first born in union reside,
And they see as they're seen, and they know as they're known;
Being equal in power, dominion and might,
With a fulness of glory and grace, round his throne.

68. The glory celestial is one like the sun;
The glory terrestr'al is one like the moon;
The glory telestial is one like the stars,
And all harmonize like the parts of a tune.

69. As the stars are all different in lustre and size,
So the telestial region, is mingled in bliss;
From least unto greatest, and greatest to least,
The reward is exactly as promis'd in this.

70. These are they that came out for Apollos and Paul;
For Cephas and Jesus, in all kinds of hope;
For Enoch and Moses, and Peter, and John;
For Luther and Calvin, and even the Pope.

71. For they never received the gospel of Christ,
Nor the prophetic spirit that came from the Lord;
Nor the covenant neither, which Jacob once had;
They went their own way, and they have their reward.

72. By the order of God, last of all, these are they,
That wilt not be gather'd with saints here below,
To be caught up to Jesus, and meet in the cloud:—
In darkness they worshipp'd; to darkness they go.

73. These are they that are sinful, the wicked at large,
That glutted their passion by meanness or worth;
All liars, adulterers, sorc'rers, and proud;
And suffer, as promis'd, God's wrath on the earth.

74. These are they that must suffer the vengeance of hell,
'Till Christ shall have trodden all enemies down,
And perfected his work, in the fulness of times:
And is crown'd on his throne with his glorious crown.

75. The vast multitude of the telestial world—
As the stars of the skies, or the sands of the sea;—
The voice of Jehovah echo'd far and wide,
Ev'ry tongue shall confess, and they all bow the knee.

76. Ev'ry man shall be judg'd by the works of his life,
And receive a reward in the mansions prepar'd;
For his judgments are just, and his works never end,
As his prophets and servants have always declar'd.

77. But the great things of God, which he show'd unto me,
Unlawful to utter, I dare not declare;
They surpass all the wisdom and greatness of men,
And only are seen, as has Paul, where they are.

78. I will go, I will go, while the secret of life,
Is blooming in heaven, and blasting in hell;
Is leaving on earth, and a budding in space:—
I will go, I will go, with you, brother, farewell.

JOSEPH SMITH.
Nauvoo, Feb. 1843.[2]

End Notes

1. Poem from William W. Phelps, between 1 and 20 January 1843, 81–82, josephsmithpapers.org.
2. Poem to William W. Phelps, between circa 1 and circa 15 February 1843, 83–85, josephsmithpapers.org.

ABOUT THE AUTHOR

CASEY PAUL GRIFFITHS IS AN ASSOCIATE PROFESSOR OF CHURCH HISTORY and Doctrine at Brigham Young University in Provo, Utah. He holds a bachelor's degree in history, a master's degree in religious education, and a PhD in educational leadership and foundations, all from Brigham Young University. He has served as president of the John Whitmer Historical Association and the BYU Education Society. Before coming to BYU he served as a teacher and curriculum writer in the Seminaries and Institutes of Religion department of The Church of Jesus Christ of Latter-day Saints. He also serves as a managing editor of Doctrine and Covenants Central, a website designed to build faith in Jesus Christ by making the Doctrine and Covenants accessible, comprehensible, and defensible to people everywhere. He lives in Saratoga Springs with his wife, Elizabeth, and their four wonderful children.

Scan to visit

https://doctrineandcovenantscentral.org/